THE UFO PARADOX

"Human experience is either real or unreal. It is either objective or subjective, this-worldly or other-worldly. No, it is not! Human experience is often far more complex and difficult to fathom than we are to imagine. Thompson knows this and shows it. *The UFO Paradox* is an effective antidote to easy explanations, simple binaries, old habits of reasoning, and dead-end thinking."

DALE C. ALLISON JR., AUTHOR OF
ENCOUNTERING MYSTERY AND
THE LUMINOUS DUSK

"This book is a call from the cosmos that is fiercely alive, weirdly involved in our own forms of culture and consciousness, and beyond any of our conventional religions and sciences. Reality is not what we think it is. Nor are we. Human beings manifest supernormal powers in a supernatural world that is much bigger than we think, and maybe than we *can* think. Keith Thompson shows us all of this, and so much more, in a new book that is now one of our finest confrontations with the baffling truth of the UFO, which is really a paradox shattering our assumptions, *whatever* those are."

JEFFREY J. KRIPAL, AUTHOR OF
HOW TO THINK IMPOSSIBLY

"Keith Thompson is both a scholar and a journalist that has been on the scene working hand in glove with many of the key investigators in this elusive field. He brings to this inquiry a deep understanding of the mythic and paranormal dimensions of reality. His exploration of the UFO mystery has been colored by an appreciation of the larger dimensions of human existence, triggered by his own near-death experience. This book has achieved something rare in UFOlogy lore: a near-perfect balance of the physical and nonphysical dimensions of the phenomenon."

JEFFREY MISHLOVE, PH.D., HOST OF
NEW THINKING ALLOWED

"Quantum mechanics, consciousness, cognition, Socrates, and a welcome dose of philosophy are all part of *The UFO Paradox*. As entertaining as it is brilliantly written, Thompson—one of the most astute writers on this topic—takes us through some of the most famous UFO cases of the modern era, giving us a fresh look at the data and how these cases touch on the most important questions of our humanity. Highly recommended."

JIM SEMIVAN, CIA NATIONAL CLANDESTINE SERVICE (RETIRED)
AND RECIPIENT OF THE CIA CAREER INTELLIGENCE MEDAL

"*The UFO Paradox* stands as one of the finest dives into the deep end of strange phenomena and all that is out there. From his own life-changing near-death experience, through the labyrinthine history of the UFO field and its luminaries, presenting a transcendent metaphysical worldview far beyond simple nuts and bolts, Thompson conducts like a maestro, synthesizing a hall of mirrors with great wisdom and a unique perspective. Utterly captivating and impossible to put down."

JOSH BOONE, FILMMAKER AND DIRECTOR OF
THE FAULT IN OUR STARS

"This exceptionally well-written book reexamines major cases and topics to explore the paradoxical character of UFOs. Calling on a lifetime of research, Thompson offers acute observations and measured criticism of today's renewed efforts to understand the nature and meaning of a phenomenon that has influenced cultures for millennia. If someone wanted to read one book on this subject, it should be *The UFO Paradox*."

MICHAEL E. ZIMMERMAN, PROFESSOR EMERITUS AT
THE UNIVERSITY OF COLORADO BOULDER AND
TULANE UNIVERSITY

"This riveting read takes us on a mind-bending trek through the UFO enigma, bringing game-changing insights from Thompson's rich experience as a lifelong UFO researcher. Digging up startling new facts on classic UFO cases, he compels us to think and challenge everything we thought we knew about UFOs—and ourselves. *The UFO Paradox* is both enthralling and deeply moving."

HUSSEIN ALI AGRAMA, PH.D., ASSOCIATE PROFESSOR
IN THE DEPARTMENT OF ANTHROPOLOGY,
UNIVERSITY OF CHICAGO

"Here we have it all—ideas about UFO/UAPS, strange ships running around our airspace, while even stranger beings seem to threaten human existence—the whole of it matching Joseph Campbell's discoveries on the power of mythmaking. Yet Thompson himself, part of an investigative team that included Harvard psychiatrist John Mack, found cases that will both shock and surprise you. Truly, there is more to the UFO mysteries than anyone ever could have predicted."

P. M. H. ATWATER, L.H.D., AUTHOR OF
THE NEW CHILDREN AND NEAR-DEATH EXPERIENCES
AND THE FOREVER ANGELS

"In the style of historian and investigative journalist, Keith Thompson details how we have gotten to the immediate question facing humanity. How shall we respond, knowing we have been and are currently in an ongoing relationship with aliens?"

PETER FAUST, M.AC., UFO EXPERIENCER AND COAUTHOR OF
THE CONSTELLATION APPROACH

"Through Greek myth, paranormal psychology, and experiences of his own and others, Thompson explores the deeper implications of the UFO phenomenon for a reevaluation of physics and philosophy. I recommend this book as one of the finest examinations of this subject I have yet encountered."

KYLEA TAYLOR, LMFT, AUTHOR OF
THE ETHICS OF CARING

"Showcases investigative journalism applied to the UFO phenomenon at its very best. It goes beyond mere reporting and presents a balanced mix of speculation, fact, intuition, and knowledge."

SEBASTIANO DE FILIPPI, MUSICIAN, AUTHOR, AND
UFO RESEARCHER OF THE CASE OF ÁNGEL CRISTO ACOGLANIS,
MOUNT URITORCO, AND THE UNDERGROUND CITY OF ERKS

THE UFO PARADOX

The Celestial and Symbolic World of Unidentified Aerial Phenomena

A Sacred Planet Book

KEITH THOMPSON

Bear & Company
Rochester, Vermont

Bear & Company
One Park Street
Rochester, Vermont 05767
www.BearandCompanyBooks.com

Text stock is SFI certified

Bear & Company is a division of Inner Traditions International

Sacred Planet Books are curated by Richard Grossinger, Inner Traditions editorial board member and cofounder and former publisher of North Atlantic Books. The Sacred Planet collection, published under the umbrella of the Inner Traditions family of imprints, includes works on the themes of consciousness, cosmology, alternative medicine, dreams, climate, permaculture, alchemy, shamanic studies, oracles, astrology, crystals, hyperobjects, locutions, and subtle bodies.

Cataloging-in-Publication Data for this title is available from the Library of Congress

ISBN 978-1-59143-488-7 (print)
ISBN 978-1-59143-489-4 (ebook)

Printed and bound in the United States by Lake Book Manufacturing, LLC
The text stock is SFI certified. The Sustainable Forestry Initiative® program promotes sustainable forest management.

10 9 8 7 6 5 4 3 2 1

Text design and layout by Priscilla Harris Baker
This book was typeset in Garamond Premier Pro with Gill Sans, Magistral, and Nunito Sans used as display typefaces

To send correspondence to the author of this book, mail a first-class letter to the author c/o Inner Traditions • Bear & Company, One Park Street, Rochester, VT 05767, and we will forward the communication, or contact the author directly at **thompsonatlarge.com**.

Scan the QR code and save 25% at InnerTraditions.com. Browse over 2,000 titles on spirituality, the occult, ancient mysteries, new science, holistic health, and natural medicine.

This is for Dorado

—◄o►—

An irregularity in nature is only the sharp exacerbation, to the point of perceptible disclosure, of a property of things diffused throughout the universe, in a state which eludes our recognition of its presence.

TEILHARD DE CHARDIN

Contents

Acknowledgments

Of the many people who contributed to this book, four deserve special thanks as true consiglieri—counselors, camerados, keen-eyed lookouts for veiled connections and audacious possibilities. Richard Grossinger, for free-ranging discussions at the outset and for shepherding the project as a Sacred Planet Book title at Inner Traditions. Michael Murphy, for spirited encouragement from beginning to end, readiness to brainstorm wide-ranging ideas, and boundless enthusiasm for exploring what we've come to call "the big vision." Jeff Kripal, for resolute empathy with the book's premise and aims, willingness to field countless questions, and excellent tips on scholarship across and beyond many fields. Nick Bibeau, for generous readings of early drafts, keen insights in extensive conversations, and contagious devotion to the craft and calling of writing.

My deep gratitude to Larry D. and Tina E. Frascella for philanthropic support that allowed me to prioritize writing this book. Kudos to the dedicated team at Inner Traditions/Bear & Company for all they did to bring The UFO Paradox to fruition; particular thanks to Ehud and Mahar Sperling, Jon Graham, Erica Robinson, Lesley Allen, Aaron Davis, Maria Farias, Manzanita Carpenter, Ashley Kolesnik, and Mercedes Rojas. An especially deep bow to my editor, Albo Sudekum, for putting the lie to John Cheever's observation that "the relationship between a writer and his editor is that of a knife-to-a-throat." Albo's graceful surgery was limited to the page and her grasp of the book's intentions made our work together mighty.

Big thanks to Esalen Institute's Center for Theory and Research for invitations to participate in symposia exploring key themes of this book, and for CTR's long-term commitment to accelerating our evolution toward a more comprehensive worldview. At a time when many think tanks and universities steer clear of new ideas because they are controversial or challenge disciplinary silos, credit to Esalen for exploring the farther reaches of human potential and societal renewal.

I am grateful to my aviator father for so generously sharing his love of the open sky; and to my friends Milena Pritel, for countless hours of conversation on the ideas and images that ride these pages, and Cary Sparks, for arriving near the end with insight and presence that helped bring it all home.

Introduction

I was twelve when I first heard of UFOs. News media ranging from
our small-town paper to prime-time national TV were lit with
reports of strange sightings in the skies over the Ann Arbor region of
Michigan. Sheriff's deputies told of seeing disk-shaped objects flashing, starlike, red and green across the dark morning sky at fantastic
speed. The media frenzy coincided with my turn to give a current
events report in my northwest Ohio classroom. I chose this UFO
sighting that stirred debate throughout the United States for over a
week. It was irresistible.

News clippings in hand, I told my classmates about a bright glowing object seen bouncing across a hollow near a marsh and becoming
airborne before disappearing like a TV screen shutting off. J. Allen
Hynek, a U.S. Air Force consultant destined for legendary status in
UFO studies, had flown in to investigate. After talking to witnesses
and visiting several sighting hotspots, Hynek stepped up to the podium
at a televised news conference and discussed a range of sightings in the
area. He made passing reference to the glowing object near the marsh,
which he speculated *could* have been, *might* have been . . . "swamp gas."

Cue pandemonium.

Hynek was mortified to watch reporters leap from their seats

1

and sprint to call their news bureaus and report (inaccurately) that he had reduced *all* of the sightings to a combination of methane and smaller amounts of hydrogen sulfide, carbon dioxide, and trace phosphine that sometimes spontaneously combusts into bright colors near swamps, marshes, and bogs. The "swamp gas" explanation would take hold as a long-running joke in UFO circles, referring to the strained attempts of reflexive debunkers to explain away extraordinary sightings, regardless of evidence. "Weather balloon" is a close runner-up in the debunking tool chest.

During his next broadcast, CBS anchorman Walter Cronkite couldn't hide his incredulity at Hynek's seemingly ham-handed dismissal of all the credible multiwitness accounts. Michigan representative Gerald Ford demanded a congressional investigation. Interviews with bewildered Michiganders were the best part. "We may be rural, but that doesn't make us rubes," was the general tenor of their pushback.

I loved it, partly because I hailed from neighboring Ohio, but also because this was a classic case of the Expert arriving to set the Villagers straight, and the Villagers responding in kind. I made no effort to conceal my populist sympathies with the local yokels.

"So you believe in aliens from outer space?" a classmate asked, as giggles rolled through the room. I didn't have firm beliefs. "Well . . . that's not my . . . some people believe that," I said.

"What do *you* think they saw?" another student asked. "No idea," I said. This wasn't a punt; I *didn't* know what witnesses had seen, but swamp gas sure didn't fit the descriptions. Somebody loudly whispered "swamp gas" and made a convincing fart sound. More laughter, mine included.

The next comment came from Gloria Lowry, our teacher.

"I think Keith is saying it's important to keep an open mind and ask relevant questions."

Wow. She didn't rescue me. She *saw* me. The way a person recognizes and acknowledges not just the viewpoint of another but their very presence as a contribution. It was a kind of benediction.

Mrs. Lowry continued: "Fine job, Mr. Thompson. You've got the makings of a good reporter, or even a scientist. Maybe a detective. Follow clues where they lead."

◄◦►

When I started tracking this phenomenon through media reports, the extraterrestrial (ET) hypothesis was the predominant interpretation for the sightings not diagnosed as hallucination, hoax, or misidentified mundane phenomena (planets, the moon, satellites, airplanes, and the like). "Have We Visitors From Outer Space?" was the question asked in 1952 by *LIFE* magazine, then America's most widely read newsweekly. The phrases *unidentified flying objects* and *UFOs* were chosen by early UFO researcher Edward Ruppelt to convey neutrality about their nature, origin, and possible intent. Even so, it wasn't long before the phrases became synonymous with "visitors from other planets" in the popular imagination. This assumption of equivalence continues to this day. "So you believe in UFOs" is almost always heard as "So you believe in extraterrestrial life," which translates to "Do you believe UFOs are visiting ET spaceships?" Then UFO proponents and debunkers take their familiar stands on the kabuki dance floor.

Jeffrey J. Kripal, author and professor of philosophy and religious thought at Rice University, often describes three levels through which the study of UFOs seems to pass. "One assumes at the first level that the UFO is some kind of physical technology, some type of extraterrestrial spacecraft whose 'tires' (or landing gear) one could presumably 'kick.'" These are the watchwords of level one: "We'll figure it out. Just wait. Keep waiting. You'll see."[2] Movies like *The Day the Earth Stood Still* and *Close Encounters of the Third Kind* instruct us to expect this. My thinking began changing as new data came into view, especially historical findings indicating that similar objects have been seen from time immemorial, with their occupants performing actions similar to the "abductions" of the contemporary UFO era. Beliefs at the heart of the saucer reports have been a mainstay of history, organized around the theme of visitation by aerially inclined beings. The broad literatures of religion and mythology feature alien-like entities with physical and psychological descriptions that place them in the same category as events in the saucer era.

Kripal describes how this sudden turn in the evidence places the phenomenon in a new and broader context, level two. Here one begins to suspect that the entire modern UFO phenomenon could be "some kind of living and tricky folklore, a mythological system taking physical shape right before our eyes, much as it has in any previous era." Because now there's not only talk of extraterrestrials and aliens, there's "also talk of angels, demons, fairies, jinn, and spectral monsters. This isn't an invasion. This is a haunting."[3]

The machinery of binary thinking dutifully replaces one monolithic story with a new one, then declares: "Closure!" Except, the phenomenal stream of evidence keeps flowing. Just as the second level of interpretation begins to gel, still more anomalies show up to expand the boundaries, and blur them as well. New kinds of physical stuff, like alleged implants in the bodies of witnesses. Saucer crash-retrieval rumors with ultra-top-secret status. Paranormal features including telepathy, precognition, clairvoyance, and teleportation into otherworldly craft. Debates about alleged leaked military documents from decades ago. Reports of human-alien hybrids borne of genetic engineering conducted in stealth by sinister aliens. *They walk among us . . .*

The mixture of data gets so wild and incongruous, it's hard to stick with a literal level one or level two reading, though partisans of various camps do dig in. "It all gets to be a bit too much," Kripal confesses. "And the mythical or symbolic phenomena just get weirder and weirder. Actually, nothing really gets explained."[4] At some point, the curtain opens to act three:

One begins to suspect that what we call "science" and "religion" are just two cultural frameworks that we have invented for our own all-too-human purposes, and that neither of them really work very well in this ufological realm. Whatever is going on with the UFO ain't science and ain't religion. What it is one no longer quite knows. All one knows is what it ain't. Well, it ain't simply objective. And it ain't simply subjective.[5]

At work on this book when I came across Kripal's model, I was struck by how closely our speculations tracked. From our differing vantage points, we had come to essentially the same conclusion: the methods of traditional science and conventional religions, and their specific ways of imagining the real, are unprepared for and ill-suited to a phenomenon that is neither simply objective nor merely subjective but is somehow both at the same time.

I'm familiar enough with the UFO field to understand this is not the kind of news that many "established" researchers find encouraging, especially those awaiting imminent resolution. When Kripal says, almost in passing, "What it is one no longer quite knows,"[6] I get even more enthusiastic to stay on this beat. But not because I'm expecting some final Disclosure of the kind that has kept ufology reciting for nearly eight decades, "Any day now, the lid on the government cover-up is gonna blow sky-high," and magically weaving every loose thread into a comprehensive and unambiguous tapestry that leaves prevailing paradigms intact. No, what keeps me at it is something else, deeper than a common panacea yet also something immediate and palpable. It has a lot to do with *grokking*.

In his novel *Stranger in a Strange Land*,[7] the novelist Robert Heinlein introduced a four-letter verb, *grok*, as in: "I grok in fullness." There's no exact definition, but the essence of "to grok" something, anything, no-thing, is to understand intuitively, to empathize or communicate sympathetically with deep appreciation. When I encountered Heinlein's novel, this strange syllable conjured a prolific sense of freedom and potentiality in the underlying nature of things. My own experiences of the extraordinary over many years have shaped my work as a writer around the idea that the limits of human growth aren't fixed, that we have unrealized capacities for exceptional functioning—and that our understanding of reality is far from complete.

As a journalist, my practice has been to write about subjects other than myself. With age comes a natural desire to put more of one's perspective on the table. Though this isn't a personal memoir, it seems fitting to relate a couple of experiences that decisively changed my life and even my sense of personhood. Doing so may help you *grok* how I came to depart from many widely held assumptions about the happenings that fly under the banner of the acronym UFO.

In my early teens, I used to climb onto the roof of our family house, unbeknown to my parents and unseen by anybody on the sidewalks and streets below. One time, lying on my back gazing into deep sky with no purpose or desire, I suddenly experienced being everywhere and nowhere at once. I was inexplicably surrounded by brilliance that blazed through me and seemed to lift me beyond space and time. At the time, religious ideas weren't prominent in my life—we were a nominally religious family; it was good for good people to be seen at church. Yet somehow I knew this power originated from a source that lies beyond each of us. It also permeates everything that is. Call it God, Spirit, Tao, Soul, Buddha Mind, Divinity, True Nature, Ground of Being, Center Court, Destiny, Patterning Intelligence, Design Mind, Collective Unconscious—or simply "life's longing for itself," in the words of Kahlil Gibran.

I was fourteen at the time. The experience left me convinced there's inherent direction and purpose in life, which had to include my own. No one knew of my time on the roof or of the vistas it opened and my sense of the possibilities that seemed implicit in every instant and iota of existence. The experience became a tacit backdrop for the flow of everyday life. I later encountered subtler versions of this presence in quiet cathedrals and chapels, in the company of ancient redwoods, in the surround of stunning sunsets and squawking gulls, in the stillness of meditation retreats, always with a sense of "being home."

Over time, I lived with a sense of split existence—part of me capable of functioning in a divided world composed of apparently separate selves, another part aware of a deeper, foundational reality that John Friedlander, an author who reframes Jane Roberts's Seth teachings, would describe in this way:

> Our lives are nested in things that are unimaginably big. No matter who you are or when you are, the whole universe wraps itself around you and re-wraps itself around you each moment. The whole universe changes its address to you each moment. No matter how small a change you make, the whole universe—and all universes— instantly change in a way that wraps around you. Not just you of course; you as part of the whole universe change and wrap yourself around every other subjectivity in the universe.[8]

Fifteen years after my rooftop revelation, the idea of separation took a second hit while bodysurfing in wild waters off the coast of Hawaii. Riptides took me under and the certainty of my death sunk in. The next thought came with identical certainty: "Wow. Dead isn't dead."

This was a time when the near-death experience wasn't yet widely known. Three years earlier, Raymond Moody had published a groundbreaking book, *Life After Life,* but I knew nothing of the phenomenon the book would bring to awareness. What's more, none of my friends could relate to the change my consciousness underwent. How unrelatable this experience was, and the confused or distressed reactions when I discussed it, led me to create a personal rule that I didn't bring it up.

The experience was a *totality-grok* beyond anything imaginable. A vast sense of presence landed like a cosmic file that has been "unzipping" ever since. In college, I had discovered a short treatise by Alan Watts, *The Book: On the Taboo Against Knowing Who You Are.* This led me to question the idea that we are separate beings unconnected to the rest of the universe. My near-death experience proved Watts had been spot on: the sense of being a perpetually struggling separate self is simply a tale told, believed, and lived as if true. Consciousness is everywhere and endless. We can't be separate from it even for an instant, though we can *seem* to be. And in so being, each of us is also a way in which Cosmos at Large takes up residence as an individual life-situation with a unique and unrepeatable point of view. All fear of death left that day, and it has never returned.

While UFO experiences and near-death experiences are not identical, and there are variances within both categories, what's common to a broad range of supernormal experiences is the emphatic sense of getting a spiritual subpoena. Once served, you can't hand the papers back. You're summoned to respond. (Exactly how?) You're expected to show up. (Where and when?) Details vary. In the face of brutal societal skepticism, count on plenty of alone time.

I quickly realized efforts to have this conversation scared people. Sometimes when my death experience came up, people would ask, "Did your life pass before your eyes?" When I answered yes, thinking this might just be the Breakthrough Conversation, it invariably became clear "life passing before your eyes" was meant only as a figure of speech. I got good at straddling worlds generally left unconnected, and I came to have a sixth sense for people who were *in on* this open secret about the way things really are. These words hit the mark:

> *Tell a wise person or else keep silent, for the mass man will mock it right away.*
>
> THE HOLY LONGING,
> JOHANN WOLFGANG VON GOETHE

So it doesn't surprise me that I came to feel at home with the stories of UFO people, even without a specific "UFO experience" to call my own. There's no single format for *cosmos interruptus*, the experience of having your core sense of reality disrupted and reconfigured. A common or shared element across many varieties is the ringing of a bell that can't be unrung. For me, the rooftop clarity and the Hawaii calamity reset the game board. When the going gets strange, I tend to get jazzed. My pizzazz levels rise. At some point, most nonfiction writers encounter a cover story that doesn't add up, some version of official reality that stirs doubts and raises questions. Identifying solely as an isolated, independent self is a hallucination that doesn't withstand scrutiny. But it's also a useful premise, as the song goes, for "living in a material world." Even now, the palpable nonsense of the Michigan swamp gas explanation decades ago is as vivid as the woodpecker's staccato tap-tapping in the tree right outside my window.

"What it is one no longer quite knows" is simply a given with the UFO phenomenon, but also—please notice—with existence at large. Open inquiry into the unknown is the flag to keep hoisting, the marker to keep planting. It is the creed I keep signing on to. For many, the idea of any "creed" is problematic. The Latin term *credo* is often translated as "I believe," but its fuller meaning is "I give my heart to."

To new students of the phenomenon, the culmination of Kripal's third level of discovery might suggest a discouraging dead end, a halt to further exploration. This need not be the case if open-minded curiosity has brought you to these pages. What can end is belief in the thought that any singular approach is likely to "solve" something like this— something that routinely and robustly transgresses the boundaries between the subjective world of mind and the objective world of matter "out there." What is this hovering, liminal "third zone" that ordinary religion and conventional science do so little to illuminate? By way of a clue, the French sociologist Bertrand Méheust throws out a highway flare:

One is not able to envisage [the UFO phenomenon] independently from our consciousness; what is more: there can be no question of eliminating that part which the human spirit adds to it; it is, on the contrary, an essential component of the phenomenon.[9]

Relinquishing the idea that UFOs can even be conceived of outside or independent of observers is not the same as locating the phenomenon solely within the human psyche, conceived of as some private interior space. In ways that push the boundaries of physicalist models of science, the phenomenon suggests a cocreative context that joins observer and observed: *us* encountering *it,* and vice versa.* "There is something about the human race with which they interact, and we do not yet know what it is," writes longstanding researcher Jacques Vallée. "But their effects, instead of being just physical, are also felt in our beliefs. They influence what we call our spiritual life."[10]

I will explore the hypothesis that the ultimate map of nature might well be the map of the collective psyche as revealed by depth psychology, a theme Carl Jung turned to in his final works, as he came to terms with consciousness as fundamental and delved into the extraordinary idea that the greater part of the soul exists outside the body. This kind of thinking changes the whole field of play. After decades of tracking this extraordinary phenomenon, sitting down to write this book has felt like beginning with the material all over again, from proverbial scratch.

"Follow the evidence where it leads." *Grokked in fullness.*

In numerous traditions, calls of many kinds often precede rites of passage and spiritual emergencies, breakdowns and breakthroughs, turning points and turnarounds, leave-takings and standstills. Calls may take the form of visions, voices, illuminations, and premonitions; sometimes they are jarring whups upside the head when subtler measures fail. The purpose of calls is to rouse individuals and communities from their

---

*The wide-ranging and observant scholar Sean Esbjörn-Hargens explores a version of this in his mutual enactment hypothesis, which is based on the idea that aspects of the UFO and aspects of our own nature bring one another into manifestation.[11]

everyday grind to a greater kind of awareness, into a broader frame of mind and heart, into communion with something larger than what they've been settling for.

This book is an invitation to imagine the UFO phenomenon as a call from the cosmos.

"Whatever or whoever is addressing us is a power like wind or fusion or faith," declares author and teacher Gregg Levoy. "We can't see the force, but we can see what it does."[12] He continues:

> Primarily this force announces the need for change, the response for which it calls is an awakening of some kind. A call is only a monologue. A return call, a response, creates a dialogue. Our own unfolding requires that we be in constant dialogue with whatever is calling us. The call and one's response to it are also a central metaphor for the spiritual life, and in Latin there is even a correspondence between the words for *listening* and *following*.[13]

"We have here a golden opportunity of seeing how a legend is formed,"[14] Jung wrote in the early flying saucer era. I heartily agree. For nearly eight decades, the curiously compelling acronym "UFO"—*as an idea at work in the world soul*—has shaped human belief and imagination in complicated ways. A robust contemporary prodigy has emerged in our midst, enticing us with the vivid ambivalence of its images, systematically resisting definitive explanation, fostering rancorous debate, comprising a provocative enigma of global proportions.

This is a chronicle of the wanderings of that prodigy.

1

Wording, Method, Sources

U.S. Air Force captain Edward J. Ruppelt gets credit for coining the terms *unidentified flying objects* and *UFO* back in the 1950s. Neutral language was needed "because so many of them didn't look like saucers,"[1] writes *New York Times* journalist Ralph Blumenthal. The public had learned about "flying saucers" from media reports of Kenneth Arnold's 1947 sighting of "nine saucer-like objects flying at 'incredible speed' at 10,000 feet altitude"[2] near Mount Rainier in Washington State.

Popular opinion holds that Arnold had described the objects in the *shape* of saucers. Not so. He said the objects moved *like* a saucer skipping across water. Jumbling the metaphoric intent of the description, reporters labeled the objects *flying saucers*. Arnold would complain that this phrase arose from "a great deal of misunderstanding," but the public had only the news story to go on, not having seen Arnold's sketches that depicted the objects with a shape Arnold described as "like stingrays."

Confusion thus got baked in to what Jung called "a modern myth of things seen in the sky." Although *unidentified flying objects* and *UFO* were intended to be relatively impartial terms, in fact they introduced new ambiguities and mixed meanings. Scholar

Sebastiano De Filippi, a world-renowned orchestra conductor and author of *The City of the Blue Flame*, surveys the opportunity for confusion:

> Contemporary science, through semiotics, teaches us that the word is a sign which carries meaning; often several meanings, but always at least one, sometimes cryptic or even prophetic (as they say in Latin: *nomen, omen*).

So, from a "word" perspective, let us consider what our object of study here is supposed to be; that is, ufology, UFOs or—at least as a starting point—the term "UFO," the popular definition in the form of an acronym created in 1952 by Edward Ruppelt. Let's see:

1. *U* stands for "Unidentified." But in which sense? And unidentified by what or by whom? Under which circumstances? Completely, necessarily and perpetually unidentified? Are not the "identified" and "unidentified" eminently dynamic categories? Yet such adjectives point toward a static definition, which seems to condemn us to cognitive failure.

2. *F* stands for "Flying." But are we talking about flights in the strict sense of the term, as if we were dealing with birds and airplanes? Or is it that UFOs rather appear and disappear in the skies? Maybe they project an image on them? (And what if they project that image into or from our inner self?) In any case, are they visible only in the heavens? We know that this is not the case: they have been sighted in the seas and on land, and leaving and entering both.

3. *O* stands for "Object." But are they actually objects? Some of them appear to be, but are they really? And even if some of them are material objects, are they all? The evidence would seem to indicate otherwise.

"Unidentified Flying Objects," we were saying. Do we possess a solid definition of UFOs in this acronym or do we just have a synthetic—useful, but limited—neologism at hand?[3]

What we have with *UFO* is a made-up word pressed into service because "so many of them didn't look like flying saucers." Even so, many of them *do* look like saucers. Others resemble lit-up triangles, cigars, eggs, footballs, spherical orbs, diamonds, ice-cream cones topped with red, and even aerial recreational vehicles. In 2021, a Pentagon task force convened. Top of the action list: come up with a new, improved three-letter abbreviation. Thus, after decades of being denied official existence, the dutiful UFO got an award (of sorts) for meritorious service: an acronym upgrade to UAP, short for "unidentified aerial phenomena."

I will generally use *UFO* and *unidentified flying objects* interchangeably, acknowledging De Filippi's sense of the quandaries and begged questions, yet mindful that both terms have become integral to how we think and speak about these extraordinary events. As for the terms *UAP* and *unidentified aerial phenomena:* though the Pentagon claims to favor transparency, these colorless neologisms almost seem designed to add layers of opaqueness. I register stylistic dissent.

Since this is a book about the UFO phenomenon, let's reflect a bit on the word *phenomenon.* A recent caller to a talk radio program commented that she was just beginning to realize how compelling the UFO subject is. Then she added, "It's just too bad there's not a better word than phenomenon. It's really not very compelling." Well, in one sense she's quite right. To take in the particulars of even a single UFO encounter is generally to be struck by vivid imagery and high levels of compelling strangeness. By comparison, phenomenon is a tame placeholder. Though as a writer I'm partial to *showing* when and how, naming names, making the case, *describing*—sometimes less really is best. *Phenomenon* is simply the Greek word for *appearance.*

In the context of this book, phenomenon refers to an object of experience, specifically awareness of something that appears and is experienced by an observer, *whatever* the object might be. *Phenomenology* is the practice of investigating and describing "that which appears" as faithfully as possible and as free as possible from conceptual presuppositions. This involves a deliberate drawing back from assumptions about what is and is not possible. A catchphrase for this approach is *zu den Sachen selbst* ("to the things themselves"), in the phrase of the German philosopher Edmund Husserl.

"I don't know exactly what happened to me that day," says Calvin Parker of Pascagoula, Mississippi, about the legendary double-abduction case. "I do know *something happened.*" Parker experienced what Harvard psychiatrist John Mack called "ontological shock," the sense of profound disorientation that goes with confronting something that radically alters one's sense of what is real. "The uncanny is that class of the terrifying which leads back to something long known to us,"[4] Freud wrote over a century ago. The theologian Rudolf Otto was partial to a classic Latin phrase: *mysterium tremendum et fascinans;* that is, a mystery (*mysterium*) as both terrifying (*tremendum*) and completely fascinating (*fascinans*).

"Phenomenon" fills the bill on all accounts, and it rolls off the tongue more smoothly than Otto's learned Latin soundbite. Resisting the natural impulse to reach for interpretation clears space for what the poet John Keats called "negative capability—that is when man is capable of being in uncertainties, mysteries, doubts, without any irritable reaching after fact and reason." Negative capability requires neither belief nor disbelief. Willingness to temporarily *suspend disbelief* is a key ingredient, as in giving over to a novel, movie, or theatrical production.

The day I presented the Hynek story to my class was the day I intuitively got it: I was an *empiricist*. The word and its liberating meanings wouldn't enter my consciousness until college, where I encountered the thinking of philosopher-psychologist William James, who believed that all of reality is made up of experience. Some experiences feel like mind while other experiences feel like matter. The difference is in feeling, not in kind. Anything that could be observed, including experience, could be looked into. The radical idea that all kinds of happenings . . . happen.

The term *empirical* derives from the ancient Greek word *empeiria* (roughly, "in test"), which translates to the Latin *experientia,* from which the words *experience* and *experiment* emerge. Empirical evidence for any proposition draws from direct observation, experience, or experiment, as opposed to being constrained by prior assumptions from theory, faith, or simple prejudice. A familiar example of the latter:

> The witnesses *didn't* see what they say they saw, in fact they *couldn't* have seen that, because what they describe *just isn't possible.*

Statements like this issue from pseudo skeptics who assert with matter-of-fact certainty that all UFO phenomena can be explained as hoaxes, hallucinations, or misidentifications of ordinary events; no other option. They then generally go through the motions of arriving at the conclusion they started with, sometimes citing "established laws of nature." These usually turn out to be subtle articles of faith confirming a favored paradigm of reality, a particular explanatory framework that they take to be *reality itself,* case closed. Ironically, many do all this in the name of empiricism, as if restoring a sense of normalcy by reciting nostrums in the name of "common sense" is critical thinking.

What it's *not*, is science. It's closer to crowd control, typically undertaken as damage prevention for a struggling worldview. Knee-jerk debunking is much like religious dogmatism, as Galileo found out when he kept seeing things through his telescope that the Vatican insisted couldn't be there. The Michigan witnesses didn't have categories for what they'd seen, but this didn't cancel that they'd witnessed something extraordinary. "Strange lights" and "aerial objects moving quickly through the air" are *observations*. Both "swamp gas" and "space aliens" are *interpretations*. This distinction locked in for me early on.

Empiricism 101: Take experiences as presented. Temporarily set aside questions of their potential truth, value, or ontology. Those issues have their place, later. Job one: Follow clues where they lead, and if this means territories not currently mapped by agents of official culture, be ready for adventure. For a long time, a prevailing account of reality might seem adequate (the sun was believed to orbit the earth), but then anomalies start gathering (hold up, the earth clearly orbits the sun and always did). Eventually, new maps of reality are drawn up showing the actual sun-Earth relationship. Learned men of the academy once reflexively debunked provincial reports of rocks falling from the heavens. (Oh, wait. *Meteors.* Never mind.)

Mrs. Lowry, my gradeschool teacher, was right. What kind of scientists, detectives, or reporters waive observations out of bounds simply because they don't fit preconceptions? Lousy ones. "We must assume our existence as broadly as we can," the poet Rilke said. To take in all that humans experience, the perplexing and most enigmatic, *even the unheard of and the seemingly impossible*, without reflexively explaining it away, "is at bottom the only courage that is demanded of us."[1]

Frequently I get asked how my views have changed from spending decades on the UFO beat. For one thing, I've come to appreciate the tension between phenomenon, which implies something singular, and phenomena as plural. Does "UFO" point to one overarching phenomenon with many different facets or to a multiplicity of phenomena for which a singular label is at best a convenience (and possibly a misleading one)? This question is inevitable when comparing modern events within the UFO frame of reference and events described in different frames of reference: mythology, primitive magic, occultism, and the fairy-faith. One of the extraordinary opportunities of modern people is the capacity to step outside one's contemporary conceptual frameworks and take a *comparative* approach toward phenomena of other cultures and eras.

For instance, the experience known as "abduction," a staple of the contemporary UFO literature, has striking parallels in these other, older literatures. Is this essentially the same experience viewed through different cultural filters, or are the likenesses largely coincidental to numerous different *kinds* of events? In 1926, Albert Einstein offered these cautionary words: "It is the theory which decides what we can observe." In other words, expectancy has ways of shaping what's perceived, especially when observers aren't even aware of the subtle ways they may be predisposed to interpret a witness report.

Many proponents of the uniqueness of UFO-related abductions insist these modern events are unprecedented; that is, they have no bona fide precursors. But it is no less obvious to other researchers that modern abduction narratives "are consistent with perplexing accounts that have come to us from earlier times, from the oldest records we have,"[5] Jacques Vallée emphasizes. Time and again we find that different witnesses and researchers *punctuate* the UFO phenomenon in very different ways, according to different conceptual distinctions they bring to UFO conversations and debates. It can sometimes seem that the UFO maps of different observers are describing fundamentally different territories!

Another way my perspective has changed since giving a report in elementary school: Back then I had no inkling of the pervasive paranormal dimensions of the UFO phenomenon, especially relative to meaningful coincidences of events separated by time and/or space, happenings that suggest secret symmetries between consciousness and matter. As a novice to the subject, I knew of reports that UFOs affect radar, cause burns, and leave traces in the ground, but I hadn't yet encountered reports of UFOs reported to "pass through walls, appear and disappear like ghosts, defy gravity, assume variable and symbolic shapes, and strike deep chords of psychic, mystic, or prophetic sentiment,"[6] in the words of philosopher Michael Grosso. My perspective has evolved with exposure to new evidence and new types of evidence.

Nor did I have the slightest clue early on about the extent to which so many UFO investigators, generally enthusiasts of the ET hypothesis, would routinely downplay and minimize the phenomenon's paranormal features through a subtle process of "smoothing" wrinkles that "didn't fit." While I could easily comprehend the sort of ingrained bias that would motivate debunkers to dismiss all UFOs as misidentifications or outright hoaxes, it took me a while to assimilate the ease with which leading ET proponents would undervalue the prevalence of out-of-body experiences, precognitions, lucid dreams, time lapses, and similar details that don't lend credence to the idea that UFOs are nothing more than the machines of advanced spacefaring visitors. "They are terrified of these phenomena," a scholar and friend said as we discussed how the mainstream of UFO research so casually disregards evidence that UFOs act like a doorway between everyday reality and a different level altogether.

At some point an act of will is required not to recognize that this mixture of objective physicality and subjective elusiveness is endemic to the phenomenon. Yet entrenched belief is a powerful force. When Vatican officials told Galileo to stop saying the earth orbits the sun and not vice versa, Galileo responded that they didn't have to take his word for it—they could have a look for themselves through his telescope. Declining his invitation on both counts, the officials promptly placed Galileo under house arrest for the rest of his life.

That seems an extreme sentence, but it was a mere slap on the wrist compared to getting hung upside down and naked in the public square and burned at the stake, the fate of sixteenth-century Italian philosopher Giordano Bruno for the heinous crime of proposing that the stars were distant suns surrounded by their own planets and raising the possibility that these planets might foster life of their own, a cosmological position known as cosmic pluralism. He also insisted that the universe is infinite and could have no "center."

Viewed as a call from the cosmos, the UFO phenomenon echoes familiar and timeless rites of passage that accompany changes of identity, status, state, and social position in cultures throughout history. Joseph Campbell's hero's journey paradigm features three broad initiatory stages that traditionally apply to individuals but also characterize societal and cultural transitions.

Separation: Detachment of individuals and groups from an existing status or set of cultural conditions; a departure from the prior state. For example, the young males in an Indigenous culture who are taken away abruptly at night by the community's adult males, who are wearing masks and ceremonial garb, and brought into a male initiatory ceremony through which the young ones leave their identity as "boy" at the door of the initiation lodge. The mothers express persuasive shock at the intrusion, even though they are in on the plan to spirit the boys away to receive essential teachings.

Transition: Entering a state of living in the margins, betwixt and between, not quite here and not quite there. The transition phase, sometimes described as a profound sense of marginality (also called liminality, from the Latin *limen*, meaning "threshold"), is characterized by a sense of flux and ambiguity about who one really is. The young male is in existential transition: no longer boy but not yet become, through specific teaching and ritual practice, an adult male member of the community. This is a time of tests, challenges, and ordeals of many types, generally revolving around transmission of the origin myths of their people, including how the first ancestors arrived (almost always from the sky).

Assimilation: Moving out of the indeterminate, transitional margins into a new state of knowing and being. Sometimes described as the stage of *aggregation or coming together*, this is a time of consummation or culmination of the entire rite. Now, the young male has earned the right to be called, and to consider himself, a man. Far from being limited to gender initiation, such ritual passages traditionally include birth and death, puberty, marriage and separation, educational and artistic achievements, athletic ordeals, and religious confirmation, including induction into mystery schools and esoteric orders.

Campbell wrote and spoke at length about the many forms the separation phase might take. In his book on the universal myth of the hero's journey, *The Hero with a Thousand Faces*, Campbell writes about the universal motif he found in world myth: "A hero ventures forth from the world of common day into a region of supernatural wonder."[7]

While some UFO cases illustrate a particular initiatory stage especially well, all three phases can be seen in each UFO encounter, just as in events of a less overtly symbolic kind in everyday life. We're often simultaneously in various phases of implicit initiation in different domains of our lives: making a chancy work transition that requires leaving a secure position; encountering flux and uncertainty in an ongoing relationship; acting on an inner call to move beyond an existing political affiliation or spiritual orientation; to name only a few possibilities.*

---

*After retiring from teaching at Sarah Lawrence College, Campbell embarked on a new career giving lectures and leading workshops, and I attended several he taught at Esalen Institute. One day during a break, I asked Campbell whether he had considered UFO encounters as illustrating his hero's journey sequence. He said he hadn't and invited me to bring up the subject at the next class session. Listening raptly and engaging the topic with characteristic insight and wit, Campbell instantly recognized numerous parallels between the UFO world and world mythology and folklore. He was struck by how UFO details like mental time-lapse, paralysis, and bodily scars resemble the patterns of worldwide shamanism and historic encounters with ghosts, fairies, witches, and demons. Nighttime bedroom invasions by strange beings reminded him of

◄◦►

Concerning my sources: Direct and paraphrased quotes of key individuals from direct conversations and interviews are drawn from contemporaneous notes and journals compiled over a long period. My broad approach draws from a variety of sources, beginning with the primary UFO literature and extending to resources from other fields that have come to seem pertinent, based on the maxim "Follow the evidence wherever it leads." I have spoken at length with countless firsthand UFO witnesses ("experiencers" is now the widely used term), as well as with many individuals who, like me, have never seen anything in the sky that didn't seem to belong there but have had life-changing encounters with *numinous* phenomena of different types. This seldom-used word, derived from the Latin *numen*, meaning "divine spirit, presiding divinity," is closely related to the English words *mysterious, holy, sacred, otherworldly, transcendent*—or, in street usage: *"Wow, there's more going on here than they talked about in Sunday school or science class."*

A farmer in Iowa hears a voice in a cornfield: "If you build it, he will come." It isn't so much that Ray Kinsella (Kevin Costner) "believes" the voice; he finds a way to momentarily suspend *disbelief,* allowing himself to ask "What if?" This doesn't guarantee that a magical baseball field will appear in *Field of Dreams.* Kinsella builds it, his neighbors think him a loon, and a young baseball player he discovers to be his father appears from beyond space and time. And by the end of the movie, the further prediction of Terence Mann (James Earl Jones) is borne out:

(Continued) incubus visitation (a demon in male form in folklore that seeks to have sexual intercourse with sleeping women). He was amused but not surprised to hear that many UFO proponents dismiss such comparisons as mere lore. "Ah yes, the legends of *my culture* are authentic compared to the mere fables of all others!" he said with delight. "This sort of literalism makes it easy to miss the common recurring mythic structure: a separation from the ordinary world, a penetration to some source of extraordinary power, followed by a life-changing return."

"People will come to Iowa for reasons *they can't even fathom*. They'll turn up the driveway *not even sure why they're doing it*. . . . People most definitely *will come*." (As the movie credits begin to roll, the line of cars extends for miles. Bring Kleenex.)

"Something is seen, but one doesn't know what."[8] That was the visionary psychologist Carl Jung's take on "the phenomenon" back in 1959. This book is a longer riff on the same point. Where better to get started than with what a pilot named Kenneth Arnold *really* saw during his famous flight in 1947 and why it matters?

2

What Kenneth Arnold
Really Saw

Everything starts with Ken Arnold.

If you know nothing else about the history of the UFO phenomenon, you might recognize his name from pop culture. The experienced private pilot who, in 1947, witnessed things moving through the sky in formation, unlike anything he'd ever observed, at speeds he couldn't explain. Who then told the world what he saw and promptly got misquoted by the press.

The phrase *flying saucer* will forever be linked with Ken Arnold. His sighting is at the heart of the "creation myth" of the modern UFO phenomenon. A creation myth is a narrative of how the world begins and how people come to inhabit it. Though in popular parlance the term *myth* often refers to false or fanciful happenings, myths also give expression to what is apprehended or experienced as fundamental reality. Myth often conveys a sense of "more real than real" that leaves language in the dust. As they describe and account for the ordering of the cosmos, creation myths speak to questions of defining importance to the society or group that shares them. They illuminate a worldview and establish a framework for the self-understanding of the culture and individual in a universal context.

Speaking mythically, the early happenings of the UFO phenomenon were *founding* events, precursors of what was to come, reflecting psychic boundaries more fundamental than temporal beginnings indicated by calendars and clocks. The events of myth, writes the Hungarian scholar Karl Kerenyi, "form the ground or foundation of the world, since everything rests on them." They are the archetypal firmament "to which everything individual and particular goes back and out of which it is made, while they remain ageless, inexhaustible, invincible in timeless primordiality, in a past that proves imperishable because of its eternally repeated rebirths."[1]

Ken Arnold's famous experience of June 24, 1947, was just such an Eternal Beginning. As the Associated Press story of Arnold's sighting of "nine bright saucer-like objects flying at 'incredible speed' at 10,000 feet"[2] percolated through the collective psyche, primordial times drew close. The significance of a creation myth's setting is almost always expressed with a dramatic sense of *illo tempore*, "At that time . . ." It is understood that the Beginning at hand is no ordinary start, but the veritable Origin of all that matters. Taken out of the idiom of contemporary journalism and framed as a creation myth with religious undertones, this is how Arnold's sighting might sound:

In the beginning were Nine Bright Objects, and Kenneth of Boise looked upon them, and he saw that their speed was truly great, and he was amazed, for he knew not what they were nor how to name them. Soon he spoke forth what he saw, and through the inexhaustible darkness there echoed Flying Saucer. In this moment, the world was born.

Kind of stilted, but at least free of "thereupon" or "thereafter." As a summary of the UFO phenomenon's debut, let's call it a passable first draft. Still, it leaves a lot out and also gets some key points wrong, and the significance of this is extraordinary. The media widely reported, for instance, that Arnold claimed he saw "nine flying saucers." But he *didn't* say that. Arnold described seeing nine remarkable objects moving *like* a saucer. A local reporter named Bill Bequette is credited with turning Arnold's passing description of how the objects *moved*—undulating across the sky, as if skipping over water, *like* a pie plate or a saucer—into a description of their supposed *shape*. Arnold actually said the objects looked like stingrays. Even so, within a matter of hours Arnold's story— trumpeted by the evocative phrase *flying saucer*, a creation of anonymous headline writers—became front-page news throughout the nation.

Simply put, reporters on the scene mangled Arnold's account. Just as the curtain was coming up on the modern UFO saga, erroneous assumptions about the nature of these strange aerial events got cemented in popular storylines, thus giving the status of authentic precedent to events that were wrongly reported in key respects.

The obvious solution: simply correct the factual record, the way honest historians would. Not as simple as it sounds. Substantive revisions to longstanding creation myths are rare. Updates should be made lightly if at all, most mythologists will say. Bumper sticker version: "Don't mess with myth!" But facts *matter*, and those first media reports got basic details *wrong*. Myths are timeless but fortunately also resilient and self-renewing. Even perennial myths sprout new branches, cut unexpected tributaries; that's how they stay *perennial*. As mythographer Joseph Campbell celebrates: "The latest incarnation of Oedipus, the continued romance of Beauty and the Beast, stand this afternoon on the corner of Forty-Second Street and Fifth Avenue, waiting for the light to change."[3]

Replenishment of a living myth often comes through disclosure of enfolded original details, hidden time-release images emerging— *storying*—as "late-breaking news." This is the case with Ken Arnold's story, thanks to decisive facts newly provided by Kim Arnold, daughter of the witness and keeper of the family archives. Fidelity to accuracy means telling new events as they become known, which will take us back to what was misreported in Arnold's original telling. Bear this in mind: in uncanny ways, the media's original misreporting would shape how the phenomenon was seen and described by future witnesses.

What then did Ken Arnold see through the portal of his airplane windshield that day? The answer will shed light on certain epiphanies Arnold chose to keep to himself and close family members during his lifetime.

In the early summer of 1947, this Associated Press dispatch came across the wire in newsrooms throughout the United States:

PENDLETON, Ore., June 25 (AP)—Nine bright saucer-like objects flying at "incredible speed" at 10,000 feet altitude were reported here today by Kenneth Arnold, Boise, Idaho, pilot who said he could not hazard a guess as to what they were.

Arnold, a United States Forest Service employee engaged in searching for a missing plane, said he sighted the mysterious objects yesterday at 3 P.M. The objects were flying between Mount Rainier and Mount Adams, in Washington state, he said, and appeared to wave in and out of formation. Arnold said he clocked and estimated their speed at 1,200 miles an hour.

Inquiries at Yakima last night brought only blank stares, he said, but he added he talked today with an unidentified man from Utah, south of here, who said he had seen similar objects over the mountains near Ukiah yesterday.

"It seems impossible," Arnold said, "but there it is."[4]

Arnold first told several people he met at the Yakima, Washington, airport of his sighting. During Arnold's subsequent flight to Pendleton, Oregon, later the same day, a member of his Yakima audience phoned details of Arnold's account to the Pendleton airport, where several skeptical reporters gathered to meet him on his arrival. At their request, Arnold repeated his remarkable tale. Because he was a well-regarded citizen—rescue pilot, businessman, deputy sheriff—"skepticism changed to wonder and the journalists reported the incident as a serious news item," writes historian David Jacobs in *The UFO Controversy in America*.[5]

Thus, a new category was born for seemingly unexplainable observations. A flying saucer could at once be unknown, yet identifiable, with the subtle connotation of artificially constructed hardware. The phrase permitted people to dismiss the very notion of an unusual object in the sky (saucers do not fly) without having to consider the context or circumstances behind the event. As Carl Jung would famously declare: "Something is seen, but one doesn't know what."[6]

Arnold appeared to realize he was in the midst of something quite extraordinary during his flight. "It is important to notice how Arnold's attention was first drawn to the presence of strange flying objects because his initial observation, to have occurred as he reported, would require an extremely bright light source to produce a noticeable increase in the light intensity on his airplane in the broad daylight,"[7] writes Bruce Maccabee in his book about the Arnold sighting, *Three Minutes in June*. Arnold had been startled by a "tremendously bright flash [that] lit up the surfaces of my aircraft."[8]

"His initial impression was that the flashes were sunlight reflected from the upper surfaces of the objects," Maccabee continues. "In thinking over the sighting in the following days, however, he became more and more convinced that the objects were not only reflecting sunlight but were almost emitting the bright, blue-white flashes that he compared to a welder's arc."[9]* Maccabee, an optical specialist, confirmed

---

*Calvin Parker, one of two Mississsippi men who reported being abducted by terrifying otherworldy creatures in 1973, would likewise compare the luminosity inside the landed craft in Pascagoula to the brilliant light of a welder's arc. Similar descriptions of UFO luminosity are pervasive in decades of witness reports. In various contemplative traditions, the capacity to perceive supersensory lights is mentioned in relationship to intense devotional practice. Distance runners, sailors, mountain climbers, and women in childbirth have also reported spontaneous illuminations, with no apparent relation to occult experience or esoteric practice. We'll look into similar demonstrations of extraordinary human capacities further along in this book.

"sunlight reflections from mirror-like surfaces of the size and distance of the objects would not be bright enough to be noticed as flashes of light on the airplane surfaces."[10]

In an interview with journalist Paola Leopizzi Harris years later, Kim Arnold disclosed that her father was "perplexed and confused about everybody's concept of aliens visiting from other planets—that type of thing. . . . [The objects] pulsated with blue/white light from the center of their surfaces similar to the rhythm and beating of our own human hearts. . . . My father believed they were alive, absolutely. . . . capable of changing their density . . . rather than anything made out of nuts and bolts. . . . He felt they were not mechanical in any sense at all."[11]

No less remarkably, Kim Arnold says her dad believed UFOs come from a larger-dimensional world, "the world where we go when we die."[12] She revealed that when her father returned from his fateful flight, inexplicable orbs of light began appearing in their house. She has also spoken about her mother's telepathic gifts and reincarnation beliefs and how greatly stressed her parents were by the way her father's experiences were contorted by the media and debunkers and by constant phone calls and the several thousand letters that her dad received.

Kim Arnold also said her father was threatened by a government operative and warned to stay quiet about what he had seen. She indicated her parents spent the rest of their lives dreading being killed by the U.S. government, whose intelligence apparatus evidently harassed and manipulated the Arnolds for its own objectives. This motif of suppression of evidence—*Keep quiet if you know what's good for you*—would assume many forms in the UFO mythos. Scholar of religions Jeffrey Kripal picks up the beat:

> And there we have it. A vision of living beings in the sky emerging from some other dimension, misreported and misperceived as flying machines likened to a little plate for your tea or coffee and immediately mixed up with the Air Force, Cold War intelligence,

the politics of the security state, thousands of visionary and erotic encounters, and an entire new demonology of invading extraterrestrials. Where to start, where to begin anew?[13]

Again, Kripal and I have arrived at the same fork in the road as two longtime observers of the phenomenon. His core question: "Where now?" My version: "What if?" Really, we're both asking what to do with this sudden clarity that the true facts of the modern UFO phenomenon's defining mythos point in a fundamentally different direction than has been assumed for close to eight decades. It's hard not to wonder how things might be different today if what Ken Arnold said (about how the objects had moved, not about their shape) had been *heard*, and if as a society we had imagined the phenomenon along the lines the once unknown pilot from Boise had kept to himself so as not to be dismissed as what Peter Berger defined as a "cognitive minority"[14] (composed at the time of precisely one person).

How might the UFO epic have unfolded if pundits in the summer of '47 saw that Arnold's so-called flying saucer vision pointed not to technology but eschatology?* What if reporters had understood that Arnold had conceived of the extraordinary aerial display more in terms of esoteric space than extraterrestrial geography?

In one respect the answer is obvious. If Arnold had climbed out of his cockpit declaring the objects seemed to be some form of living, pulsating energy somehow connected to what we call death, comedians would have had an even greater field day at his expense. Conceivably, his future flight privileges would have hinged on passing a psychiatric exam. Arnold acknowledged that "half the people I see look at me as a combination of Einstein, Flash Gordon, and Screwball"[15] based solely

---

*Encyclopaedia Britannica: "In the history of religion, the term *eschatology* refers to conceptions of the last things: immortality of the soul, rebirth, resurrection, migration of the soul, and the end of time. These concepts also have secular parallels—for example, in the turning points of one's life and in one's understanding of death."

on mistaken media reports that he had seen flying objects shaped like saucers.

Would a convincing modern creation myth have formed around a pilot's sighting of undulating stingray-like objects rapidly soaring over Mount Rainier? Not likely.

The two levels of the UFO story—extraterrestrial and esoteric, technological and eschatological—come together and coexist *allegorically*. This is to say, the UFO narrative juxtaposes two thematic levels: a primary or surface plot where words give every sign of meaning what they say and a secondary plot conveying meanings of another kind and often telling a different story altogether. Meanings at the secondary level get transmitted intuitively, never referred to explicitly; the primary story never refers to the secondary level. Debates are explicit. In the secondary plot, think implicit possibilities, tacit realities, facts by connotation, veiled horizons, secret truths.

According to Angus Fletcher in *Allegory: The Theory of a Symbolic Mode*, "Allegory says one thing and means another. It destroys the expectation we have about language, that our words 'mean what they say.'" An allegorical work, then, goes along saying one thing in order to mean something beyond that one thing, in order to imply something or many things not stated in the primary or surface story. In the sixteenth century, the literary scholar Henry Peacham described allegory as a kind of 'aenigma . . . which for the darknesse, the sense may hardly be gathered.'"[16] Fletcher makes a similar point when he describes allegory as "a fundamental process of encoding our speech."[17]

By holding together two levels of meaning in this way, UFO events generate a powerful response in the psyche, precisely because neither level can be completely reduced to the other. A defining characteristic of pure allegory, Fletcher notes, is that its formal, or literal, surface level doesn't explicitly demand to be interpreted for hidden meanings, for it often makes "good enough" sense by itself. "But somehow this literal surface suggests a *peculiar doubleness of intention*, and while it can, as it were, get along without interpretation, it becomes much richer and more interesting if given interpretation."[18] (Emphasis added.)

The reader of Orwell's *Animal Farm* comes to recognize that the tale about barnyard animals presented literally corresponds to a secondary plot about the dangers of authoritarianism. In a strict sense, the surface story of any allegory, although apparently primary, is secondary to the deeper meanings of the obvious yet invisible substory. "Allegorical stories exist, as it were, to put secondary meanings into orbit around them; the primary meaning is then valued for its satellites,"[19] Fletcher observes. And yet children are fully capable of reading *Animal Farm* as nothing more an imaginative yarn comparable to the tales of Dr. Doolittle, a fictional physician who shuns human patients in favor of animals, with whom he can converse in their own languages.

Here Fletcher's insight stopped me in my tracks. In the UFO allegory, the surface-level debate that goes on in the public square inevitably casts a spell that masks deeper and more difficult questions about the very nature of reality. The great abundance of controversy (the arguments about flyovers, landings, close encounters, secret rumors and rumors of secrets, strained official denials, and, of course the alien abductions) practically instructs the reader to go beyond the increasingly baroque surface into the depths. In this way, allegory *casts its spell*—but not by conveying that there's *nothing* to the surface arguments about what UFOs are and where they are from but instead by making clear that there's *something else* to be seen and understood.

Ultimately, what gets communicated beyond words is that finding answers about the nature and origins of extraordinary Otherworld beings almost certainly will require us to come to terms with *who and what we are*, or the farther reaches of our own nature. For in the most surreal close encounters involving transgressions of time and space and apparently "super-normal" human capacities, the events take place on the common ground of shared nature. How otherwise could the encounters even register as experience? What is the common nature we inhabit, such that interaction occurs?

For decades, conventionally minded UFO researchers have proceeded on the assumption that if UFOs are real physical objects, this could only mean they must be extraterrestrial in the ordinary sense of the term. Simply put, this conflates perception and interpretation. If extraordinary events in the sky are chronicled not only in our time but in earlier eras as well, and if their occupants have performed similar actions along similar lines of behavior, it does not automatically follow that they are "simply" interplanetary visitors starting after World War II. The assumption is an interpretation masquerading as an obvious fact, and as longtime UFO investigator Jacques Vallée never tires of remarking, other interpretations cry out:

> In attempting to find an adequate framework, it is useful to speculate about variants of current physics in which apparent miracles could occur without violating physical laws and in which psychic phenomena should be the rule rather than the exception. In such a physics, UFOs could come from earth without necessarily being human inventions, or they could come from another galaxy without necessarily being spacecraft.[20]

In debates between advocates of the view that the ET hypothesis is the only reasonable interpretation of UFOs and scientists who waive away all UFO reports as hoax, hallucination, or misidentification, partisans of both camps have tended to minimize such speculations. Significantly, the two sides tend to share an unspoken presumption that all the features of the UFO phenomenon mystery should be explainable without challenging our concepts of reality. The preponderance of evidence over a long passage of time makes this presumption unlikely, for this is a phenomenon that readily emerges as a physical event entirely capable of manipulating its environment, while in the next moment "it can evaporate into thin air, leaving not a trace of what was a moment before an immense and overwhelmingly real experience," as Whitley Strieber puts it. "How can this be?" Strieber asks.[21]

How, indeed? The question points to the likelihood that the many and various threads of the modern UFO phenomenon are part of a larger and more complex tapestry.

Jeffrey Kripal asked, "Where to start, where to begin anew?"[22]

We can only start *here* (with the evidence we have now), while acknowledging having been *there* (when mistaken assumptions ruled for a while). Knowing where we are and where we've been go hand in hand. To ask new questions requires being clear about the recurring dynamics that keep leading to the same stalemate.

In case after UFO case, something remarkable is experienced. Witnesses speak of it. Various agents of official culture dismiss their accounts. Time and again, this exchange reaches the same impasse: evidence from The People on one side, dismissive rejoinders from The Authorities on the other. In the fertile void of this deadlock, extraordinary possibilities—about the nature of mind and matter, spirit and soul, heaven and earth, human nature and the destiny of the universe—enter the debate. The traditional celestial UFO is thus transformed into a metaphysical one.

Gradually, it begins to dawn that the issues in play in the UFO controversy have *always* been metaphysical, in the sense that they raise fundamental questions about the very basis of existence. These issues are tough to discuss when there's a missing ingredient of openness to evidence that whatever's afoot seems to trump the explanatory power not only of physics but logic itself. The phenomenon's very ways of revealing itself involve elements of strangeness so ludicrous as to further conceal it. The case of a 60-year-old Wisconsin chicken farmer is a case in point.

In 1961, Joe Simonton reports a silvery, saucer-shaped object "brighter than chrome" about 12 feet high and 30 feet in diameter hovering close to the ground. One of three occupants about five feet tall who appears to "resemble Italians" exits the craft holding up a jug apparently made of the same material as the saucer. He motions to Simonton in a way that indicates he needs water. Upon returning from indoors with a filled jug, Joe sees that one of the men inside the saucer is "frying food on a flameless grill inside the saucer." When Joe motions that he is interested in the food, one of the men hands him three small cookies perforated with small holes.

Then the men reenter the craft and close the hatch. The object rises about 20 feet from the ground before taking off due south with a blast of air that bends some nearby trees. When Joe eats one of the cakes, it "tasted like cardboard." The Air Force subsequently determines the cake to be composed of hydrogenated fat, starch, buckwheat hulls, and soybean hulls—all common terrestrial ingredients. Speaking for the Air Force, investigator J. Allen Hynek concludes: "There is no question that Mr. Simonton felt that his contact had been a real experience."

But this isn't the end of it. Hynek's Air Force superiors subsequently say Simonton, who lived alone, has had a sudden dream while awake, and then the dream somehow gets "inserted" into his normal surroundings, while Simonton is oblivious to the whole process.[23] The response sounds like a discarded story idea that science fiction writer Philip K. Dick never got around to writing about a bureaucrat in a military uniform sent out to a Wisconsin farm with a clipboard to conduct fieldwork unrelated to either military or psychological training. "Close enough for government work," as Ronald Reagan used to quip.

The larger point is that in a very real sense, the phenomenon "hides" precisely in the dark cracks that open between a witness's experiential certainty that something extraordinary took place and the formulaic, offhanded dismissals issued by various authorities. Meanwhile, the phenomenon goes along doing what seems to be its job: nourishing within the collective psyche a free-floating expectation of unspecified yet inevitable contact between humankind and an elusive yet widely posited otherkind. Because an anomalous encounter can be experientially realistic while still leaving big questions unsettled, the nature of *contact* and *otherkind* remain open to limitless conjecture.

Are we dealing with interplanetary visitors? Denizens of realms once considered "spiritual"? Subtle-material beings echoing daimons of ancient Greece, angels of Christianity, jinn of Islam? Projections from Jung's collective unconscious? Military psyops? Mass delusion, hoax, misidentification of ordinary objects? Waking-Daydream Chicken Farmer Syndrome?

As the various experts—governmental, military, academic, scientific—refuse to consider reports involving absurd entities and paradoxical scenarios, witnesses and the public reach for larger explanations. As one school of researchers presses its claim that aliens are implanting physical probes in the bodies of human abductees, powerful mythic images take root in the culture's subconscious. As ET stalwarts await the Big News ("any day now, the lid on the government cover-up conspiracy's gonna blow sky-high"), UFOs consolidate their status as a cosmic chameleon darting back and forth between mind and matter, improvising brazenly with the core elements of each realm, making known their top-secret truths to high-level official bureaucrats (says the cover-up legend) but not to the rest of us.

Small wonder Ken Arnold kept details of his seminal sighting to himself and his family, along with deeper intuitions about its meaning. "If I saw a ten-story building flying through the air I would never say a word about it."[24] The successful businessman and deputy sheriff had tasted the derision so often bestowed on witnesses who describe phenomena that don't officially exist, couldn't have happened, that's that. Checkmate. Stalemate. Deadlock.

◄o►

The impasse is safeguarded by deeply engrained binary thought-forms: reality must conform either to matter *or* mind, literal *or* metaphoric, world *or* imagination, no other choice. The UFO has a genius for triggering tacit orthodoxies shared by conventional religion and establishment science—each camp being wary of Jung's big idea in the modern era— and echoed by ancient philosophers like Plotinus and Paracelsus: that the whole of Psyche contains vibrant and sometimes terrifying dimensions that ego identity struggles to face, let alone resolve on its limited ground.

Because this applies as well to the extended psyche or mind at large, known to the ancients as the soul of the world (Anima Mundi), the apparent absurdities of the UFO phenomenon point to the irrationality of our contemporary worldview when faced with sudden dimensionality and perplexing depth. Philosopher Bernardo Kastrup frames the stakes:

> Do the calls of the absurd offer clues? The absurd is, and has always been, an intrinsic part of our world. As a culture, we ignore its significance at our own peril. After all, there may just be profound meaning in the absurd.[25]

A genuine anomaly is not some new ontological category; it's simply a feature of reality that happens not to conform to expectations of a particular theory. When sufficient anomalies raise valid questions about the adequacy of a paradigm or worldview, a new and more inclusive explanation is called up for duty. Skepticism that explains away anomalies because they threaten the coherence of a given paradigm— skepticism that fails to challenge assumptions about what's allowed to be so—is the craft of ideologues. For at least two centuries, dogmatic scientific physicalism feigning observational neutrality has obscured recognition that mind and world are, in fact, continuous with one another—indeed, recognition that the sole given datum of existence is conscious experience. Kastrup is very clear about this:

Consciousness—whatever it may intrinsically be—*is the only carrier of reality anyone can ever know for sure.* It is the one undeniable empirical fact of existence. After all, what can we really know that isn't experienced in some form, even if only through instrumentation or the reports of others? If something is fundamentally beyond all forms of existence, direct or indirect, it might as well not exist. Because all knowledge resides in consciousness, we cannot *know* what is supposedly outside consciousness; we can only *infer* it through our capacity for abstraction.[26]

What began with Ken Arnold was told partially. Eventually came a retelling, a new beginning. And with that comes an invitation to return with curiosity to the one question that led Darwin to gather fossils, Jung to probe myth, Einstein to ponder relativity, Siddhartha to leave home, and Ken Arnold to think deeply about nine luminous, blue-white, streaming, pulsating, seemingly alive, rapidly soaring object-beings near Mount Rainier: *What is going on here?*

3

A Modern Saga Takes Shape

In strict historical terms, the popular view that the UFO phenomenon began with Arnold's sighting is mistaken. Starting the year before and continuing until 1948, witnesses in Sweden and Finland reported seeing strange, cigar-shaped objects flying close to the Soviet border, leading United States Army intelligence agents to fear that these "ghost rockets," as they came to be known, might be Soviet secret weapons developed in collaboration with German scientists. Fully 20 percent of these sightings found no explanation. During World War II, pilots reported unusual balls of light and disklike objects following them—in some cases, "dancing" on the wingtips of their aircraft—as they flew bombing runs. The origin of these phenomena likewise remains a mystery.

Half a century earlier, between November 1896 and May 1897, thousands of people in 19 mostly western and midwestern states reported seeing dirigible-type cylindrical airships sailing through the skies. Because this was five years before the Wright brothers' famous experiments with heavier-than-air flight at Kitty Hawk, these reports caused a sensation not unlike the early response to flying saucers. Today's UFO researchers remain characteristically divided concerning this late nineteenth-century phenomenon, some attributing the sightings to contagious rumors and deliberate hoaxes, others arguing that at least some of these aerial events emerged from the same mysterious dimensions beyond time and space as did their eventual descendants, flying saucers.

But in terms of what Jung was to describe as "a modern myth of things seen in the skies," there's no doubt Kenneth Arnold's legendary sighting indeed marked the beginning of the UFO phenomenon. A widely published Gallup poll of August 19, 1947, less than two months after Arnold's sighting, revealed that 9 out of 10 Americans knew about the flying saucers, whereas considerably fewer had heard of the Marshall Plan for the postwar reconstruction of Europe. The Age of the Saucers had arrived, and in no small way.

The summer and fall of 1947 featured a rash of public activity that would center the phrase *flying saucer* in the public imagination. Consider this succession of responses that appeared in the aftermath of Arnold's sighting:

A preliminary study of UFOs has "not produced enough fact to warrant further investigation," according to an official U.S. Air Force statement on July 4. The same public statement notes that the Air Force would *continue to study* several sightings of interest in Texas and the Pacific Northwest.

> Nine shiny objects flying at a high rate of speed, such as described by a Boise, Idaho, pilot, were reported by W. I. Davenport, a carpenter, to have been sighted here yesterday" (Associated Press, June 26, Kansas City).

> Reports of flying saucers subsequent to Kenneth Arnold's sighting were caused by a "mild case of meteorological jitters" combined with "mass hypnosis," according to Gordon A. Atwater, astronomer at the Hayden Planetarium (*New York Times,* July 6).

FLYING SAUCERS SEEN IN MOST STATES NOW *(San Francisco Chronicle* headline, July 7).

RAAF CAPTURES FLYING SAUCER IN ROSWELL REGION. NO DETAILS OF FLYING DISKS ARE REVEALED (Roswell, New Mexico, *Daily Record* headline, July 8). "The many rumors regarding the flying disc became a reality yesterday when the intelligence office of the 509th Bomb Group of the Eighth Air Force, Roswell Army Air Field, was fortunate enough to gain possession of a disc through the cooperation of one of the local ranchers and the sheriff's office of Chaves County, *(San Francisco Chronicle,* July 9; picked up by the Associated Press, the *New York Times* wire service, and the prestigious *Times* of London).

A private pilot named Vernon Baird reports knocking a "pearl gray, clam-shaped, craft resembling a 'yo-yo'" out of the sky over Montana. The story is carried by newspapers throughout the nation. In a one-paragraph report the following day, Baird admits he fabricated the story while shooting the breeze with other pilots around the hangar. He promises not to do it again.

Flying saucers belong in the same category as the Loch Ness Monster, insists Dr. Newbern Smith of the United States National Bureau of Standards (*New York Times,* December 27, 1947).

A savvy press agent advertises a radio program featuring the "Flying Saucer Blues."

Significant episodes of these early years occurred entirely behind the scenes. As with secret government activity in general, the impact of this classified transaction would eventually return to the public domain, where it would echo at various levels and bring new interpretations and storylines into the controversy.

On September 23, 1947, Lieutenant General Nathan F. Twining, the first U.S. Air Force general to serve as Chairman of the Joint Chiefs of Staff, responded to a Pentagon request for a UFO update by writing a memo saying that "the reported phenomenon is something real and not visionary or fictitious."[1] Citing reported operating characteristics (including extreme rates of climb, maneuverability, and evasiveness) as indicating possible manual control, Twining recommended that a detailed, classified formal study of the disks should begin at once. Twining's memo led to the establishment of a classified Air Force project to determine whether flying saucers posed a threat to national security. "The attitude toward this task varied from a state of near panic early in the life of the project, to complete contempt for anyone who even mentioned the words 'flying saucer,'"[2] recalled Captain Ruppelt in his classic account of the period, *The Report on Unidentified Flying Objects.*

Project Sign, located at Wright Field and known publicly as Project Saucer (yet another sign of the "doubleness of intention" we explored in the previous chapter), began on January 22, 1948, two weeks after military and civilian witnesses sighted a UFO that looked like "an ice cream cone topped with red" over Godman Army Air Field in Kentucky. Four National Guard P-51 planes were scrambled to take a closer look. The flight leader, Captain Thomas Mantell, radioed Godman Tower that "it appears to be a metallic object . . . tremendous in size . . . directly ahead and slightly above . . . I'm trying to close in for a better look."[3] That was his last radio contact with the tower.

Later that day, Captain Mantell's decapitated body was found in the wreckage of his plane near Fort Knox. Subsequent investigation indicated that Mantell had most likely blacked out from lack of oxygen and suffocated before the crash. But what had Mantell seen and chased? The air force's preliminary verdict—*Mantell had died while chasing the planet Venus, which he had mistaken for a flying saucer*—met with hoots of derision from the press and much of the American public. The hoots became howls of outrage when subsequent investigation showed no meaningful correlation between Venus and the object. Three years later, the navy revealed that a top-secret, high-altitude, photographic reconnaissance Skyhook balloon, capable of expanding to a diameter of 100 feet, had been in the area. It was determined that this was what Mantell had pursued.

But by then it was too late for the air force to rebound from its fateful assertion that Mantell met his death en route to Venus. In the interim, filling a void left by the military's unconvincing response, a vivid legend had taken hold: *a man had died in a dramatic encounter with a UFO, and the air force had conspired to conceal the truth.* Whether this legend was strictly or even loosely true is beside the point, in terms of the legend's primary effect on the collective imagination. The legend held.

The provocative notion that the government had definitive answers that it systematically kept from the public was now in place. For decades to come, this theme would capture the energies and passions of a vocal cadre of civilian researchers, whose cries of "Cover-up!" served as a lightning rod for a percentage of followers inclined toward conspiracy theories (for some, the more elaborate and less verifiable the theory, the better).

Six months later, things got worse for the air force when Clarence Chiles and John Whitted, pilot and copilot of an Eastern Air Lines DC-3, flying at 5,000 feet between Montgomery and Mobile, Alabama, reported seeing a torpedo-shaped, wingless craft over 100 feet long, powered by jet or some other type of power and shooting flames from the rear some 50 feet, according to Captain Chiles. The massive object, with two horizontal rows of large square windows, reminded Whitted of "one of those fantastic Flash Gordon rocket ships in the funny papers'" as it streaked past their aircraft at nearly 700 miles per hour at 2:45 a.m.

The Pentagon responded by claiming the pilot and copilot (and one passenger who awoke in time to catch a brief glimpse) had seen a weather balloon, but this explanation was abruptly withdrawn. Air force consultant J. Allen Hynek remarked that no astronomical explanation was possible for the pilots' descriptions. UFO archskeptic Donald Menzel, a distinguished Harvard astronomer, dismissed the sighting as an unusually bright meteor embellished by flight-weary imaginations, but the pilot and copilot vehemently disagreed. The air force eventually adopted Menzel's theory, listing the object as a fireball.

Notwithstanding their increasingly strained assurances that all was well in the sky, Project Sign's staff were plainly worried about the public relations fallout from the Mantell and Chiles–Whitted cases. Deciding a bold move was in order, the Sign staff wrote a confidential "Estimate of the Situation" memorandum documenting the history of UFO sightings and concluding, for the first time, that UFOs were extraterrestrial in origin. Chief of Staff General Hoyt S. Vandenberg, the memo's intended recipient, rejected this hypothesis for lack of evidence and returned the document to Sign headquarters with an order to burn all copies. Consequently, those Sign staff members who held to the extraterrestrial hypothesis lost influence to those who believed UFO sightings could and would be explained in mundane terms.

Many students of early UFO events aren't aware that a third hypothesis emerged in addition to efforts to explain the events as either extraterrestrial or simply mundane. In 1948, the air force commissioned a report analyzing the likelihood that the strange aerial events could have off-planet origins. J. E. Lipp, the report's author, left no doubts in his conclusion that "[a]lthough visits from outer space are believed to be possible, they are believed to be improbable. In particular, the actions reported to be 'flying objects' during 1947 and 1948 seem inconsistent with the requirements for space travel."[4] The report addressed not only the physics of space travel but also reasoned speculations about the motivations of extraterrestrial visitors:

> The lack of purpose apparent in the various episodes is also puzzling. Only one motive can be assigned; that the space men are "feeling out" our defenses without wanting to be belligerent. If so, they must have been satisfied long ago that we can't catch them. It seems fruitless for them to keep repeating the same experiment.[5]

Lipp's report also focused on what he considered a key issue: the distribution of sighting reports. "As far as this writer knows, all incidents have occurred within the United States, whereas space men could be expected to scatter their visits more or less uniformly over the globe."[6] He concluded the likely origin of the objects to be earthly, whether physical or psychological. Though there were non-U.S. sightings Lipp apparently didn't know about, his analysis shows that early military speculation about UFO origins was not limited to misidentified mundane objects or extraterrestrial origins. In the report, Lipp emphasized the apparent absurdity of aliens "repeating the same experiment," a theme later UFO researchers would echo concerning alien kidnappers supposedly conducting the same rudimentary medical experiments over and over.*

In February 1949, Sign issued a report concluding that there was insufficient evidence to prove the objective reality of UFOs (welcome news for debunkers), while admitting that the study was unable to find a "reasonable and convincing explanation" for 20 percent of the sightings. This conclusion greatly encouraged proponents. On December 16,

---

*"What kind of doctors are these," Jacques Vallée would ask years later, "who need to induce such trauma in hundreds of patients to collect a little blood, a few embryos? . . . Using the advanced paralyzing devices they possess, it should be simple for them, if they were an extraterrestrial task force, to raid the blood bank of any modern research hospital where they would also find collections of frozen embryos at various stages of development" (Vallée, 1988, 268).

1948, the military study received a new code name, Project Grudge—a name that, if unintentionally, mirrored the air force's barely concealed contempt for its subject. Grudge was charged with finding an explanation for every sighting received, by way of assuring the public that the air force was indeed on top of the situation. "Instead of seeking the origin of a possibly unique phenomenon, as Sign had done, Grudge usually denied the objective reality of that phenomenon,"[7] notes historian David Jacobs.

Project Grudge's first attempt to shape public opinion by cooperating wholeheartedly with the author of a two-part *Saturday Evening Post* series was a notable failure. Although the articles explicitly sought to debunk UFOs and to mock the people who reported them, author Sidney Shalett conceded that explanations for a few sightings had not been found. A few days after the second installment hit the newsstands, UFO sightings reached an all-time high. In response, the air force issued a lengthy news release repeating its increasingly familiar mantra: *All UFOs can be explained as hoaxes, hallucinations, and misidentifications.*

Instead of reassuring the public, this sequence only raised new doubts. For the first time, civilians began studying the UFO phenomenon for themselves, marking a new chapter in the unfolding UFO epic. Civilian interest shot up when, six months after its inception, Project Grudge revealed that 23 percent of the sightings it studied remained unidentified. The Grudge staff decided to try a new tack, arguing that the very reporting of UFOs constituted a danger to national security. By this logic, it was but one short step further to Grudge's recognition that the continuing existence of a UFO investigatory body could only *encourage* such reports. Project Grudge folded on December 27, 1949.

The focus of the simmering UFO debate shifted to publishing when the January 1950 issue of *True* magazine featured a sensational article by retired Marine Corps major Donald E. Keyhoe. Short on facts and high on speculation, this widely read and controversial article interpreted the new official silence on UFOs as clear evidence that the air force was hiding something big. To Keyhoe this could be only one thing, stated in the author's characteristically unambiguous terms: "For the past 175 years, the planet Earth has been under systematic close-range examination by living, intelligent observers from another planet."[8] This assertion and others like it were based primarily on reconstructed conversations with anonymous individuals supposedly "in the know," conversations that resembled dialogue from the less distinguished detective novels of the period.

"Charley, there's a rumor that airline pilots have been ordered not to talk," I told Planck. "You know anything about it?"

"You mean ordered by the Air Force or the companies?"

"The Air Force and the C.A.A."

"If the C.A.A.'s in on it, it's a top level deal,"[9] said Charley.

Keyhoe later expanded his article into an influential and no less sensational book, *The Flying Saucers Are Real*, which sold 500,000 copies.

At roughly the same time, a popular author named Frank Scully wrote a melodramatic book called *Behind the Flying Saucers*. Scully chronicled the alleged air force capture of three landed saucers and several four-foot-tall dead aliens. Although the story turned out to be bogus, its impact—like that of Keyhoe's article and book—was enormous. Scully will be remembered in the annals of saucerology for introducing themes that would become staples in an ever-widening UFO mythology: crashed saucers, alien corpses, and elaborate cover-ups of the truth awaiting unveiling by intrepid investigators.

In short order, there followed several national magazine articles on the subject: *Time*, asserting that all UFOs were actually Skyhook balloons; *U.S. News and World Report*, announcing that all saucers were actually navy secret weapons; and *Cosmopolitan*, scathingly depicting people who reported UFOs as "true believers," "screwballs," "gagsters," and members of the "lunatic fringe."

These early book and magazine treatments—like the emotionally unsatisfying air force verdicts on the Mantell and Chiles-Whitted cases and the official admission that a persistent percentage of sightings eluded definitive identification—offered little to clarify the remarkable happenings variously called flying saucers and UFOs. Neither did they do much to discourage public fascination with the charges and countercharges leveled between proponents and skeptics (most of the latter aiming to debunk UFOs as a whole).

To the contrary, the emerging controversy simply enhanced the mythic status of an apparently new class of events that seemed to travel in the interface between mind and matter: a "twilight zone." A strangely consistent plot was beginning to take shape.

The early happenings of the UFO phenomenon were "first events" in both a mythological and historical sense. History and mythology are supposed to be separate fields, with, on college campuses, separate departments and professors. It's more accurate, however, to cast the fields as two genres in juxtaposition, two frames of references based on different ways of knowing and different styles of imagining a phenomenon's early appearances and, in a real sense, its ongoing stagecraft. The fence that separates *mythological* and *historical* also keeps them connected. But the border is porous, yet another example of the trickster impulse of Hermes prevailing over Apollo's insistence on clear-cut categories.

In chapter one, we explored Kenneth Arnold's sighting as the defining event of a creation myth—a narrative of how a world begins and how people and events come to inhabit it—the world of the modern UFO phenomenon, a cosmos organized around compelling sightings of strange, *unknown* objects with their very own taxonomy.

Arnold became ufology's de facto archetypal ancestor, primal progenitor, canonical First Man, but of course he was never so identified in these terms in media reports. And the creation myth records that Arnold's nine saucer-shaped objects took their place as accepted facts within the founding legend.

Key details had gotten muddled. Arnold reported objects that *moved* like saucers, as opposed to being *shaped* like saucers. It can seem a minor point, but as with the doctrine of stare decisis ("to stand by things decided") in legal jurisprudence, the motifs of a creation myth are intended as precedents to guide future behavior. *"As it was for the First People in the Beginning, so it is now and shall always be."* This, of course, isn't to say the Arnold sighting provided an explicit precedent to which UFO research must conform; this would be to literalize a mythopoetic reality. The dynamics of myths as precedent are subtler.

A writer named Martin Kottmeyer couldn't resist noting that, based on mistaken news reports that Arnold had seen objects shaped like saucers, "People started looking for flying saucers and that is exactly what they found. They reported flat, circular objects that look like flying saucers are expected to appear. The implications of this journalistic error are staggering in the extreme,"[10] Kottmeyer declared. Besides indicating a cultural origin of the entire flying saucer phenomenon—he says—this affair inserted a first-order paradox into efforts to interpret UFOs in extraterrestrial terms.

"Why would extraterrestrials redesign their craft to conform to Bequette's error?"[11] Kottmeyer asked with a scarcely concealed wink, referring to the local reporter who wrote those first misleading accounts.

The intent of Kottmeyer's question was to show the psychosocial dynamics of UFO sightings—new witnesses report saucers based on reports of earlier witnesses seeing the same shape. In this vein, the psychologist Jerome Bruner once conducted an experiment designed to investigate what he called "perceptual readiness," the tendency of people to hold expectations about their environment that predetermine to some degree what they perceive. Bruner showed subjects two sets of playing cards, one with colors reversed and one normal, at speeds of a fraction of a second.

Not surprisingly, subjects had greater difficulty identifying the color-reversed cards. But what especially interested Bruner were the lengths to which subjects went to reinterpret and "regularize" their perceptions to fit with their prior expectations about the nature of playing cards. One subject reported that the red six of clubs was indeed a six of clubs, but there was a pinkish illumination inside the instrument that presented the cards to view. There was, of course, no such coloring inside the device.

"All this is banal enough but the implications are anything but that," Bruner said. "For it means that perception is to some unspecifiable degree an instrument of the world as we have structured it by our expectancies. Moreover, it is characteristic of complex perceptual processes that they tend where possible to assimilate whatever is seen or heard to what is expected."[12]

The analogy between this experiment and the ongoing UFO "test" seems obvious, yet there is an important difference as well. After Bruner's experimental trials, his subjects were able to examine both sets of cards and scrutinize the display instrument, then compare those confirmable physical parameters against their own observations. Next, they could explore the implications of any variance between test constraints and their responses. Thus, they could gain new insights into the subtle assumptions guiding their moment-by-moment experience of living.

In contrast, after a UFO experience, what are the agreed-upon points of reference? Who will come forward with concrete criteria showing what was *really* happening during the "test" so that subjects can separate how much of "it" was really "it" and how much of "it" was really "them"? A common refrain within the UFO debate is that "the facts speak for themselves." But nothing was clearer in these early days of the phenomenon than that the "facts" (and the values concealed within) spoke differently to different listeners, so that even the supposedly "hardest" of physical evidence (such as UFO photographs) remained open to vastly different interpretations among well-credentialed optical physicists on both sides.

Yet there was another possibility lurking in Kottmeyer's satirical question, one he didn't mean to lay on the lectern for serious consideration as a genuine skeptic, as distinct from a vitriolic debunker who ignores evidence and attacks character. Precisely by engaging critical reasoning, genuine skepticism sometimes opens doors to scenarios beyond boundary fences assumed by the very doubts they raise. For starters, we can enjoy Kottmeyer's wit. Then, we can agree Bruner's thinking about "perceptual readiness" is relevant to how past UFO reports can shape ways in which future sightings get interpreted. There's also a third step: Kottmeyer's question can be given respect in its own terms. Indeed, "why would extraterrestrials redesign their craft?"

Let's go there.

Since we can only speculate about origins, the question about motivations of supposed extraterrestrials applies equally to potential interdimensional dwellers from beyond time-space and to possible time travelers from the future, two widely held hypotheses. "Why *would* they" is the gist of the inquiry. Kottmeyer's use of "would" indicates a possible consequence of an imagined event or situation. In simple logical terms, *would* implies *could*, and both terms assume capacity to act. To be *able* through acquired knowledge or skill, through the purposeful activity of some cause—now we're talking agency, the capacity to act based on choice.

And look where this lands us: smack in the middle of a conversation about possible nonhuman intelligence. It matters not that Kottmeyer never refers to this possibility. He walks us right up to the river's edge, perhaps hoping satire will keep us on safe shores, but his logic for crossing over is inescapable: Why *would* they redesign suggests that they *could*, which is agency, and that's intelligence talk. Commonly agreed characteristics of intelligence include the capacity to think, reason, understand; also, conceivably the capacity to enact intention and purpose consistent with the properties of the nine objects Arnold observed and reported seeming to be pulsating, shimmering, living beings capable of changing their density.

Since we've taken the plunge, let's swim. By Kottmeyer's (unintended) construction, intelligence would do this because it has the capacity; this leads to *why*. Because it can? But that's about capacity, let's get to motivation. Why would sentient nonhuman intelligence change its form after its movements were misreported as its shape? What does this suggest if not *interactivity*—some manner of interface already in place, *them* responding to *us* responding in the first place to *them*. Contact as already happening, as distinct from something to occur in some indeterminate future.

This thought exercise doesn't require erasing Kottmeyer's intended irony for a literal explanation of the sort that might start with, "This explains why extraterrestrials *actually* revamped their craft after the initial reports." Kottmeyer's insightful satire gets to stay, because it's good stuff. Teasing out his rhetorical logic shows he has unknowingly created a clearing that reveals a defining feature of the phenomenon as *activity*. In fact, a rather spectacular clearing in which to behold and reflect upon *whatever this is, doing whatever it is doing, in ways that it does.*

The UFO is a protean shape-shifter.

The Greek god Proteus was the son of Okeanos and Tethys. His dwelling place was the depths of the sea, whose changeability he mimicked in his remarkable capacity to change himself into myriad shapes and forms—a lion, panther, swine, serpent, or, if desperate, the contour of water or fire—in order to avoid those who would press him to demonstrate his prophetic powers. As the psychologist James Hillman put it, Proteus's "ceaselessly changing image that could take on any shape or nature represented the multiple and ambiguous form of the soul."[13]

To say that Proteus enters the UFO story from the annals of myth (just like Hermes) is to use a personified figure of speech to illustrate a wider, more inclusive frame of reference beyond everyday language. Myths are root metaphors, fantastic accounts, elaborate tales, symbol systems not to be taken literally but viewed as "imaginative agents" that open new entry points to terra incognita.

Ufologists seeking to pin down the UFO's extraordinary nature—its "prophetic powers"—have found themselves rewarded, often to their dismay, with a treasure trove of imaginal richness: Arnold's splendid image of nine celestial objects undulating, like saucers skipping over water . . . Captain Mantell's fateful pursuit of an object described by witnesses as an ice-cream cone topped with red . . . a torpedo-shaped wingless craft trailing a massive flame as it caromed by an Eastern Air Lines flight over Alabama . . . balls of light dancing on the wings of aircraft during World War II . . . "ghost rockets" over Sweden and Finland. UFOs have also been reported in the shape of stars, cigars, spheres, fireballs, dumbbells, footballs, hats, diamonds, plates pressed rim to rim, and washtubs.

But there are also limits to this god's expressiveness. A passage from Homer's *Odyssey* states that those who seek to learn from Proteus must "grasp him steadfastly and press him yet the more." Joseph Campbell offers this important detail: "This wily god never discloses even to the skillful questioner the whole content of his wisdom. He will reply only to the question put to him, and what he discloses will be great or trivial, according to the question asked."[14] Philosopher Ludwig Wittgenstein joins in: "We have to remember that what we observe is not nature itself, but rather nature exposed to our method of questioning."[15]

From this perspective, each hypothesis that attempts to explain the UFO phenomenon—extraterrestrial visitors, denizens of other dimensions, misidentification of Venus, time travelers back from the future, Russian weapons, U.S. weapons tests, products of disturbed minds, and so on—is the product of a particular and limited question put to the UFO by particular observers with particular assumptions and, in Jerome Bruner's phrase, different "expectancies." Project Sign staffers looked at the data and "asked" the UFO phenomenon ("Proteus") whether its origins were extraterrestrial. This question was posed so as to stipulate a range of possible answers, as most questions do and as clever lawyers understand when putting strategic questions to witnesses who have sworn to tell the truth. ("Are you still beating your wife?")

The UFO phenomenon "answered" Project Sign's question not in ultimate or definitive terms but according to specific criteria introduced by specific observers with their own agendas. From this point, it was but a short step for investigators to forget that the resulting answers came into view as a result of particular questions based on particular distinctions, and then for them to embrace the assumption that they now had a view of the UFO "as it really is." General Vandenberg asked a particular question—ET or not?—and received the answer *not*. Other observers got the opposite answer during the first few years of the UFO's presence at the edge of reality.

Thus, by focusing largely on the question of extraterrestrial origins—a question whose answers could only be a matter of conjecture, short of the proverbial landing on the White House lawn—it was possible for many answers satisfying many different questions to be presented. This should never surprise us, wrote the Enlightenment philosopher Giambattista Vico, "since human knowledge is nothing else than the endeavor to make things correspond to one another in shapely proportion."[16] Here, Vico anticipates an idea that the twentieth-century psychologist Jean Piaget would develop at length:

knowledge (or what is put forward as "known") can never be merely the result of passive receiving but necessarily originates as the product of an active subject's activity or constructions. Questions seeking a true and certain picture of the world almost always open to multiple conjectural interpretations.

No wonder, then, that the UFO debate that began in 1947 often resembled trench warfare in the decades to come. Proteus felt no obligation to advise his questioners about whether their question about "his" origins was futile. He showed no interest in suggesting that focusing on other questions—such as the idea that UFOs could represent unknown dimensions of material or psychological (or both: psychophysical) reality—might ultimately prove more fruitful. Such counsel would have been more likely from Apollo, bearer of light, order, and clarity; and this god showed no sign of being anywhere near the UFO neighborhood (although the longing for his presence amid the tumult was great).

Instead, by using the specific questions of his unknowing disciples to put forth aspects of his whole wisdom—"great or trivial"—Proteus remained true to the tasks steeped in his mythic nature as a shape-shifter, keeper of a divinely ambivalent (*ambi* = many, *valent* = strengths or powers) ground. Because the major players in the UFO epic were interested in final and definitive answers to their questions, the secret presence of Proteus could only bring havoc to the festivities. "Nothing personal," this god says with a wink, but not to offer justification or reassurance. He doesn't show up to negate any particular UFO narrative; in fact, he's happy to convey to advocates of particular hypotheses that their accounts are *fitting*—but so are the views of other explainers with very different views. The search for definitive, iconic truth can, and usually does, open to many *viable* answers.

By analogy, a key is understood to *fit* if it opens a lock. The fit describes a capacity of the key, not the lock. Other keys might open the same lock—viability in action. Many different narratives can "solve" the

UFO mystery, in the eyes of various proponents whose explanations are so different that an outside observer can easily wonder if they're describing the same phenomenon.*

In mythic pantheons throughout the world, each divine person carries a particular *necessity*, a specific sense that things must "play out" in a certain way. Shorthand for this sense of the inexorable: the Fates. Sometimes the ancient playwrights would introduce characters so named, identifying them by function: *that which must be.* Proteus conjures multiplicity, while Hermes the swift-footed messenger and guardian of thresholds masterfully reroutes communications through twisted pathways, shortcuts, and parallel routes, always with quicksilver nuances of the uncanny. And Apollo invokes rational order, absence of ambiguity, the necessity of clarity and precision—"let there be order in the court."

The gods and goddesses of a pantheon are interrelated (literally often relatives) yet also interlimiting (think political arguments at holiday gatherings). The divinities are also *mutually entailing*, insofar as a pantheon acknowledges many different and sometimes conflicting directions in the psyche and celebrates multiple sources of meaning, direction, and value. Though the phrase *human nature* can be spoken as if it is a known quantity, it must ultimately include the sentient human being as a whole, a volatile complex of somatic, energetic, vital, emotional, cognitive, volitional, and transpersonal dimensions. If our nature is this mixed, imagine anything less multifaceted for UFOs.

Figures of myth are characteristically depicted as quarreling, cheating, vulnerable, seeking revenge, tearing apart, and being torn apart—

---

*"Thanks to professional burglars we know only too well that there are many keys that are shaped quite differently from our own but which nevertheless unlock our doors. . . . All of us—scientists, philosophers, laymen, school children, animals, and indeed, any kind of living organism—face our environment as the burglar faces a lock that he has to unlock in order to get at the loot" (Watzlawick, 21).

yet somehow the center holds and things that fall apart come back together. Evidence of "mythic patterns" is plentiful among competing UFO researchers as they contend to form a consistent *mythos*, or plot. The very effort to do so forms a mythos of its own: an epic drama of individuals seeking to make meaning of epic events and experiences in which (to borrow an apt phrase from the psychologist James Hillman) "the supposed surety of facts and illusions of fiction exchange their clothes."[17]

Leaping off the pages of myth, Proteus is metaphoric of modes of perceiving and imagining adequate to the phenomenon's multidimensionality. It is becoming increasingly clear across numerous fields of study that mere goal-directed rationality—unaided by art and literature, dream, religious and mythic imagination, and paradigm-challenging evidence for supernormal phenomena—greatly narrows the depth and scope of nature across the ontology game board. Proteus sounds a call to expand the horizons of reality and explore aspects of "all and everything" that may just fall outside the purview of conventional scientific assumptions that blithely write off the significance of consciousness and its many allusive forms: metaphor, analogy, riddle, symbol, myth.

By the end of the saga's first act following Arnold, the intrepid UFO found itself the subject of seemingly unbounded speculation as it went about wildly transgressing the boundaries between mind and matter, spirit and soul, symbol and substance, stealing shamelessly from the repertoires of each. During the break before the next act, ufologists had only to get together backstage and agree on methods suited to dialogue with a phenomenon whose appearances were too compelling to be ignored, yet also too absurd to be taken entirely at face value. The meeting never happened because its necessity wasn't apparent to the majority of UFO detectives who, after all, were predisposed to find evidence that proved their pet theory, the single key that would open the lock.

Proteus occasionally wondered whether those who had elected to follow his tracks could be enticed to shift their *own* shapes, to expand their horizons beyond the dreary one-dimensional debate that had emerged so far. He had his doubts. But in the confusion of the moment, one thing was clear: the shape-shifter would keep his own scope both broad and deep. He was enjoying the general pandemonium.

4

Morning in Zimbabwe

The air was warm and dry, the sky mostly clear. About sixty students of Ariel primary school, a mixed-race private academy at Ruwa, a rural community in the northeastern region of Zimbabwe, were at recess on the playground. Emily Trim remembers catching a glimpse of something silvery shining over a nearby field. Other students saw it too. Some began screaming excitedly, but many stood in stunned silence as a strange craft hovered before their eyes. There were other, smaller craft drifting around the larger one. Humanlike figures with big heads and pale faces and black eyes, seemingly clad in black bodysuits, appeared outside the craft, cavorting strangely in the grassy field where the kids were used to playing games.

"I saw one of these men by the spaceship," Emily recalls. "And there was another one running, running in the grass. He ran normally, like us, but bouncy, as if a human were drunk on the moon. Not as much [gravity] as a human on the moon. When the man ran his distance, he stopped and looked at us for a while, and then he ran back."[1] One of the men seemed to run repeated stretches in slow motion, as if the scene were being rewound and replayed.

Emily remembers the strange man watching her and classmate

Lisil. They felt they were almost within reach of the strange visitors. Emily still thinks about the being's large dark eyes.

The adult staff were at a meeting inside the school. When students came into the building clearly upset about what they had seen, most teachers assumed they were playing a game and didn't take them seriously. As the pandemonium grew, the adults went to find out what was happening. The sighting on September 16, 1994, was quickly reported on ZBC radio, which is where local UFO researcher Cynthia Hind heard about it. She came to the school on September 20 to speak with students and ask them to draw pictures of what they had seen. This interview took place soon after the 1994 encounter:

HIND: Did you all see something?

CHILDREN: Yes.

HIND: What's your name?

DANIEL: I, I, I'm Daniel Mandy and, and I saw this, this silver thing in, in amongst this clump of, of trees with this one thing sitting on, on, on the side and, and another thing sort of like running up and down the, the top.

BART: It had a, a long top and it then it was flat like that along the sides.

HIND: What was around the sides?

BART: Just a, um, sort of like a platform coming down the side.

HIND: Platform. Did you see anything else?

BART: Yes. We saw a black man running around. Just . . .

HIND: A little man or what?

BART: From where we looked, he was about this small [points to his shoulders], but we were quite a way away. So he was about half-sized.

HIND: What did you see?

STUDENT: I saw something silver on the ground amongst the trees and a person in black. And that's all I saw.

HIND: You saw a person alongside the silver thing?

STUDENT: Yes.

HIND: Have you heard about UFOs before this?

STUDENT: No.

HIND: You didn't know anything about it? So it was something quite new to you?

STUDENT: Yes.

HIND: Were you afraid?

STUDENT: Yes.

HIND: Nobody should panic. We don't know what it is . . .

"I believe they saw what they said they saw," Hind told reporters. "I think that perhaps some have been influenced by others and they've added a little bit here and a little bit there, but basically they put in their drawings many things that I don't think that they could know about. . . . As an investigator, I've learned that if they tell exactly the same story, then there's corroboration, they've got together and they're doing it. But if they tell a similar story but from different viewpoints, to me, that's the truth."[2]

Tim Leach, BBC correspondent in Zimbabwe's capital city, Harare, heard about the sighting when he got a call from the nation's chief immigration officer. "What are they talking about?" he said in a media interview. "I had no experience of UFOs or anything like that, apart from seeing Steven Spielberg's film, *Close Encounters of the Third Kind* or whatever. I just thought they're all bonkers! I was just a hard-assed journalist, skeptical as, as everybody would be! What is this? I want to know. I mean, the BBC want to know. What is going on here?" When

Fig. 4.1–4.3. Drawings by unidentified students at the
Ariel school in Ruwa, Zimbabwe.

Photos courtesy of Archives for the Unexplained, Norrköping, Sweden.

Leach spoke with Cynthia Hind, she suggested that he call John Mack, who was by now the world's most high-profile UFO investigator. It was morning on America's East Coast, so Leach left his contact numbers and a short message:

> Tim Leach from BBC Television News in Harare, Zimbabwe. Message for Dr. John Mack. This concerns a UFO sighting over a school where it hovered, landed, a black man got out. But of course, we're having difficulty being taken seriously despite it being the BBC. Please call me as soon as you can. Thank you.[3]

Fig. 4.4. The striking episode of a UFO landing and alien contacts
with children remains unexplained.
Photo courtesy of Archives for the Unexplained, Norrköping, Sweden.

When Mack called back, Leach told him, "Listen, I don't know
what's going on, but this is way outside my normal ball game. What do
I do?" Mack said, "As soon as I can break away I'm coming over." That
satisfied Leach, who later told an interviewer: "With his credentials as
head of the Department of Psychiatry at Harvard, I sat up and took
notice. That took it to another depth."[4]

Embroiled at the time in Harvard's investigation of his alien abductions research, and in need of distraction, Mack began going over
reports faxed from Zimbabwe. Two days before the Ariel school events,
hundreds of people all over the country reported bright lights moving

across the sky. Witnesses from fishermen to farm workers to pilots and technicians told of seeing a silent, bright white object with an orange-red tail, about the size of a Boeing 747. "Some thought it was about to crash, but it leveled off, flying at treetop level and rising to avoid the hills at Lake Kariba on the Zambian border northwest of Harare. Two people viewing it from underneath said it had a flat belly. One thought he could see two engines in front."[5]

When he made the 7,000-mile trip to Africa, Mack met with Ariel headmaster Colin Mackie.

"Do you think it's possible that one imaginative child had a story and kind of stirred the rest of them?" Mack asked.

"No, I don't believe it," Mackie said. "I honestly believe they saw something, but for me to actually draw a conclusion as to what it is, I don't think I could do that at this point in time."

"How many of them reported seeing the craft?"

"Probably in the region of about sixty," Mackie replied. "More of them could have seen it and they're just too embarrassed to talk about it. Or we haven't, actually, haven't had the grade ones and twos involved."

"How long would you estimate that the scene actually lasted?

"It took over about ten to fifteen minutes."[6]

Then Mack spoke with Lisil:

MACK: What were you doing at the time?

LISIL: Well, I was playing at, in the playground and then we just, we saw something silver and then we quickly ran to the log, to the logs. And then we saw a silver thing. And we saw a man standing next to it.

MACK: And what did he look like?

LISIL: Well, he had big eyes that, like, pointed. . .

MACK: Did you look into the eyes? I mean, could you make, did you have a sense that you were . . .

LISIL: No. All we saw was his eyes. They were black.

MACK: Black. But, like, were [the eyes] looking at you [as] you [were looking] at him?

LISIL: Seemed that he was looking at all of us.[7]

Then Mack spoke with a student named Haley:

MACK: Haley, something scared you. Is that right?

HALEY: Yes.

MACK: What scared you?

HALEY: The noise.

MACK: What noise?

HALEY: The noise that we heard in the air.

MACK: You heard a noise in the air?

HALEY: Yes.

MACK: What was it like? Like a roar or a buzz or a hum, or what kind of a noise?

HALEY: It was like someone was blowing a flute.

MACK: And that scared you?

HALEY: Yes.

MACK: Mm-hmm. And what did you do when, when you were afraid?

HALEY: Um, I ran away from it. We told the teacher, but she said just forget about it.[8]

Mack noted that the subject of not being believed came up with student after student. "People [who] have these experiences are very serious about them. And I think that generally speaking, when something powerful, important, exciting, scary has happened, that it's useful to talk about it, to have open discussion. And it doesn't mean you have to impose a point of view. It's not about what we believe; it's what their experience is and how they find the adults around being receptive to that experience."[9]

Journalist Tim Leach was finding the story harder to deal with than the most intense war scenes he had covered. "It's a dirty subject. If you want to sustain a career in the BBC after having been in many war zones, you don't suddenly come up with a UFO story which was absolutely waterproof. Then they just said, no, Tim's suffering from the stress and the strains of all the war zones he's done. He's lost the plot. He's gone bonkers. I think that's when my career with the BBC ended. Gone. I think I lost my credibility because you don't talk about these things."[10]

Joseph Campbell observed that when protagonists of myth receive a call to adventure, sometimes their response is to refuse the summons. "The myths and folk tales of the whole world make clear that the refusal is essentially a refusal to give up what one takes to be one's own interest."[11] To say yes to a call as an opening to destiny, or simply some greater life, requires some turning away from what's familiar and secure. A certain existential arithmetic brings reckoning with what a call will demand, the price to be paid for following it. This can mean letting go of life as you know it in the name of a sensed larger life, with no guarantees as to outcome. You'll get to know living in the margins.

It isn't unusual that a specific life event might not register as a call (in Campbell's sense) when the event happens. Emily Trim was eight years old when she locked eyes with the bouncing alien figure that emerged from the craft. "My family's religious and we came to Africa for mission work," Emily says. "My brother and sister also attended Ariel. They were very traumatized about the event. Talking about it in a religious environment wasn't something that was allowed to be done. I was very quickly removed out of the situation, so it was pack up everything, and we flew [home to] Canada. I didn't get to have the opportunity of growing up with the friends in that environment who had had that occur to them."[12]

Two decades later in Toronto, Emily wasn't in top form. Struggling with future plans, goals, and work, she ended a relationship after being engaged for six years and moved in with her parents, who had become more understanding. The childhood experience at Ruwa was her initiatory separation from a world-picture that had made sense; she was now clearly betwixt and between. Then came a letter in 2019 from an Ariel friend:

> Dear Emily, I hope this finds you well. As you may have seen on our Facebook page, next month we will be celebrating our 25th year as a school. I know it's short notice coming from Canada, but we'd love to have you join us. If you can't make it, know that you are always welcome to visit your old home. Love, Judy.[13]

"It brings up a lot for me," Emily says, looking at the letter. "It's a reminder of pain, of holding something inside. I don't want to hold onto those feelings anymore. I kept it quiet for a really long time. This journey, it's literally to pick up the pieces and put them back together." The original definition of adventure, as in Advent marking the coming of Christ, referred to "something about to happen." Emily suddenly felt new hope that outweighed anxiety; this was a good sign. Says author Gregg Levoy: "It's this adventurous hope—perhaps even the blind spiritual instinct that tells us our lives have purpose and meaning—that propels us to make sacrifices on behalf of calls."[14] Emily began planning her return to Ariel school.

Emily and her classmates agreed to have their reunion recorded for a documentary titled *Ariel Phenomenon*, directed by American filmmaker Randall Nickerson:

EMILY: I mean, you just felt nobody really cared. Who do you talk to? How do you understand it? The people in my life that were supposed to be the closest and the support system, it didn't feel like it was there.

EMMA: There was nobody there to say, "Now it's OK to talk about it." So we never did. And as children, you have a huge imagination, so you see those sort of things and not know what they are. And you, you're left with this, well, "Where am I?" limbo state of "Am I safe or am I not safe?" So it was, I think, a protective mechanism, block it out, turn it off, don't, don't go back to it.

NATASHA: You know, deep down, okay, fine, it's always there, it happened. Now I got scared. For me, it's like the feelings that exist that are real. And yes, I may have been a child, but still, it was another thing, too. So, yeah, it's kind of hard to talk about it. It is.

EMMA: Because it's not something that I bring up to anybody ever. My husband doesn't even know about it.

EMILY: Oh, true expression of how it felt at times. It's really, really difficult to face yourself. That's a scary time. Very, very scary time. A lot of my drawings of the incident were done in black at first, because I think that's how I was really feeling . . . hands over my eyes trying to hide away from everything that's been going on. It got really, really dark.[15]

In the immediate aftermath of the sighting, Emily had tried to describe to Mack her communication with the beings. "I think they want people to know that we're actually making harm on this world and we mustn't get too technologed," Emily said.

"How did that get communicated to you?" Mack asked.

"It came through my head," she said.

"Through your head? Did it talk, like, through words or . . . ?"

"My conscience, I think . . . While I was . . . While the being was looking at me."

"While it was looking at you," Mack repeated quietly.

"It was like this lake of calmness in his eyes," Emily continued.

I was compelled to look at him. It wasn't like I wanted to look away from him. Time became very still and very bizarre. . . . I think that he was saying to me, beware of the technology. Don't go into it too heavy because it's, it's not going to be good for you. It was only when I was looking at him and his face and his eyes that I got that. As soon as I looked away from him, that's when all of reality and, and everything that was happening came back, too. And that's when I realized that something really strange is happening here.[16]

The big turning point for adult Emily came when she connected with a former school acquaintance who welcomed her back to Ruwa and offered to introduce her to local spiritual leaders. "You can visit all the sacred places." This felt right to Emily. While a student at Ariel, she had had very little direct contact with the Indigenous culture. She was taken to meet Duke Musonza, son and apprentice of village chief Goromonzi.

"I can conclude that there are spiritual messages that you have to deliver," Duke told Emily.

"I'm supposed to talk about with, it's not, you know, not for . . . " Emily was at a loss for words.

"You don't have to keep it for yourself," Duke said.

"Yes," Emily said quietly.

"You have to share it," Duke emphasized. "And by sharing, then you can be able to change people's hearts and minds. So, you have to speak out. If they don't hear you speaking, maybe you have to shout. You have to shout. The significance of children is that they are not yet exposed to the world, and they communicate better with the spirits and nature. So, it's always good to have children. If you want a message to be delivered, it has to be delivered to children because the child grows with the message."[17]

Emily seemed to have an intuition of this when she confided to John Mack years earlier, "I think it was quite unusual that the aliens came at the same time that the teachers were in the staff meeting."[18]

"The child grows with the message." Eight-year-old Emily felt certain she had gotten a message from the black-eyed beings about humans "making harm on this world." She had also gotten a clear message from her devout parents that *we don't talk about things like that.* For a long time, Emily didn't. "You shall know the truth," Flannery O'Connor once said. "And the truth will make you odd."

In Campbell's terms, Emily hadn't refused the call; her parents had done so as her proxies, based on what they believed best. And this is Campbell's description of the effect: "One is bound in by the walls of childhood; the father and mother stand as threshold guardians, and the timorous soul, fearful of some punishment . . . fails to make the passage through the door and come to birth in the world without."[19] But even the apparent constraints and obstructions belong to an odyssey's telos or purpose; indeed, they help fulfill it. A calling may be hijacked, deferred, or recurrently overlooked. Sooner or later, it will out. The calling makes its claim. The *daimon*—fate, necessity, innate image—does not go away.

Nearly 25 years later came Judy's letter of invitation. This inspired Emily's return trip to Ruwa, where the words of Duke ("You have to speak out") broke the spell of enforced silence. "Don't speak of this," her parents had instructed. "Shout it loud," Duke countered. The parental denial, intended to eradicate Emily's experience, ironically served as a container for the experience to ripen until she was ready to take it on in Africa. There she was able to merge with it, and then to emerge. As T. S. Eliot foretold: "And the end of all our exploring/Will be to arrive where we started/And know the place for the first time." Think of what happens for a caterpillar in the chrysalis.

UFO historian Jerome Clark has called the Ariel incident the "most remarkable close encounter of the third kind of the 1990s."[20]

Debunker Brian Dunning described the affair as either one of mass hallucination or outright fraud, claiming that by interviewing the children in groups, Cynthia Hind unknowingly encouraged copycat accounts of the event.[21]

Paul McHugh, MD, professor of psychiatry at Johns Hopkins University, said Mack's interest in UFOs made him "embarrassed for the profession and a little worried about John himself." Describing Mack as a man "who tends to take on enthusiasms," McHugh announced: "This time he's gone too far. We hope he'll pull himself together, come back."[22] *Return home, heretical son; repent and all will be forgiven.*

"There's a lot of harrumphing that goes on," Harvard law professor Alan Dershowitz said in response, chiding the intellectual intolerance of Mack's critics. He was amused that at Harvard, lauded for its divinity school, "Theology is okay, but extraterrestrials, no. Angels, yes. Extraterrestrials, no." Dershowitz said he took at face value Mack's statements that he "is inquiring and probing and he has the right to be wrong. The most fundamental right that any academic has is the right to be wrong. Prove that he's wrong. That's the job of other academics."[23]

For his part, Mack was circumspect, yet also relieved when Harvard's investigation of his research reaffirmed his right to pursue the subject of UFOs or any other controversial topic in a professional manner. "In the beginning of my going public with this, I received absolutely no general acceptance," Mack noted. "There were no particular advantages to be gained and every disadvantage. And there were assaults from every direction in terms of the main part of my profession. If it was an opportunity, it was an opportunity to commit professional suicide."

Why is it, Mack wondered, that "we tend to want to shrink this vast, fascinating, powerful phenomenon to our notions of reality rather than being able to stretch ourselves to expand what we know and to admit that we don't know and to open up?"[24]

When Emily Trim returned to Zimbabwe and was given one of her childhood drawings of the craft and the aliens, she said she would put it with the more than 300 art pieces she had created in recent years. "I don't know what it means for me further down the road, but I feel more confident. A calling doesn't have to declare *what* "it" is to confirm *that* it is. Consider this parallel. Amateur night at Harlem Opera House. A shy 16-year-old steps timidly onstage. The crowd is told: "The next contestant, Miss Ella Fitzgerald, is gonna dance for us. . . . Hold up. . . . Correction, people. Miss Ella has changed her mind. She's not gonna dance, she's gonna sing."

Young Ella gave three encores and won first prize. But "she had meant to dance,"[25] just as Emily had meant to lie low in Canada. Instead, Emily "sang." The Greek philosopher Plotinus believed we each embody our own central premise that tolerates some wandering and drift, but not too much. He, and Plato before him, held that the innate image—*paradeigma*, the basic pattern encompassing one's entire destiny—is a spark of consciousness that takes an interest in what we do because (this is the part that turns modern psychology on its head) it chooses us from the start, for its reasons. Here's what finally landed for Emily:

> It's a stepping stone forward to go out, show my art, share my story, and feel good about it. With my family, they've been extremely supportive throughout this whole thing. And they've understood that this is something that I've had to go through. My mother has started speaking a bit about it. My father for the first time at the dinner table brought it up. But I don't know if this is something that they'll ever be able to accept completely, but I know that they love me and they trust me. They know because they were there that something happened.[26]

5

Detecting Signals of
Transcendence

When I began noting and looking into parallels between UFO encounters and the odysseys of the world's mythic traditions, there was no way around reckoning with the fact that, in our age, *myth* and *mythic* have largely become synonymous with something inaccurate or patently false, something mistakenly taken as fact. To a person whose life is upended through an encounter with a phenomenon that doesn't officially exist, a person who wants most of all a convincing explanation, the idea that decisive insight might come from myth and religion, or from *Grimms' Fairy Tales,* seems misguided at best, possibly completely haywire.

Joseph Campbell's use of "hero" can be perplexing for subjects of an unwanted episode that leaves their life compass spinning wildly and that seems to bear no relation to the idea of an accomplishment. I've lost count of the number of close-encounter witnesses who have told me, "It's like I was at the wrong place at the wrong time." The main decision after such an encounter is whether to tell even one other person or accept for oneself that *this is what happened.* The idea that they have embarked upon some ceremonially magnificent "hero's journey" just doesn't compute.

I get it. We're conditioned to think of a hero as an extraordinary person who sets out to accomplish extraordinary feats. By contrast, the subjects of close encounters usually speak of going about the business of living when something nearly beyond their comprehension intervenes. What I'm proposing is that this very sense of becoming an involuntary witness to the impossible resonates with Campbell's depiction of figures from myth and folklore living ordinary lives moments before being faced with life-changing circumstances. He makes a compelling case that "it has always been a chief function of mythology and rite to carry the human spirit forward," and "it may well be that the very high incidence of neuroticism among ourselves follows from the decline among us of such effective spiritual aid."[1]

The essential power of mythic narrative lies not in providing "the" meaning of life in general or a philosophy based on religious answers passed from on high; its potency is its capacity to speak to the innate image or idea that guides a life. For example, the myth that each person enters the world *called* is told differently by different cultures at different times. A common theme is that even "accidents" are taken to be meaningful. But this idea doesn't depend on belief. Just to consider the possibility without prejudice is to attend to life in new ways. It is to be willing to listen for what the sociologist Peter Berger called "signals of transcendence," phenomena that are "found within the domain of our 'natural' reality but that appear to point beyond that reality."[2] Berger believed our natural sense of affinity with a larger transcendent order is increasingly marginalized by the growing influence of secularization. This happens not so much to churches and other religious institutions, but "to processes inside the human mind . . . [as] a secularization of *consciousness*"[3] where the normal state of everyday awareness approaches "the same conception of reality as that held by a slightly drowsy, middle-aged businessman right after lunch."[4]

With this diminished state as society's de facto baseline of normalcy, Berger says:

> Whatever the situation may have been in the past, today the supernatural as a meaningful reality is absent or remote from the horizons of everyday life of large numbers, who seem to manage to get along without it quite well. This means that those to whom the supernatural is still, or again, a meaningful reality find themselves in the status of a minority, more precisely, a *cognitive minority*—a very important consequence with very far-reaching implications.[5]

By *cognitive minority*, Berger means a group of people whose view of the world contrasts significantly with the one generally taken for granted in their society, a group formed around a body of anomalous "knowledge." The quotation marks indicate that the "knowledge" always refers to "what is *taken to be or believed as* 'knowledge.'" The use of the term is neutral on the question of whether or not a socially held body of "knowledge" is actually true or false. The status of a cognitive minority not only allows for but encourages identity with others who share the same status of "knowing" certain truths about the world, just as others who don't share the supposed knowledge don't accept the minority's views as truth.

Acceptance or nonacceptance of a given truth claim generally comes down to consensus, which in turn depends upon the perceived plausibility of the claims in the eyes of various participants. What one person alleges to be knowledge, another person may call mere belief. To a greater degree than we usually acknowledge, plausibility is achieved not through definitive logical proofs but through tacit processes of negotiation. Knowledge is *socially* acquired, is in need of *social* backing, and is thus susceptible to *social* pressures. This goes to the heart of the Ariel incident, where the young witnesses didn't pause to consider whether the possibility of not being believed should keep them from reporting what they saw. As they stood transfixed on the playground, none of them could have known the continuous questioning they were in for would effectively make the sighting itself continuous—a one-time event that would replay in all subsequent efforts to explain what exactly they had seen and how it could have been real. Ken Arnold, constantly pressed to retell his story, was caught up in the same dynamics, as a cognitive minority of one.

The term *supernatural* of course comes heavily freighted with associations of phenomena outside or beyond the natural world. Here, to the contrary, I'm using supernatural to mean synonymous with supernormal and paranormal, indicating something like "of the natural world not yet explainable by existing science." Understood in this way, the term closely resembles the "otherness" of direct religious experience. Historian of religion Rudolf Otto, in *The Idea of the Holy* (originally published in German in 1917), attempted what many still consider a definitive description of the sacred (that is, the reality that human beings encounter in religious experience) as "totally other" than ordinary, taken-for-granted human phenomena.

Precisely in this "otherness," the sacred impresses as an overwhelming, awesome, irreducible, and strangely fascinating power. This primal sense of *otherness* is a feature of a wide variety of UFO-related experiences, from unexplained sightings of aerial objects in daylight and anomalous nocturnal lights, to landings by apparent craft that include humanoid creatures, to interactions with such beings, including abductions and quasi-medical examinations to be explored in the pages to come.

In the nearly eight decades since the phrase *flying saucer* became part of the cultural lexicon, a robust debate has ensued along lines that mirror Berger's description of how knowledge of unapproved or nonofficial truths is held by subcultures within a larger culture where direct apprehension of such truth isn't the norm and is likely to be considered an aberration from "the stuff the rest of us believe." Recall an early scene in the 1977 movie *Close Encounters of the Third Kind* in which a tense conversation takes place among the pilots of two commercial aircraft and the airport controller concerning unknown aerial objects described by the pilots:

Supervisor: Ask them if they want to report officially.

Air traffic controller: TWA 517, do you want to report a UFO? Over. [No response.] TWA 517, do you want to report a UFO? Over.

TWA pilot: Negative. We don't want to report.

Air traffic controller: AirEast 31, do you wish to report a UFO? Over.

AirEast pilot: Negative. We don't want to report one of those, either.

Air traffic controller: AirEast 31, do you wish to file a report of any kind to us?

AirEast pilot: I wouldn't know what kind of report to file, Center.

Air traffic controller: AirEast 31, me neither.[6]

"I wouldn't know what kind of report to file" is the pilot's frank acknowledgment that to go on record would likely result in his being seen as claiming unapproved knowledge, effectively relegating him to the status of a cognitive minority. In short, he'd be considered a weirdo. The pilot might expect to "be listened to with shocked surprise or tolerant amusement," Berger notes. "Attempts may be made to 'educate' him, or he may be encouraged to exhibit his exotic notions and thus to play the role of ethnographic specimen.[7] This is an uncomfortable status to say the least, for the majority refuses to accept the minority's descriptions as true knowledge. Culture doesn't lack for examples of holders of majority viewpoints being intolerant and sometimes repressive toward cognitive minorities who give witness to officially forbidden viewpoints.*

---

*"The last thing I wanted life to bring me was this unending sense of rejection, and the feeling that I'm considered either a charlatan or a lunatic, especially when what I have to offer is potentially so important and so valuable." Whitley Strieber's sentiment speaks to the complex emotions of many UFO experiencers.[8]

Consequently, when it comes to interpreting transcendent experiences that aren't supposed to even be part of the modern world but nonetheless continue to be, ". . . today no meaning is in the group—none in the world: all is in the individual," says Joseph Campbell. When collective rites no longer exist and the problems of life transitions devolve entirely upon individuals to work out for themselves, extraordinary encounters once considered ceremonially significant tend to be viewed as nothing more than points of sickness and anxiety for the individual. Campbell continues:

> One does not know toward what one moves. One does not know by what one is propelled. The lines of communication between the conscious and the unconscious zones of the human psyche have all been cut, and we have been split in two.[9]

While seeking adventure or a diversion or perhaps by accident or simply following a routine, like outdoor play during recess, a protagonist has somehow gone beyond "the world of common day into a region of supernatural wonder."[10] The reality of that region didn't simply recede for the Ariel students when classes resumed or when reporters faded away. Many felt as if their lives had come to a stop. That was Emily's experience when she returned to Canada with an understanding that what had happened was best left in the past. Yet unfinished experience continues to move toward completion or fulfillment. When Emily got the invitation to the Ariel reunion, she said yes. When she was invited to meet African sacred teachers, again she said yes. It felt right, so she made a trip by car beyond the boundaries of the childhood playground.

This was an act not of will but of faith. It was also an act of solidarity between young-adult Emily and eight-year-old Emily. As an example of a signal of transcendence, Berger cites a child who awakens at night with terror, perhaps from a bad dream, seeking reassurance from a parent who assures the child by word and gesture: Don't be afraid—everything is in order, everything is all right. "The reassurance, transcending the immediately present for two individuals and their situation, implies a statement about reality as such," Berger writes. "The formula can . . . be translated into a statement of cosmic scope—Have trust in being."[11]

Emily was keeping faith with herself at the deepest levels.

A UFO experience, or a related paranormal, parapsychological, or paraspiritual experience, is significant in that it doesn't fit the pattern of daily life, especially in a secular culture committed to the assumption that any intelligence perceived to exist in the cosmos can only be projected by the human mind. Tulane University philosopher Michael Zimmerman calls this "naturalistic humanism,"[12] a worldview in which ordinary individuals have little incentive to seek, long for, pray for, or even anticipate experiences that point beyond the absolute privileging of the human in the cosmic scheme. Such experiences come spontaneously, uninvited, and unexpectedly.

Often, before a witness begins trying to interpret what's going on, there's a sense that the visitation hails from a source other than the normal rational world we take for granted. This was indeed so for many of the Ariel witnesses. Ancient Greeks and Romans, Babylonians and Hebrews, Egyptians, as well as Europeans of the Middle Ages, assumed such encounters represented divine intervention in their lives and devoted themselves to discerning its promptings. Fate, character, genius, daimon, soul, and destiny (and of course, calling) all speak to its autonomous potency. In Campbell's framework, this prompts a Call to Adventure, signifying that:

> [D]estiny has summoned the hero and transferred his spiritual center of gravity from within the pale of his society to a zone unknown. This fateful region of both treasure and danger may be variously represented: as a distant land, a forest, a kingdom underground, beneath the waves, or above the sky, a secret island, lofty mountaintop, or profound dream state; but it is always a place of

strangely fluid and polymorphous beings, unimaginable torments, superhuman deeds, and impossible delights. The hero can go forth of his own volition to accomplish the adventure, as did Theseus when he arrived in his father's city, Athens, and heard the horrible story of the Minotaur; or he may be sent abroad by some benign or malignant agent, as was Odysseus, driven about the Mediterranean by the winds of the angered god Poseidon. The adventure may begin as a mere blunder, as did that of the princess in the fairy tale "The Frog Prince"; or still again, one may be only casually strolling, when some passing phenomenon catches the wandering eye and lures one from the frequented paths of man. Examples might be multiplied, ad infinitum, from every corner of the world.[13]

I quote this passage at length because of the many parallels between the call to adventure in mythology and numerous examples from UFO lore of individuals summoned "from within the pale of society to a zone unknown . . . a place of strangely fluid and polymorphous beings, unimaginable torments, superhuman deeds, and impossible delights."* Popular reports have accustomed us to UFOs seeming to disappear "above the sky." And there are a good many impressive reports of luminous disks retiring "beneath the waves."

Separation from familiar reality is how it starts, often with lights, buzzing sounds, sudden failure of machinery, and onset of terrifying paralysis amid otherworldly creatures who don't seem to represent the community's charity drive. An otherwise ordinary person just passing by a moment earlier is now navigating a bewildering labyrinth with no exit signs. In the ancient traditions of alchemy, success with separation, which begins with some fateful call, is considered essential for

---

*"Delights"? While it's true that many experiencers report unmitigated trauma, others describe positive, life-transforming effects from their interactions with otherworldly agents. Responses tend to fall on a full spectrum ranging from terror to transcendence.

giving birth to a new consciousness. Times of intense crisis, for an individual or a community, are requisite for re-creation. The workings by which order is birthed from the womb of confusion are analogous to those in which cosmos is born of chaos in creation myths, says Gregg Levoy in his book *Callings*:

> In the primary creation myth of Western cosmology, the very first call came through the voice that said "Let there be light," and there was light, the words then becoming flesh. Every call since then has also been a call to form, a call to each of us to materialize ourselves.[14]

Ken Arnold was surprised by what he witnessed because, as a skilled pilot, he knew what to expect as normal in the skies. Consternation can be collective, as with military officials and civilian air traffic controllers who realized they weren't tracking anything ordinary, but who also knew they'd pay a social price if they pressed the point. The Ariel students didn't face those pressures until later, when they began to realize what they had reported placed them in a special category of observers who had seen something that separated them from everyday assumptions about what can happen on an ordinary playground. No one voiced this disorientation quite like a girl named Dorothy when she spoke nervously to her dog at the outset of their own decampment from the known: "Toto, I have a feeling we're not in Kansas anymore." This is the recurring theme of sudden departure from consensus reality: all bets are off.

6

The Rockefeller Disclosure Initiative

I didn't expect a phone call from Laurance Rockefeller about UFOs in the summer of 1993, but I wasn't altogether surprised when it came. I knew he was interested in the subject and especially concerned about government overclassification of UFO-related documents. He was familiar with my work (*Angels and Aliens*) on parallels between contemporary UFOs and various phenomena that have shaped our mythologies, philosophies, and religions. Different divisions, same team. It turned out he was calling to brainstorm a plan of attack. I was all ears.

I had long admired Rockefeller as one of America's preeminent conservationists. Our paths had crossed briefly a decade earlier when I contacted him about pending federal legislation that many believed would turn a beautiful stretch of the California coast into a theme park in the name of protecting it. Owing to this brief encounter, Rockefeller and I had some positive history. Going forward to UFOs, we were on speaking terms.

"Well." I remember this is how he started the conversation. "I've been reading some things you've written, Mr. Thompson. You take what I would call a big-picture approach." I asked him to say more about that and to please call me Keith. "Then you'll call me Laurance, and we'll have the formalities settled," he responded warmly. "I noted a phrase you used, 'the pattern that connects.' You're looking to find out how UFOs are related to other anomalies. That's what I mean by big picture. Is that a fair summary?"

I considered it both fair and accurate and touched on a few correspondences between UFOs and religious miracles, the otherworldly journeys of shamans, near-death experiences, and the entire inventory of paranormal phenomena. How does this all hold together? Is there one underlying core phenomenon? Are there other dimensions pouring into our physical world? Or are we just profoundly out of sync with the true makeup of our immediate reality?

"This puts the UFO situation in a larger context," Rockefeller said. Then a pause, as if collecting his thoughts. "It seems you don't have many enemies in this field."

"That's easy." I don't go out of my way to pick fights, and I keep my distance from researchers who claim to be rock certain of what this is all about. It's possible for a hypothesis or perspective to be true, yet partial.

"What do you make of the abductions?" he asked.

I gave him an overview of my thoughts as described in the following chapter. Abductions by otherworldly beings are commonplace in world folklore. Crossbreeding between humans and otherworldly beings is a recurring theme in world mythology and religions. Obvious question: Where are the hybrid babies? This isn't to dismiss what abductees report. They're describing experiences that shouldn't be explained away, nor taken at face value.

"Well," he again said, as if planting a flag, the way the comedian Jack Benny would punctuate his laconic comments. "There's much to be understood. I've come to think some of the current views about abductions are headed down a blind alley. It seems John Mack at Harvard is asking better questions."

"Agreed," I said. "Mack has more questions than answers."

"That's terribly important," Rockefeller said. "False certainty is a constant danger in these territories." Another pause. "I have a particular endeavor in mind, one that's rather focused. I'm hoping you might agree to participate." He said he had gotten to know the Clintons, Bill and Hillary, president and first lady. He was planning a back-channel initiative to encourage President Clinton to get more UFO-related government information into the public domain, consistent with protecting national security. He said he had no doubt the subject was highly overclassified and it was time to start leveling with the American people. He also was of the mind that the Roswell affair was a good place to start, 45 years after the controversial crash of whatever-it-was in the New Mexico desert.

Step one: he planned to convene a private retreat at his Wyoming ranch where a small group of researchers and thinkers would devise and implement a strategic plan to further the cause of UFO disclosure at the White House level. Would I be willing to join in? "Count me in," I said. He told me to expect a call with details about dates and travel. "One more thing," Rockefeller said. "If possible I'd like you to come out to Jackson Hole a day before the gathering." He wanted to talk about the larger patterns in the evidence, as well as how the UFO controversy might be shaping human belief. "Sounds like a plan," I said.

After the conversation, I thought about the promise of Rockefeller's plan, and the potential drawbacks. Rockefeller was a classic "big fish," a person with enormous influence owing to his legendary family background. Precisely because he could pick up the phone and get through to presidents, it would be natural to hold high expectations about what the outreach could lead to. Rockefeller obviously understood this as a mixed blessing better than anyone.

I was on board with his civic-minded conviction that excessive secrecy works against the public interest, but I was also mindful of long-term hopes within the UFO community that a single individual with high cultural capital (and, ideally, considerable personal wealth) would be all it would take to "crack the UFO case, once and for all." This trope from bad detective fiction has become an article of faith for many in the UFO field. From conversations with intelligence officials with a genuine interest in anomalies, it is conceivable that much of what government officials may be hiding is embarrassed bewilderment about maneuvers such as those described by Luis Elizondo, former head of the Pentagon's once hidden UFO study:

> Imagine a technology that can do 6-to-700 g-forces, that can fly at 13,000 miles an hour, that can evade radar, and that can fly through air and water and possibly space. And oh, by the way, has no obvious signs of propulsion, no wings, no control surfaces, and yet still can defy the natural effects of Earth's gravity. That's precisely what we're seeing.[1]

Government, civilian and military, is supposed to be *in charge*. There's little reason to expect a Pentagon press secretary to tell reporters anything like this: "Something beyond astonishing has been entering and leaving our airspace with impunity for quite some time now, and darned if we have a clue what's going on, but we'll keep you posted." What we've gotten instead from government for decades are variations on this looped message: *Everything's fine, people. Return to your little lives.*

What made the Rockefeller initiative new and hypothetically different was the possibility that President Clinton might be in a position, and could be willing, to send some ripples into the federal bureaucracy and at least start a process toward greater disclosure . . . but disclosure of precisely *what*? If government accounts of what happened at Roswell have been a series of layered lies crafted to mislead, what hypothetical chain of events would motivate the current keepers of the lies to step up and simply say "Never mind." It's the liar's paradox in spades: "Yes, I was lying yesterday. But you can trust me now for sure."

With all these considerations, I had no reservations about accepting Rockefeller's invitation. Not expecting his phone call was the least of it. I also hadn't expected to be pursuing the UFO phenomenon over the long period since a sixth-grade class report. I had come to believe there was no guarantee that consistent efforts to get the phenomenon to "make sense" would necessarily lead to definitive answers. For as Jacques Vallée has observed, it's entirely conceivable:

> [T]hat the universe might contain intelligent creatures exhibiting such an organization that no model of it could be constructed on the basis of currently classified concepts. . . . The behavior of such beings would then necessarily appear random or absurd, or would go undetected, especially if they possessed physical means of retiring at will beyond the human perceptual range.[2]

No matter whether the phenomenon is natural or artificial in nature, Vallée concluded, "we are presented with the dual possibility of long-term unsolvability and of continued manifestation."[3] That a new myth should be nourished on this duality is entirely predictable, he added. Indeed, the consistency of UFO observations, combined with their irreconcilability with current scientific knowledge, creates a logical vacuum that the human imagination cannot but seek to fill with its own hopes and fears.

What a brilliant place to hide, deep in the creases of currently accepted scientific concepts! The narrow ways we have learned to interrogate the phenomenon practically ensure that its displays must appear random or absurd, or simply fail to be detected, or be subject to infinite speculation in the province of Proteus and his trickster soulmate Hermes, fleet-footed messenger and spanner of thresholds. Awkward and sometimes outlandish dismissals from supposed arbiters of reality in science and academia only send UFO paradoxes underground into the collective psyche, where their symbolic portents become all the more powerful as drivers of culture.

The same holds for those evergreen rumors of crashed and recovered spacecraft and efforts to reverse engineer them at an ultrasecret wing of Area 51 . . . and continuing buzz about creepy alien corpses preserved in jars stored in dark recesses of the byzantine military-industrial complex . . . and credible reports of military officials scouring the desert floor for scraps of whatever had crashed outside Roswell . . . and alleged threats to locals that if they dared keep any of the material they could get in *really big trouble.*

I was eager to get into all of this with my unexpected host and to spend time brainstorming in the wilds of Wyoming with fellow heretics with expertise in various facets of the mystery. There seemed a real prospect of moving the football down the field. It was also possible the meeting would founder on the unproductive shores that Vallée had described. What would be the best way to minimize the chances of that? Participants could always bring new and daring questions and dial down presumptions of certainty.

Rockefeller's first outreach to the Clinton White House was in a March 29, 1993, letter written by Henry L. Diamond, Rockefeller's attorney, to Jack Gibbons, PhD, special assistant to the president for science and technology. The letter stated that Rockefeller, described as "a leading U.S. conservationist, businessman, and philanthropist," was "anxious to have a brief meeting with Dr. Gibbons (Special Assistant to the President for Science and Technology) to discuss the potential availability of government information about unidentified flying objects and extraterrestrial life." Rockefeller was prepared to tell President Clinton the following:

> There is a belief in many quarters that the government has long held classified information regarding UFOs which has not been

released and that the failure to do so has brought about unnecessary suspicion and distrust. Many believe that the release of such
information, if it exists, on a basis consistent with national security
considerations, would be a significant gesture which would increase
confidence in government.[4]

Rockefeller arrived with a briefing paper for Gibbons written by
award-winning journalist Richard Farley based on his 20 years of active
UFO inquiry. J. Allen Hynek and prominent ufologist Jacques Vallée
were the chief contributors to Farley's thinking. Gibbons informed his
visitors that in his three months as science advisor he had no knowledge
of any information on UFOs being withheld from the public. (In other
words, no keepers of secrets had volunteered any secrets.) About a week
later Rockefeller wrote Gibbons, thanking him for the chance to present
their case for "UFOs and Extraterrestrial Intelligence." Rockefeller
said Scott Jones would be sending along an annotated bibliography as
important background source material on UFOs, as apparently prom-
ised at the briefing. In a May 26 letter to Jones, Gibbons revealed he
had received the bibliography, along with a number of books from the
Jones Foundation Library. Gibbons told Jones he was reading the UFO
books and would return them when he was done.

Documents obtained by Canadian UFO researcher Grant Cameron
indicate Gibbons had recommended that the UFO issue be handed off
to Secretary of Defense Les Aspin for action, even though some members of Gibbons's team wanted to keep UFOs in their jurisdiction.
Meanwhile, Aspin was encouraged by Melvin Laird (former secretary
of defense in the Nixon administration) to send UFOs back to Gibbons
and the president for action. In a letter dated April 13, Rockefeller noti-
fied Gibbons that Scott Jones was "planning to convene a small group
to discuss the state of knowledge about UFOs and ETI in an informal,
non-public way." Gibbons or one of his staffers would be welcome as an
observer. One of Gibbons's staff members scribbled in the margin of the

letter, "I would be willing to go if JHG [John H. Gibbons] OKs it."[5]

Several weeks later, Rockefeller officially invited Gibbons to join the informal roundtable discussion that was to be held September 13–15, 1993, at Rockefeller's JY Ranch in the Bridger-Teton National Forest near Jackson Hole, Wyoming. Neither Gibbons nor staff elected to attend but asked to be kept informed.

As requested, I came to the ranch a day before the start of the roundtable. A ranch hand showed me to a rustic cabin with décor right out of the Old West and suggested I might want to rest up from the trip. I told him I'd like to roam around a bit, and he assured me there was plenty of room for roaming. I found a trail through woods, rocks, streams, and meadows with glorious autumn foliage, all leading to a vantage point over an expanse of water known as Phelps Lake that opened to a cavernous joining of rock and sky called Death Canyon. I spent at least an hour in quiet reverie before ambling back toward my cabin and noticing Rockefeller approaching on a different path. He wore khakis, a casual jacket, and western hat, carried a sheaf of papers under one arm, and with his free hand poked the ground with a classic walking stick. Think Henry Fonda in *On Golden Pond*, with hints of an older Spencer Tracy. Rockefeller was 83.

After a brief exchange of greetings, we delved into UFOs. He wanted to know how I came to be interested in the subject. I said the Michigan case explained away as swamp gas had been my beginning. "Oh, yes, that was quite the circus, wasn't it?" he said with a chuckle. Rockefeller traced his interest to being raised with a "commitment to participate." This meant more than simply taking up duties or tasks; it involved engaging wholeheartedly in family, community, and society. He described this with a reverence that implied a bond with the very spirit of life. Though his brothers were known for political careers, LSR (as he was known to friends and family) had cut his own path through his involvement in humanitarian endeavors. Rockefeller had answered an early call, and it had stayed throughout his life. Long before Socrates and Plato came Heraclitus, who spoke three little words, "*Ethos anthropoi daimon*," frequently rendered as "Character is fate." *Ethos* usually gets translated as "ethics," but the more ancient source is closer to "habit" or "custom." Rockefeller was accustomed to participation. It was kind of his *thing*.

He credited studies of values and purpose at Princeton, which led to an undergraduate degree in philosophy. "UFOs are an intersection of philosophy, science, and religion," he said, adding: "And of course, government is in the mix, which is what we're going to be exploring this weekend." He asked how I had gone from the Michigan case to what he again called my "big-picture perspective."

I said I had read widely in philosophy and psychology in college, as Rockefeller had. Alan Watts's book *The Wisdom of Insecurity* turned me on to the idea that the main source of insecurity is our trying so hard to feel secure. Abraham Maslow's books stood Freud on his head by showing spiritual and existential needs are primary human matters. As for UFOs, after Michigan I'd paid close attention to news coverage. I assumed UFOs would probably be explained sooner than later. Somehow this prompted Rockefeller to say, "I would like to see UFO investigations take on greater scientific rigor, like the field of near-death research." Nodding agreement, I brought up my experience. He said he had friends who had come back from death or its brink, and he'd like to hear what happened.

Rockefeller had no way of knowing this was not something I spoke of freely. I had learned to keep quiet about Hawaii for much the same reason I made a point not to discuss my unexpected rooftop recognition of *just this*—the immediacy of this present moment, this open aware presence that is seamless and ungraspable, radically alive and full of everything, elusive of all conceptual formulations. Even though near-death experiences now were part of popular culture, I had not paused to review my long-standing self-protective strategy of not talking about my "big" experiences, due to the uneven or negative reactions I had grown to expect, even from well-meaning friends whose voices I still hear: "You nearly drowned; that's a major trauma; get therapy and things will be normal (again)." Rockefeller's simple invitation to tell him what had happened felt like an opening to the Breakthrough Conversation I had somehow stopped expecting.

I told him about the moment in the waters of Hawaii when I was sure I was going to die. The day before, I had run the Honolulu Marathon with several close friends. We had driven north to Oahu's legendary Sunset Beach to get in some epic bodysurfing. *IF IN DOUBT, DON'T GO OUT!* Beach signs warned about Sunset's famously fierce breakers, but I wasn't a bodysurfing novice and didn't intend to head far away from shore. The grandeur of completing a 26.2 mile race only made the prospect of engaging huge waves all the more exhilarating. The air was balmy, and the salty water still warm by December standards. I remember it being around noon.

Enjoying the buoyancy near shore, I swam out to catch a breaker. Out and back several times, a little farther each run. I knew to stay tuned to the waves coming in. What I didn't know was the importance, let alone the force, of the currents coming back from the beach under those waves, out toward the horizon. Somebody calls my name, and I give thumbs-up and begin heading back to quieter waters. The rip currents have a different idea, carrying me out with astonishing swiftness, while larger waves keep breaking against me yet not bringing me closer to shore. I paddle hard in that direction but can't make headway, and get trounced from behind by a breaker and slammed against the ocean floor. Returning to the surface gagging from swallowed water, I hear my name again. No thumbs up this time. The shoreline is moving rapidly in the wrong direction. The rip current sucking me out is relentless. My legs feel like lead from the marathon; treading water is harder with each kick. More shouting from shore as another wave crests over my head. *I'm close to drowning.* Then the biggest wave yet takes me under and into a spin. Tumbling through a field of darkness I don't know which way to go for air. *Now I'm going to die.*

I felt myself leaving my body through the back of my head. From some vast vantage point, I looked down at my friends on the shore, who were focusing their worried attention on the body of a swimmer I paradoxically recognized as Keith. My body was maybe 200 yards offshore, struggling in loud and tumultuous waves. While out of body and witnessing the scene from above, I heard my friend Mary Payne speaking to a friend by her side: "Why didn't he listen? I told him the water was too rough." I tried to let them know I was still "here" but not as the body flailing in the surf. My message wasn't heard. Suddenly, blackness with a swooshing sound that grew steadily to the roar of a freight train, and a sense of being propelled through a vortex at great speed with spectral flashes of color and light reflecting off "walls" that appeared to be alive and breathing. With this came astonishing tranquility and joy. *"This may destroy me, but it can't hurt me."*

In what seemed an instant, I was again seeing through the eyes of my body—the body that had been wrestling with the waves. Somehow these waves carried me into a calm cove near shore. People I gradually recognized as my friends waded toward me, urgently repeating a single syllable, "Keith." I grokked that this word referred to me as an exhausted sentient individual, just as the words Mary, Jim, and Moore referred to their separate selves. After a semblance of normalcy returned on shore, my friend Moore said, "Man, you came pretty close to giving it up out there." I told him, "I did, but came back." When I gave details, everybody looked at me like I was delirious. I only knew everything had changed.

The next day I told Mary there was something I needed her to know, so we went for a walk. I told her I'd heard what she had said on the beach. When I quoted her exact words ("I told him the waves were too rough . . ."), her face paled. We both understood what it meant. It should not have been possible for the struggling swimmer to hear her subdued remark from a great distance. Likewise, my experience of seeing the swimmer's body from a panoramic vantage point beyond the body. At the time, I only knew that the reality game board was bigger than anybody had clued me to expect.

Like most people, I had never given thought to the "nature of consciousness." I would probably have said awareness is on when the body is alive, off when the body dies. As with my rooftop experience a decade earlier, everyday language isn't of much use for conveying a dimension of reality where time and distance play no role; where consciousness is everywhere and endless. Where the sense of "I" as a field of spatially unlimited subjectivity can easily take up residence as seemingly separate embodied forms.

Especially, where "dead isn't dead."

Rockefeller listened to this story intently, then cracked a smile. "I can understand why you haven't been thrown off by the paranormal aspects of UFOs, with that experience." After a pause, he asked, "So you believe consciousness survives permanent death?" I said yes, consciousness also precedes birth, in the sense of being the ground of everything. "But I can't give you proof," I said. "None asked," he responded.

We both looked at the mountain peaks bathed in crimson sunlight. I asked Rockefeller if he was aware that a large number of what appear to be solid spacecraft materialize instantaneously before witnesses, and then disappear before their eyes the way old TV screens faded to a single dot on being turned off. "Fascinating," he said. "And yet these apparent craft do sometimes leave landing marks and radar evidence and sometimes burn the skin of witnesses. So, it's a physical phenomenon in some sense, would you agree?"

Indeed, physical some of the time, or physical in *some sense*, switching between phases of manifestation and disappearance. This is a phenomenon that doesn't obey the strict separation between the subjective, psychological world that's supposed to stay inside our minds and the objective, physical world that's supposed to stay out there. We talked about the need for a framework that includes *all* the data, including new thinking about different degrees or grades of materiality. I mentioned the many traditions of the world that speak of subtle matter and subtle-bodied beings. Could subtle matter be a link between UFO phenomena, paranormal apparitions, the dead, and unknown aspects of our own nature? "And we haven't begun to grapple with the significance of consciousness," I added.

I said the field needs broad empiricism* that views many different kinds of phenomena together, from UFOs to near-death experiences, shamanism to religious miracles, folklore to paranormal research, and then looks for how these distinct areas may be connected. From there, look for the patterns that connect these realms that seem disparate.

"That's maybe a lot for the White House," I said, thinking I'd probably been talking too much. Rockefeller held up an index finger, as if saying, "Hold up." After maybe twenty seconds of silence, he continued. "The ideas are important, but yes, too much for the White House. If we come in with metaphysical guns blazing, we'll be easily rebuffed. We must be *strategic*." His strong inclination was to present President Clinton with a narrowly focused proposal to begin creating greater government transparency. "If we can get the disclosure ball rolling . . ."

He didn't need to finish the sentence. He clearly felt the goal should be to get an audience on a specific set of issues that don't require a larger

---

*In *Religion, Philosophy, and Psychical Research,* British philosopher C. D. Broad writes: "Philosophy involves at least two . . . closely connected activities, which I call Synopsis and Synthesis. Synopsis is the deliberate viewing together of aspects of human experience which for one reason or another are generally kept apart by the plain man and even by the professional scientist and scholar. The object of synopsis is to try to find out how these various aspects are inter-related. Synthesis is the attempt to supply a coherent set of concepts and principles which cover satisfactorily all the regions of fact which have been viewed synoptically."

paradigm of reality. One foot in the doorway today, widen the opening tomorrow. Start by urging disclosure of what no longer needs to be concealed. An unknown factor: whether government actors would willingly relinquish control of whatever they are sitting on, whether it was evidence of crashed saucers or simply their befuddlement about the true nature of the phenomenon.

Rockefeller opened up his accordion file folder, and pulled out a worn copy of *The Art of War* by Sun Tzu. "There are many gems here," he said, reading aloud: "*The most difficult things in the world must be done while they are still easy, the greatest things in the world must be done while they are still small.*" Looking up from the page, he said: "The president's term is still young. He has called for greater openness across the board. Let's give him a chance to claim a win."

Then he glanced at his watch. "Maybe that's enough for now?" he said. I nodded as we stood up, both of us looking at the illumined mountain peaks. "The wonder never ends," he said. We shook hands and my host turned toward the path. "To be continued," I said. "Oh, yes," he said.

The conference started the following evening when everybody had arrived at JY Ranch. Participants made presentations on their primary research and thinking, followed by group brainstorming. There was agreement and disagreement on key points and a collegial agreement that deliberations would be off the record in the spirit of encouraging candor.

The roundtable ended with an understanding that Rockefeller would continue engaging with Jack Gibbons of the White House Office of Science and Technology, and that the most productive approach would be to prioritize getting the facts out about a single UFO case, with hopes that success with one significant case might have a cascading effect. Rockefeller still felt the Roswell incident of 1947 was the case to go with. He was more than a little surprised

Fig. 6.1. September 14, 1993, at JY Ranch near Jackson Hole, Wyoming. Researchers who came together with Laurance Rockefeller and associates to discuss strategies for the Rockefeller Disclosure Initiative. Left to right: Henry Diamond, Dr. Steven Greer, Dr. Bruce Maccabee, George Lamb, Robert Bigelow, Linda Moulton Howe, Leo Sprinkle, Keith Thompson, Dr. John Mack, Laurence Rockefeller, C. B. "Scott" Jones, Anne Johnie Jones, Robert Teets. Photographer: Marie "Bootsie" Galbraith.

when Jack Gibbons subsequently wrote Rockefeller to encourage the quest:

> We believe that your approach of starting by addressing a specific incident is an important and reasonable way to begin the process of declassification in this area.[6]

In a letter to Gibbons, Rockefeller moved quickly to lock the science advisor in to the agreement:

> If it actually was UFO related, it could be used to start the process of reversing the government's 40-plus years of denial on the subject.

If it can fully be explained as not UFO related, it would be a significant contribution to the field, and perhaps even contribute to more rigor in research on the subject.[7]

Rockefeller's hopes were high when, in May 1994, President Clinton's general counsel Robert G. Damus sent out a memorandum to agency heads declaring intent to enforce Clinton's proposed declassification executive order titled "Declassification of Selected Records within the National Archives of the United States." Four months later, those hopes were dashed when the air force issued a press release announcing its final conclusions:

> The Air Force research did not locate or develop any information that the "Roswell Incident" was a UFO event nor was there any indication of a "cover-up" by the Air Force. Information obtained through exhaustive record searches and interviews indicated that the material recovered near Roswell was consistent with a balloon device of the type used in a then-classified project. No records indicated or even hinted at the recovery of "alien" bodies or extraterrestrial materials.[8]

Rockefeller's point man on the project, Scott Jones, expressed immediate disappointment at what he saw as the air force's assumption that the UFO issue could still be "managed" so as to maintain secrecy. It was clear to Jones that Clinton had the authority to demand a full briefing, but nothing of the sort would ever come if Clinton seemed to signal he could take it or leave it.

Rockefeller himself responded with characteristic diplomacy and grace. "I hope we made it clear that we were very grateful for your initiative in stimulating the recent Air Force Review of the Roswell incident," he wrote in a letter to Gibbons. "Although many who are students of UFOs felt that the report was not complete, your leadership in bringing this about was an important step." He told

Gibbons he would be continuing "our citizens' reconnaissance of the extraterrestrial intelligence phenomena" and that he wanted "to take the opportunity of keeping you informed and from time to time seek your counsel."[9]

Disclosure activists perked up the following year when a report by the Government Accounting Office on the Roswell incident revealed that all outgoing messages from the Roswell Army Air Field generated during the period surrounding the event had gone missing. The circumstances of the disappearance were unclear, including when the files had disappeared. Maybe the 1950s. The '70s? Rumors began circulating that the Rockefeller inquiry had set off a panic among current caretakers of the cover-up; they must have gone into full delete mode to make it harder to get to the facts about whatever had crashed at Roswell in June 1947. Then it was revealed that the missing messages extended as far as March 1945 to 1950.

Crashed-saucer proponents interpreted this to mean the cover-up custodians wanted to be thorough, so they had decided to scoop up everything from two years before to about two years after the crash. This hypothesis was a key that opened the desired lock: smart conspirators are painstaking. Any alternative keys? It's not hard to imagine systematic, long-term embezzlement of government funds at military installations, with deletion of records to cover tracks. Mere speculation, of course. If getting to the bottom of it were up to me, I'd send Jack Reacher a bus ticket to Roswell.

Rockefeller had made clear from the start that he was playing a long game. He viewed the apparent setback as an opportunity to regroup. The goal had been to open a door, and he'd succeeded. More from Sun Tzu's *The Art of War*: *"Walk in the path defined by rule, and accommodate yourself to the enemy until you can fight a decisive battle."*

Laurance Spelman Rockefeller had ended this phase of his pursuit just as he had begun it: as one for whom *participation* joins obligation as service and opportunity as adventure. This italicized word and the largeness it signified for him came up in our final phone conversation a few years before his death in 2004. "It matters to me less than ever where they're from," he said, "whether outer space or hidden dimensions right here. What's clear is they have access to greater realities than we understand. Just as we humans have depths we don't realize."

"It's like the phenomenon is inviting us to participate," I said.

"Yes. In the largeness of existence," he replied. "I hope you'll keep asking questions." I knew he would as well. I can still hear his quiet words as we stood watching the glowing mountains of Wyoming:

"The wonder never ends."

7

The Alien Abduction Impasse

The letter dated February 28, 1992, began "Dear Colleague, We are organizing a scientific conference to assess the similarities and differences in the findings of various investigators studying people who report experiences of abduction by aliens, and the related issues of this phenomenon.

"One of the features of this conference," the letter continued, "will be an abductee panel with abductees drawn from the community. If you have investigated an abductee who is thoughtful and articulate and has had particularly interesting and/or manifold experiences, please send us his/her name and a brief paragraph about why this person would be a desirable participant." The five-day conference would be held at the Massachusetts Institute of Technology (M.I.T.) from June 13 through June 17.

Signed by Harvard psychiatrist John E. Mack, the letter ended with this handwritten PS: "Very much hope you can make it. You have a lot to offer. JEM."[1]

I crossed paths with John Mack for the first time at the Esalen Institute at Big Sur, California. Before Mack got interested in the subject, I'd convened a 1986 conference there called The Further Reaches of UFO Research, bringing together a cross section of UFO thinkers and investigators to brainstorm the phenomenon. The following year, while a participant in an Esalen symposium called Frontiers of Health, Mack met Stanislav and Christina Grof and got acquainted with the practice of holotropic breathwork.* When Mack became a regular participant in breathwork modules, Stanislav handed him a chapter I had written for the Grofs' forthcoming anthology, *Spiritual Emergency: When Personal Transformation Becomes a Crisis*. The piece was based on a talk I had given at an annual UFO and abductee conference in Laramie, Wyoming, convened by Leo Sprinkle, PhD, a University of Wyoming professor whose research went back to the 1960s. The talk outlined likenesses between traditional rites of passage and UFO encounters, as discussed earlier in this book in chapter 1, "Wording, Method, Sources." *New York Times* journalist and author Ralph Blumenthal picks up the story in his biography of Mack, *The Believer*:

> Mack had no idea why Grof would give him Thompson's chapter. He read it with skeptical interest, all the while asking himself, "But is it true?" Were people being contacted by humanoid beings? He saw that Thompson had skirted the question phenomenologically, but he still couldn't help wondering. Mack was still wondering later that year when he went back to California for another breathwork module, heard . . . about prominent abductions researcher and author Budd Hopkins, and, somewhat to his own surprise, sought him out. . . . "One of those dates you remember that mark a time when everything in your life changes."
>
> It was his own call to adventure.[2]

---

*Psychiatrist Stanislav Grof and his wife Christina Grof developed holotropic breathwork, a technique in which breathing is regulated by rhythmic music with the aim of inducing an altered state of consciousness to facilitate emotional and spiritual healing and personal growth. Mack credits the method with opening him to dimensions of awareness that went well beyond the concepts of his formal psychiatric training. Years later he would say everything went back to the Grofs. "They put a hole in my psyche and the UFOs flew in."

When we spoke for the first time about the UFO phenomenon, Mack said that if he hadn't come across my published talk, he thought it unlikely he would have started down the road of investigating the reports of people who claimed they were taken against their will by alien beings.

"Are you giving me credit or blame?"[3] I asked ironically.

"Credit for now, subject to review," he said, laughing. I had long admired Mack as a prominent activist for nuclear disarmament and for his Pulitzer Prize–winning biography of T. E. Lawrence (of Arabia), *A Prince of Our Disorder*. My thoughts would often return to our first conversation as Mack became increasingly famous as the Harvard psychiatrist who studied the subject of alien abductions, especially when Harvard launched a critical inquiry into Mack's research. The chief investigator, Professor Arnold Relman, had assured Mack the committee's job was not "to conduct an inquisition into your beliefs and opinions—that is none of our business."[4] When the investigation even-

Fig. 7.1. Dr. John E. Mack of Harvard University shown with Digger, the coonhound his son Kenny rescued from a shelter.

Photo courtesy of John E. Mack Archives, LLC.

tually took on a decided inquisitorial tenor, Mack would think himself foolish for overlooking that it was Relman who brought up the possibility of an ideologically driven investigation in the first place. "Detectives would call that a clue," he said.

Mack was well aware that his interest in alien abductions would prompt disdain and probably opposition at Harvard, where, as with many elite universities, the call to "celebrate diversity and inclusion" doesn't always extend to minority *viewpoints*. He told me he didn't really care, as he planned to follow the advice of Thomas Kuhn, an old family friend and author of *The Structure of Scientific Revolutions*, who cautioned Mack to "hold on to the null hypothesis as long as possible."[5] In other words, until evidence to the contrary appears, assume that his observations could be explained in conventional terms. Consider any other hypothesis as something to be *dis*proved. Kuhn urged Mack to postpone conclusions until and unless Mack felt certain he had at least three smoking guns. In the meantime, gather evidence.

We talked about how the abductions debate is usually assumed to come down to a single question: "Are they *real* or *unreal*?" Mack understood that I had temporarily set aside this question to make a case for structural parallels between abductions and initiatory rites of passage. UFO discourse has a way of congealing into binary choices that present themselves with an unspoken sense of necessity to *make a choice right here, right now, go no further until you decide.* I had discovered that the pressing call to answer this or that UFO quandary can simply be noticed and left to itself. The UFO field needs a "waiting room" that encourages abiding with such questions, on the assumption that more will be revealed as the phenomenon continues presenting itself.

At the time of our first conversation, Mack's psychoanalytic training and practice had led him to a dual-role approach: he was investigating the nature of the events through interviews and hypnotic sessions with experiencers, while also serving as a clinician of sorts to the same individuals, often simultaneously. Mack had been tutored in the investigatory methods of Budd Hopkins and David Jacobs, both of whom had concluded that abductions are unquestionably physical rather than merely psychological or symbolic events. The two had moved beyond "what if this is true?" and were focused on finding new subjects with abduction claims to bolster their established conclusions. This was the approach that Thomas Kuhn had urged Mack to avoid. From his study of paradigm shifts in science and society, Kuhn realized it is human nature to prefer mental shortcuts. This allows quick judgments to be made, usually at the cost of disregarding information that contradicts existing views.

Mack and I found common ground on a number of issues. The abductions are real because they happen—but they "happen" in what sense and on how many levels? What is the nature of reality such that events of this kind *could* occur as reported? UFO narratives in general, and abduction reports in particular, are frequently punctuated by quick cuts: "Suddenly I was inside . . ." or "The next thing I knew . . ." or "I don't remember how I . . ." Scholar Peter Rojcewicz calls UFOs a "blurred-reality genre"[6] that to some extent manifests in physical reality but doesn't leave unambiguous traces and thus maps poorly onto material physics.

What's not at question, we agreed, is the reality of extraordinary *perceptions*. There are valid differences about how best to interpret the perceptions. They can't just be papered over. Neither of us could name a single field of human endeavor where progress results from lockstep thinking. We didn't have definitive answers. We were both hoping for better questions, and knew there had to be many we hadn't imagined.

J. Allen Hynek would likely have given Mack the same advice as Thomas Kuhn. Though health issues kept Hynek from attending the Esalen UFO conference I convened, he kindly agreed to speak with me by phone from his home in Scottsdale, Arizona. We discussed not only the current state of UFO research but also his memories of key turning points in his perspective toward the phenomenon. As we talked about the earliest reports of abduction, I asked if he could recall his visceral response to those early reports, and their implications for further study of the phenomenon as a whole.

"I remember my feelings at the time quite well," he said with laughter.

"My gut response was, 'Oh, isn't this just *great*.'" Hynek said this sardonically, and continued:

> It was one thing to take seriously reports of aerial objects that gave the impression of being under intelligent control, but now there were reports of credible humans interacting with humanoids. This complicated the whole picture, yet there was no more of a logical basis to refuse consideration of the reports than to ignore UFO reports as a whole. It never occurred to me or Jacques [Vallée] that deliberately rejecting legitimate data was an option. How could we square that with authentic science? We were suddenly faced with reports of luminous beings that found walls no impediment to passage into rooms, and who appeared to take control of the witnesses' minds. If this is an advanced technology, then it must encompass paranormal factors as much as our own technology includes semiconductors and holograms.
>
> Is it proper to consider the abductions event-level happenings in the same sense that we are speaking by telephone at this moment? Or do these humanoids and UFOs represent a parallel reality that somehow manifests itself to a few of us as limited episodes? This wasn't the first time, and it wouldn't be the last, that science faced data that don't fit conventional models. In any area of basic research, various hypotheses can and must be eliminated when found inadequate. But just ruling the data of a phenomenon out of bounds in advance is never honorable. And it is entirely appropriate to speculate without reaching definitive conclusions.[7]

Close encounter classification was first proposed by Hynek in his 1972 book, *The UFO Experience: A Scientific Study*.[8] UFO sightings are placed into two distinct categories: distant sightings and close encounters. The following categories identify the criteria for each classification within the close encounters scheme. The "close" range means the witness estimated the UFO to be no more than 500 feet away.

- Close encounter of the first kind (CE1): A UFO is witnessed that has no interaction with the environment and leaves no traces.
- Close encounter of the second kind (CE2): A UFO leaves physical traces or has physical effects on the witness and may have interaction with animals or objects.
- Close encounter of the third kind (CE3): A human can see occupants in the UFO or around the UFO, if landed.
- Close encounter of the fourth kind (CE4): Abduction or direct contact, including verbal or telepathic exchange. This category includes cases where witnesses experience a marked transformation of their sense of reality, sometimes including medical procedures, artificial insemination, semen removal, object insertion, and so on. Close encounters of the first three kinds were already part of Hynek's taxonomy when the abductions necessitated a fourth category.
- Close encounter of the fifth kind (CE5): A witness claims to initiate and establish communication with a UFO or nonhuman intelligence through meditation or focused attention.

The first speaker at the M.I.T. conference is Mark Rodeghier, director of investigations for the Chicago-based Center for UFO Studies, the most prominent of the UFO research organizations. Rodeghier's topic is "A Set of Selection Criteria for Abductees." He has three minutes to talk and two minutes to answer questions.

Placing a transparency on the screen of an overhead projector,

Rodeghier begins speaking. "In order to qualify as an 'abductee,' a person must be (a) taken against his or her will, (b) from terrestrial surroundings, (c) by nonhuman Beings." Quickly replacing his first transparency with a second, Rodeghier continues: "The Beings must take a person to (a) an enclosed place, (b) nonterrestrial in appearance, that is (c) assumed or known to be a spacecraft by the witness."

Third transparency. "In this place," Rodeghier continues, "the person must be either (a) subjected to a physical examination, (b) engaged in communication, verbal or telepathic, or (c) both."

Fourth transparency. "These experiences may be remembered (a) consciously or (b) through methods of focused concentration, such as hypnosis."[9]

Next up is Thomas E. Bullard, a professor of folklore whose presentation is an update of his now five-year-old research paper "On Stolen Time: A Summary of a Comparative Study of the UFO Abduction Mystery." Bullard announces that the number of cases he has cataloged since his 1987 summary has risen to 725; but he is less exacting than Rodeghier about what should be considered an "abduction." He reports coming across about 80 cases where witnesses have seen luminous or glowing orbs in their rooms, and he has also gathered what he calls "psychic abductions"—narratives by people about experiences that are "close" to being abductions but fall short of being physical events. There are also what Bullard calls "voluntary entry" cases. In these instances, individuals seem to welcome visitation, and for that reason, he says, "they shade into 'contactees' in that they develop a long-term, nonprofit relationship with the aliens."[10]

After a break, Budd Hopkins, dean of UFO abduction investigations, strides to the podium. The author of two books on the subject (*Missing Time* and *Intruders: The Incredible Visitations at Copley Woods*), Hopkins is not given to understatement, as indicated by his characterization of abductions as "the most portentous phenomenon science has yet to produce." Abductions most often take place at night when people are sleeping, Hopkins declares. "The person is first paralyzed—although there seems to be different degrees of paralysis, people can generally move their eyes. Most abductees Hopkins has dealt with are then either lifted up a beam of light or floated up accompanied by the entities into an awaiting spacecraft, "a journey that for the most part, it seems to me, goes astonishingly unnoticed by people outside whom one might otherwise expect to witness it,"[11] notes Courtlandt Bryan, an open-minded yet seasoned journalist and author set to write a book about the conference.

Using interviews and regressive hypnosis with hundreds of abductees or "experiencers," as they are sometimes called, Hopkins became well known for reporting cases in which a woman is somehow impregnated and the embryo is then removed by UFO entities and given up to surrogate alien parents, who purportedly have the ability to communicate telepathically with the "transgenic" (human-alien hybrid) child. According to victims' reports, as stated by Hopkins, the human parents are allowed to see the child during continuous, deeply traumatic abductions that they are powerless to prevent. If people have had one abduction experience, Hopkins said, then they will have others.*

John S. Carpenter, a Missouri-based clinical social worker, came to the conference because he had studied abduction reports expecting to find evidence of psychopathology that would explain the reports. He came up empty-handed:

> I fully expected to have to wade through a variety of psychological
> issues first—including fantasies of hysterical individuals, dramatic

---

*According to abductions researcher David Jacobs: "Abductions sometimes take place in 'clusters.' They may increase as the child approaches and goes through puberty, continue through the teens, and then abruptly stop. Long periods of time may pass without an abduction and then they begin again—intensely. Sometimes the abductee can have as many as one experience every few nights for a week or two. For some women, frequency is linked to their menstrual cycle. Abductions increase during ovulation and decrease during menstruation. The frequency of abductions for men has not yet been adequately researched, but it appears to be less predictable than for women."[12]

confabulations from Borderline Personality Disorders, dissociative episodes as with Multiple Personalities, attention-seeking antics of sociopathic characters, intricately-woven psychodynamics of those traumatized in childhood, and the space-age delusions of insecure individuals, influenced by extraterrestrial themes and speculations in all of the media.

"But to my astonishment," Carpenter continued, "none of these expectations has become valid in my research so far,"[13] and this was after he had interviewed police officers, schoolteachers, college professors, business people, and community leaders who claimed to have had abduction experiences. John Mack stood up to point out that among the abductees who have sought his counseling, none showed a "desire to be perceived as an experiencer."[14]

By the end of day three, journalist Bryan found himself struggling with all the complexities: "I realize *I don't know what to believe!* How does one explain the similarities in the abductees' stories—the consistency of detail, structure, scenario?"[15]

There are also *inconsistent* details, which Mack addressed when he sat for an interview with Bryan after the conference. "I'm struck by the fact that there seems to be a kind of matching of the investigator with the experiencer," he said, noting that abductees he works with often emphasize positive psychological and spiritual effects of their experience, while the abductees of Budd Hopkins and David Jacobs describe their experiences as nearly always traumatic.

"The experiencers seem to pick out the investigator who will fit their experience," Mack observed.

Bryan asked, "Could you have that backward?" Isn't it equally possible that Jacobs and Hopkins "may pull out of their experiencers what they want to see?" Mack responded, "People said that of them at the conference; I can't say that."[16]

Ironically enough, some of the best evidence that top abduction investigators actively *work* their experiencers for preferred outcomes comes from their own accounts of the research methods they follow. Their bias is often concealed, especially to themselves, by their certainty that they have taken strides to be unbiased. David Jacobs is such an investigator.

Now a retired associate professor of history at Temple University, Jacobs wrote his dissertation on the controversy over unidentified flying objects in America. A revised edition of his dissertation was published to acclaim as *The UFO Controversy in America* by Indiana University Press in 1975. When he later found himself curious about abductions, he wanted to be sure that abductees were fundamentally different from "people [who] have always claimed that many sorts of strange events have happened to them."[17] This includes people who claim to have lived past lives, communicated with denizens of the spirit world and even Space Brothers, or "had near-death experiences with religious implications."[18]

A college freshman taking an introductory science methodology course would quickly spot the fallacy of Jacobs's automatic assumption that "psychology rather than objective reality would explain these stories,"[19] and for this reason such phenomena could safely be set aside from serious consideration. That near-death experiences should have "religious implications" strikes Jacobs as especially beyond the pale. His main interest was to find out quickly whether or not the alleged abductions might merit the same proper disdain. Read his account of his preliminary exposure to abductions reports:

> The problem was that when I read abduction accounts I could get no real sense of the progression of events from beginning to end. Most of the reports consisted of snippets of stories, beginning in some logical order but then either ending abruptly or swerving off into wild, fantastic flights of fancy.[20]

The "problem" for Jacobs is that abduction narratives seem to be just a series of unrelated episodes: *this* happens and then *that*. There are no signs of the structure of causation expected of "realistic" narratives that typically feature an exhaustive working out of what Aristotle called "necessary or probable sequence." This element is what causes otherwise random successive episodes to "make sense," as in a page-turning detective thriller or a historical narrative. "Character A does one thing which, perhaps only much later, is shown as affecting Character B in a probable or 'realistic' way," observes literary scholar Stuart Miller. "The reader's response to such a 'model' realistic plot is an ordered response to an image of order."[21]

There are obvious parallels between realistic genres of narrative and the world of modern science and philosophy. In both realms, order, probability, and predictability reign supreme. Jacobs candidly discloses this is what he is looking for, and what he not only wants but needs to find, if he is to undertake a serious study of abductions. He could not make things plainer: "As a historian, I required a chronological narrative." Jacobs continues:

> I needed a clear idea of exactly what the abduction accounts consisted of. I wanted to learn the details on a careful, rigorous, second-by-second basis, beginning with an abductee's first feeling that something extraordinary was happening to him and ending when the event was finally deemed to be over. I needed to be sure of my evidence.[22]

In short, he wants to make sense in terms of his own expectations of plausible order. But, again, all he sees in abduction reports are fragments that express anything but order—and this is crucial: fragments that express anything but order *as Jacobs defines order*. Compare Jacobs's sense of order with Peter Rojcewicz's characterization of phenomena that "raise the question of whether or not an event takes place in an intermediate realm which doesn't manifest exclusively in a physical objective way or leave a trace." Rojcewicz is describing a *different kind of order*, which to Jacobs would not be order at all, for without limitations of probability and realistic causation, the door is left ajar to the fantastic, the random, the weird. This opens the door to the intuition that the world could be without fundamental order; the world might be chaotic, again as Jacobs defines order and chaos.

At the M.I.T. conference, journalist Bryan declares himself "leery . . . of Dave Jacobs's attempts to impose a historian's order on what, to me, appears utterly chaotic: the abductees' efforts to come to grips with what they believe has happened to them."[23] But to Jacobs it seems self-evident that he should be able to use his professional training as a historian of conventional events to come up with the real facts about alien abductions that reflect a world structured by probable laws resembling modern science and realistic narrative. If he knew in advance that the basic plot structure he would encounter in abductions would closely resemble that of magic realism (think the novels of Gabriel Garcia Marquez, Isabel Allende, Salman Rushdie), Jacobs might be less interested in tracking abductions. Almost certainly, he'd take a hard pass.

This is not to ascribe to Jacobs unique narrow-mindedness. His views exemplify core precepts of the Enlightenment, according to which the material world is *manageable* and can be studied and thoroughly understood by means of empirical science limited to gross sensory information, as distinct from integral or inclusive empiricism in which realms of visionary illumination (including subtle-material phenomena) can likewise be studied and chronicled as aspects of reality. In Jacobs's implicit worldview, it was an advance when the Renaissance and the Reformation devalued and sidelined aspects of reality that aren't reducible to discernment by the five senses. Sidetracked in this way, larger-dimensional, extrasensory, supernormal, or primordial religious experiences (even when these are felt and cognized as constructive and life-changing) are to be considered merely speculative and mythic (in the narrow or eliminative sense) and, finally, declared *unreal*. This approach is sometimes referred to among philosophers as "eliminative materialism," based in empiricism limited solely to physical evidence.

By taking "mind stuff" off the table in advance, Jacobs is confident he can pursue the pragmatic satisfactions of discovering how the *real* mechanics of this planet work. Almost certainly Jacobs would recoil at the idea that this eliminative move on his part was inherently ideological or faith based in ways comparable to the Vatican's demand that Galileo disregard the view of the heavens made available through his telescope. The ideological component in the two scenarios consists of this unstated stricture: Observations must be limited to predetermined categories of allowable phenomena. *Yes to empiricism, just not too much.* *

So Jacobs's dilemma at the outset is that he has no way to know how to achieve the certainty he desired. But his uncertainty doesn't last for long.

> I knew that if I were to make sense of what was happening, I would have to do abduction research myself. This meant I would have to learn hypnosis . . . By 1985 Hopkins was doing his own hypnotic regressions, and he invited me to sit in on his sessions. I discussed hypnosis techniques with him and other researchers. I read books about hypnosis. I attended a hypnosis conference. I learned about the dangers and pitfalls of hypnosis.[25]

Learning hypnosis was *imperative*, Jacobs says. But where was it written that hypnosis is an indispensable investigatory tool, simply because it was part of the abductions methodology of a few other researchers? Jacobs is describing the methodology he assumes he would have to follow to replicate the findings of his mentor Budd Hopkins. Once he sets up shop, his next concern is how to avoid getting mired in

---

*The philosopher Alfred North Whitehead's summary of this limited empiricism: "At this moment scientists and skeptics are the leading dogmatists. Advance in detail is admitted; fundamental novelty is barred. This dogmatic common sense is the death of philosophical adventure. The universe is vast."[24]

false patterns. Remarkably, he decides to exclude from his data pool all "one-of-a-kind accounts—no matter how dramatic." For he takes it as axiomatic that "no reliable inferences can be drawn from them without confirming testimony from other abductees."[26]

This comes close to saying that any time a new finding is recognized, it must be discarded simply because there's no other like it. By definition, this precludes the discovery of evidentiary patterns that diverge from previous ones. How far would Charles Darwin have gotten if he had stipulated in advance that every fourth fossil he came across in the Galapagos islands would have to be discarded if it didn't match the prior three?

Here's the three-part clincher. (1) Jacobs quickly discovers he has special prowess in identifying details in abductee narratives that are obviously untrue ("unknowing confabulations" is his phrase). (2) Jacobs learns to eliminate such details on the spot because they don't fit the broader emerging patterns of evidence. (3) The criteria for trustworthy abduction details will be the extent to which they de facto "make sense" to Jacobs in consultation with his mentor, Budd Hopkins. Seldom is the circular thinking of confirmation bias quite so round and smooth or the elimination of cognitive dissonance quite so comprehensive. It escapes Jacobs entirely that abductions conceivably could represent new ontological territory—a different *kind* of order—not yet mapped by science or society. Or, the seemingly new territory could be ancient but largely forgotten due to a long period of dormancy. His sole focus is how to situate abductions phenomena into his existing paradigm as a historian of realistic events.

"I noticed that the abduction accounts were forming themselves into distinct patterns of reality," Jacobs says after he has begun working with people who claimed abduction experience. "Practically all the abductees said that they were experiencing similar physical, mental, and reproductive procedures."[27]

"Abduction reports were forming themselves." This description of sim-

ply *finding* patterns greatly downplays his role in *forming* them according to the specific criteria he brings to the table. The near-unanimity of abductees follows inevitably from Jacobs's a priori elimination of abductees with divergent stories and from his similar dismissal of abduction themes from folkloric sources preceding the saucer era. How much potentially relevant evidence did Jacobs leave "on the cutting room floor" when he edited out details that didn't fit the predominant Hopkins-Jacobs alien profile: thin, grayish-colored beings 3½ to 4½ feet tall, called the Greys and occasionally assisted by beings colloquially known as the Talls?*

I don't doubt that Jacobs in good faith believed the data shaping his emerging mythology was solid; that is, direct and unfiltered, free of researcher error in translation or other bias. What I am suggesting is that Jacobs places himself at the mercy of a data-filtering mechanism so subtle he is simply not aware of his role in creating and implementing it. In other words, the clarity and coherence he sees in his emerging findings better describe the clarity and coherence of his mental picture *projected onto the data*. In further words: Jacobs *brings* to the data the order he purports to *find*.

In his book *The Threat*, Jacobs asserts that when his subjects reported "out-of-body experiences" on the "astral plane," experiences such as intuitive communications with animals, visions of extraordinary radiance, encounters with deceased relatives or friends "reassuring them that 'Everything is all right,'" or seeing religious figures—such as guardian angels or the Devil—it was proper for him to conclude that these interpretations represented nothing more than the sincere, unconscious efforts of an "unaware abductee" attempting to "explain their strange

---

*Here is a relatively short list of widely reported alien types besides Greys and Talls: Insectoids, Reptilians, Hybrids/Clones, Dwarfs/Short Non-Greys, Giants (8–12 feet+), Sasquatch/Bigfoot, Cetaceans (resembling marine mammals like porpoises and whales), Amphibians, Felines, Canines, Mer-peoples, Spirits/Ghosts, Energy/Light Beings. Additional frequently reported types: Human-looking and Mini-humans. In retrospect, the bar scene in George Lucas's first *Star Wars* movie was remarkably prescient.

experiences in ways acceptable to society."[28] When these temporarily self-deluded subjects subsequently became aware that they were actually abductees, only then were they set free, Jacobs says, to discard such false religious and paranormal interpretations. By this extreme reductionism, William James's classic study *The Varieties of Religious Experience* should be dismissed as a compendium of false interpretations used by victims of alien abduction to avoid coming to terms with the terrible truth. A truism often attributed to psychologist Abraham Maslow comes to mind for Jacobs's methodology: "When the only tool at hand is a hammer, every problem tends to look like a nail."

And, speaking of axioms: our college freshman quickly learns that what human beings "know" is never merely the result of passively receiving information from an objective environment; knowledge is necessarily the outcome of an active subject's *constructive activity*: sensing, selecting, sorting, and so forth. Jean Piaget puts the matter this way: "Intelligence organizes the world by organizing itself."[29] The perceptive Italian philosopher Vico never tired of reminding fellow knowledge seekers that it should not surprise them if the world they experience and get to know seems stable and coherent, since that world is necessarily constructed by themselves (ourselves).[30] Indeed, our word *fact* comes from the Latin *facere*, to make.

I'm aware that readers devoted to Jacobs's work might have appreciated a "trigger warning" at the start of the preceding section, for it must seem my skepticism toward his methods means I think his findings should be dismissed, just as Jacobs rejects the possibility of afterlife phenomena. Not so. My reference to Jacobs's "mythology" is in line with Bernardo Kastrup's idea that myth consists of words that encode "a certain way of interpreting consensus reality so as to derive meaning and affective charge from its images and interactions."[31] I certainly don't embrace popular notions that myth means "inaccurate" or "patently false." The territory is far richer and more nuanced.

Kudos to Jacobs for constructing a sincerely held, highly coherent, indeed, close-to-airtight picture of abductions data, based on criteria he brings to the conversation.

The purpose of my critique is to suggest that when the witness reports Jacobs deemed unreliable are not summarily eliminated, the full reality of abductions might turn out to be far more complex, and ultimately even weirder, than his highly structured findings suggest.*

Concerning Jacobs's claims of human-alien hybrids and implants placed in human bodies by aliens, neither am I implying that these frequent motifs in abductee narratives are simply concocted by Jacobs (or Hopkins). The concern is how to interpret these motifs—precisely what evidentiary status to afford them—given that Jacobs freely acknowledges:

> The aliens themselves were enigmatic. I did not know whether they ate or slept, or had any kind of life outside the abduction context. The same was true of the hybrid babies, toddlers, adolescents, and adults; their lives were a mystery. . . . I was also puzzled about why abductees were subjected to strange *staging* and *testing* procedures in which they acted out a scenario with aliens or found that they could operate complex devices or perform tasks they do not remember having learned.[33]

"Staging" and "testing" are interesting words in this context—and revealing. Abductees sometimes report being given a task and observed carrying it out. The aliens are described as seeming interested only in observing abductees' emotional response. In the spirit of speculation,

---

*"The real UFO story must encompass all of the many manifestations being observed," writes John Keel. "It is a world of illusion and hallucination where the unreal seems very real, and where reality itself is distorted by strange forces which can manipulate space, time, and physical matter—forces that are almost entirely beyond our powers of comprehension."[32]

suppose these apparent tests are themselves staged to appear authentic, for the purpose of observing abductees' responses to tests they assume to be genuine. Question as thought experiment: What if abductees are chosen to witness presentations of imagery that the aliens (or the intelligence behind the UFO phenomenon *manifesting as* aliens) intend for abductees (and researchers) to *absorb* and *believe*?

From this standpoint, could it not be the case that abductees indeed see what they see, because what they see is what they are deliberately *shown* by an intelligent metaphenomenon that generates such culture-specific happenings with the aim of influencing the arc of human belief? Jacques Vallée muses whether "an advanced race somewhere in the universe and sometime in the future has been showing us three-dimensional space operas for the last two thousand years, in an attempt to guide our civilization? If so, do they deserve our congratulations?"[34]

The theme of hybrid offspring from pairings between humans and otherworldly beings is a mainstay of religions and mythologies throughout the world. Abduction is a standard theme in traditional fairy tales (which must be distinguished from the abridged versions that come to us "sanitized" to meet the nursery-rhyme standards considered appropriate for modern children). In the older abduction motifs, young ones are also taken, and a fairy child, called a changeling, may be substituted for a human child. An obvious implication is that, if such activity in modern UFO literature is assumed real, it therefore doesn't lack precedent, as Jacobs and Hopkins insist it does. An implication more appealing to debunkers, of course, is that both modern and ancient reports are cut from the whole cloth of sheer nonsense. But this is neither my point here nor my claim. Like John Mack, I want to highlight our recurring impulse to "shrink this vast, fascinating, powerful phenomenon to our notions of reality rather than being able to stretch ourselves to expand what we know and to admit that we don't know and to open up."

True to his nature, Hermes would be quick to point out that there's a third interpretive option, beyond either literal readings or simplistic debunking. Recalling Hynek's invitation to think outside the boxes, such pairings can also be interpreted *symbolically*, as foreshadowing of human mind meeting cosmic mind; or indeed, they can be taken to indicate that the meeting is already accomplished, as an aspect of latent human potential. The recognition of a reality ordinarily concealed before being apprehended as our true nature, our immortal soul, our "original face," is implicit in much Hindu, Buddhist, Jewish, Christian, and Islamic thought. Jacobs obviously prefers a literal reading consistent with his materialist commitments, so, in fairness, let's follow his lead.

Presuming actual human-alien hybrids ("hubrids" in Jacobs's phrase) do walk among us and their goal is to make themselves known, I wondered whether a 23andMe genetic test would likely produce anomalous genetic results. When I put this question to Dr. Garry P. Nolan, professor in the department of pathology at Stanford University School of Medicine, this was his response:

If it was seeable by 23andMe, it would have been seen. In fact, 23andMe is crude compared to the analyses which have been done. Graduate students and postdocs go over those public datasets of millions of people's genomes. No one has seen anything that smacks of hybridization or totally novel gene sequences not seen in other people. You can be sure that someone would have noticed it (unless such alleged hybrids have been consciously avoiding detection). Remember—the algorithms are sophisticated enough to detect Denisovan and Neanderthal genes in our DNA. That said, there's more than enough sequences of humans available that if there were true "hybrids" it would have jumped out at people by now. So, my conclusion is that hybridization is not a real thing.

The best way to think about it is twofold:

First, selective breeding over thousands of generations of humanity can accomplish more than any single genetic intervention. Look at what we've done with wolves and dogs over a few thousand years. A superior intelligence could have done the same thing with us and we would not even know it. I am not saying it has happened, I am just saying that seeing that a certain tribe succeeds, or a certain individual marries another is a great way to play if you have near infinite patience. Witness the Bene Gesserit—the social, religious, and political force in Frank Herbert's fictional Dune universe—in their quest for the Kwisatz Haderach, a term for miraculous travel between two distant places in a brief time. It took them 10,000 years of selective breeding to get Paul Atreides. Frank Herbert had a good sense of timing for genetics even if his work was fictional.

If some alien civilization *did* feel a need to "engineer" our genomes, it would need to be done at a far subtler manner than what we generally think of as genetic engineering. It would need to be done at a near epigenetic level—which is a level of intervention that we do not have in our toolkit yet, and likely will not for several decades at least. For instance, where is the gene for "nest building" in birds? There is none. The instinct and motor patterns for this are not found in any single gene. It is distributed across likely millions of places in bird chromosomes and so subtly intertwined in the 3D architecture of DNA that our most sophisticated AI could not find it. The reverse: to encode something like that would require a level of knowledge we don't have, but that said it would be undetectable to us.

So, while 23andMe is the right thought process, it is not able to see something we have not seen to date. More than willing to be proven wrong, but it's not likely.[35]

Jacobs insists that the alien-human hybridization process is now so far advanced that the hybrids now "look very human," so much so that "if properly attired and wearing dark glasses, they could 'pass,'" although they might be "off" in their appearance by having "too much black in their pupils or lack eyebrows or eyelashes." Although "it is unknown precisely how many stages of hybrid development exist, the evidence points inexorably to the development of an increasingly human-looking and human-behaving hybrid armed with the aliens' ability to manipulate humans."[36]

It must be acknowledged that Jacobs tempers his certainty about what "the evidence points inexorably to" by acknowledging that his thinking "makes me seem as if my quality of mind is lacking and my judgment is severely impaired. It destroys my credibility in virtually all other areas of my intellectual life, and did so as a professor of history." Jacobs candidly admits that "the majority of evidence for the alien abduction phenomenon is from human memory derived from hypnosis administered by amateurs," and "it is difficult to imagine a weaker form of evidence."[37] He adds: "But it is evidence and we have a great deal of it," but "still, readers must be skeptical of what I say and of what all others say in this tangled arena of alien abductions, hypnosis, popular culture, and memory."[38]

Implicit in Nolan's analysis: If the humanoids that play such a prominent role in the case studies of Jacobs and Hopkins are real, their existence poses a steep challenge to the Darwinian theory of evolution. It is highly unlikely that beings so similar to us could have independently evolved on another planet. But is it necessary to limit evolutionary possibilities to the Darwinian "database"? In the ancient Vedic worldview of India, living beings are conceived as souls dwelling within bodies. Known as the *atma* and *jivatma*, the soul is endowed with the faculty of consciousness. The body consists of a gross body composed of familiar physical elements (as visible in a mirror or on a driver's license) and a subtle body made up of energies that can't normally be detected by our current scientific instruments.

The conventional scientific view is that such energies do not exist.

According to Vedic understandings, however, these energies naturally interact with gross matter and can exert a powerful influence upon it. I will take up ideas along these lines in the following chapter.

It seems fitting to conclude these ruminations by returning to the famous Betty and Barney Hill abduction case, which stands out for its resilience within the cosmos of ufology. Like Kenneth Arnold's sighting 14 years earlier, the legend of the Hills became timeless from the moment it entered the collective imagination. The Hill case stands as a primordial precedent—the mythic First—for future alien abductions, just as much as Arnold's sighting represents the mythic Origin of flying saucers.

Budd Hopkins acknowledged as much when he stepped forward to affirm the logic behind the Hill case's *ideal* status. In his book *Missing Time*, Hopkins adopted the Hill case as a model and primary reference point for his research with abductees. If a particular case follows the basic outlines of the Hill encounters, according to Hopkins, it thereby merits designation as either a likely or a definite abduction. In mythic terms, this statement holds particular appeal as a foundational judgment in its insistence that once a precedent is established, more authenticity will likely follow.

But there's a catch. The converse of Hopkins's theory necessarily follows: If any aspect of the Hill case doesn't conform to the abduction prototype, then any of the rest of the abduction model is up for revision, much the same as with the Arnold case when new and pivotal details surfaced many years after his sighting was misreported by the media.

What is the essence of the Hill case as widely reported over many decades?

During the night of September 19, 1961, Barney and Betty Hill, an interracial couple, are driving back home on an isolated road in central New Hampshire. They see a strange light that resembles a falling star but moves differently. The light seems to follow them and steadily grows closer. They stop and use binoculars to get a better look, but then get back in their car and continue their journey. When they have traveled 35 miles farther, the Hills find they cannot explain how two hours have elapsed, nor can they recall what had happened during that period.

Two days later, Betty leaves a message with the nearby air force base and gets a return call the following day. Betty describes what they had seen, making no mention of the presence of beings. The official she speaks to explains the sighting as a likely misidentified planet. Betty goes off to the local library and checks out a book about UFOs by retired marine pilot Donald Keyhoe, who argues in the book that the Department of Defense was hiding evidence of technologically advanced aliens.

When the Hills begin having strange dreams, they consult a respected psychologist and undergo hypnotic regression in 1964, nearly three years after their sighting. While in trance, the Hills for the first time describe being abducted by strange beings and taken aboard a spacecraft where they undergo some sort of strange medical examination. Under hypnosis, Barney identifies the aliens as having wrap-around eyes. Twelve days prior to the hypnotic session, an episode of the TV series *The Outer Limits* had featured aliens with the same sort of eyes. In other details, the TV aliens seemed to resemble the UFO pilots of Barney's description.

In their account of the event prehypnosis, "the Hill couple did not clearly see a craft." While conscious, they described seeing something with their naked eyes and with binoculars that "appeared to be flashing thin pencils of different colored lights, rotating around an object which at that time appeared cigar shaped."[39] As told under regression, the "spaceship" was actually perceived as an orange ball of fire. Author Eric Ouellet notes this is typical of the most common form of earthlights, which are believed to be produced by the grinding of tectonic plates or landscape features that produce or contain gravitational or magnetic anomalies. Some who interact with these luminous orbs describe them as intelligent or sentient and sometimes malevolent. The Hills settled on the spaceship interpretation, thus cementing it as part of the myth.

Though well-known pro-ET researchers have claimed that the UFO was tracked on radar on the night of September 19 over central New Hampshire, subsequent research by David Webb and John Oswald in the 1970s found no evidence of a link between the radar tracking and the Hills incident.[39] What about the magnetized marks that appeared on the car? Given the orange ball of fire they described under hypnosis, "then perhaps the 'perfectly' round and magnetized marks noted by Barney and Betty on their car could be explained by the impact" of earthlights, Ouellet speculates. "In any case, those marks do not constitute a proof of any ET involvement."[40]

So far, this exchange illustrates the familiar point-counterpoint argumentation that so often leads to impasses in which established opinions get to hang tight. But there are other details in the Hill case that have not been widely reported, and they bear striking parallels to discrepancies between what Kenneth Arnold actually sighted in 1947 compared with what the media misreported. The psychiatrist and parapsychology researcher Berthold Schwartz discovered that after their New Hampshire encounter, Betty and Barney Hill:

[B]egan to experience poltergeist phenomena in their home. Betty would find her coats unaccountably dumped on the living room floor even though she had left them in the closet. Clocks would stop and start mysteriously, or their time settings would change. Water faucets would turn on when nobody was there, and electrical appliances would break down and then work perfectly well without repair.[41]

Recall that Kim Arnold described inexplicable orbs of light appearing in the Arnold house after her father returned from his fateful flight.

She also spoke about her mother's telepathic gifts and reincarnation beliefs. It turns out that Betty Hill had a history of paranormal experiences, including precognitive dreams in high school in which she foresaw the deaths of school friends in automobile accidents. Many of her family members were reportedly psychic.

These remarkable details were not widely known at the time the Hill case became iconic as the prototypical alien abduction case, just as Kenneth Arnold's description of nine luminous, blue-white, streaming, pulsating, seemingly alive, rapidly soaring object-beings near Mount Rainer did not make it into media accounts, which inaccurately reported that Arnold saw nine objects *shaped like* saucers. Nor did the 1947 media stories report that Arnold believed UFOs come from a larger-dimensioned world, "the world where we go when we die." This information wasn't available because Arnold waited many years to disclose it.

Here is the significance of the parallel between the Arnold and Hill cases as precedents: In both narratives, certain primary perceptions (luminous, pulsating blue-white objects for Arnold; orange ball of fire for the Hills) became conflated with a particular popular interpretation or storyline that emphasized that ET craft were very likely seen, as opposed to the perceptions being considered in terms of the longer, larger history of visionary encounters. This flouts the elementary principle of parsimony, which in logical reasoning stands for identifying the simplest, least complicated explanation of a situation or observation that accounts for all observations without embracing unnecessary or peripheral assumptions. Parsimony doesn't mean taking some hypothetical fastest route in a way that eliminates observed details; it means finding the most efficient, effective, and comprehensive path to account for a body of data. If there's a simpler yet equally thorough solution, this is the desired choice.

With both the Arnold and Hill cases, a parsimonious eye sees that the ET interpretation was layered upon primary perceptions of *light*.

At the heart of UFO accounts, a relatively small number of interactions are consistently described. An apparent object or light appears in the sky or, less specifically, in the spatial environment of a witness or witnesses. This object or light (or combination) affects people, animals, machines, or other physical surroundings in an unusual way. Frequently, but not invariably, some form of interaction occurs between human witnesses and either occupants of the apparent craft or beings that appear out of vast luminosity. Sometimes communication takes place, verbal or nonverbal; occasionally, the beings perform "operations" on the human witness; often a voyage to "other realms" takes place inside a strange craft.

But parsimony is not an ironclad rule. It can simply be set aside. Doing so allows for the preceding UFO characteristics to be dropped into a storyline of post–World War II events starring outer space visitors. Striking resemblances between modern UFO events and encounters with numinous beings from myth and folklore can thus be kept out of view. When the resemblances are pointed out, they can be declared irrelevant—along with likenesses between the aerial effects reported by abductees and the flights of seventeenth-century witches. What about parallels between bedroom intrusions by UFO beings and evil spirits said to descend upon and have sexual intercourse with women as they sleep, reported in cultures around the world for millennia? These too can be ignored. What relevance should be given to the fact that the majority of modern abductees are women?

The most famous proponent of such historic and cross-cultural comparisons, Jacques Vallée, wasn't invited to speak at the M.I.T. conference. He had told the planners he would be willing to appear at the end of the event to comment on broad comparisons between ancient and modern encounters. The planners declined his offer, perhaps sensing the potential complications of a heretic inside the temple of inquiry?

A full survey of Vallée's writings gives no reason to think his purpose would have been to reduce contemporary abductions to "mere" folkloric status. For decades, Vallée has sought to broaden the conversation beyond the contemporary saucer frame to include historical and cultural parallels, including reports from history and folklore indicating that a time dilation effect (in which time inexplicably passes more slowly in parallel worlds than in the ordinary world) bears resemblance to the "missing time" motif of modern abduction narratives. Vallée would likely have urged participants to recognize signs that UFO reality could be much weirder that they were allowing themselves to imagine. It would have been true to form for Vallée to call for expanding inquiry to meet the robustness of the phenomenon. "My view of the phenomenon has evolved," Vallée states, "beyond classic physical and biological parameters to a reality in multiple layers: it melds the pre-existing grid of its logic with the consciousness of the observer, manifesting a 'display' of arbitrary complexity."[42]

From a sheer evidence-gathering standpoint, the wider context would have made considerable sense. If investigation of modern alien abductions is comparable to a crime scene investigation, as Jacobs and Hopkins frequently state, why would competent forensics investigators choose to rule out of bounds in advance databases covering periods that precede the modern age of saucers? In fairness, Vallée understood that contemporary abduction researchers already face ridicule for giving credence to reports of diminutive aliens known as Greys literally kidnapping helpless humans with impunity. It wasn't hard to understand why today's researchers might prefer not to add in angelic and demonic encounters from the Middle Ages or humanoid races mentioned in Vedic literature. It was difficult enough even for tenured professors to deal with professional disdain for the implications of the current reports.

After the M.I.T. conference, Mack reflected on what he saw as one of the gathering's unresolved contradictions. "Some of the investigators . . .

want to have it both ways. They want to treat this as a literal phenomenon of hybridization and genetics in our physical world. . . . But in treating this phenomenon in that manner, they're not really looking at the shattering implications of this for the nature of our reality, or the fact that this means we're in a relationship that has some meaning beyond this.

"In other words," Mack says, "I don't see how, on the one hand, you can say this phenomenon shatters our notions of physical reality and then treat it entirely literally in terms of our physical reality." In a 1994 interview with *New York Times* magazine writer Stephen Rae, Mack recounted an argument he'd had with Jacobs. Mack had said, "David, how can you say this is the real experience, the reproductive baby-making aspects, and the rest is secondary when we don't know what reality any of this is taking place in?"[43] He elaborated on this point a year later in his book *Abductions*:

> The UFO abduction phenomenon appears to originate from an unseen reality, but "crosses over" into the physical world. It presents us with severe methodological problems, for we do not know just how to study a matter which shows up in the material world but does not seem to be *of* that world. . . . The fact that what experiencers are describing simply cannot be possible according to our traditional scientific view would, it seems to me more sensibly, yes *rationally*, call for a change in that perspective, an expansion of our notions of reality, rather than the "jamming" of "data into existing categories" that some critics would have us do.[44]

Mack appeared to be speaking to those who would dismiss abductions reports entirely, as well as to others who not only take today's reports entirely at face value but also dismiss the idea of mythic and folkloric phenomena as genuine precedents. Both groups generally accept the "existing categories" into which abductions do or do not easily fit. In the final analysis, Mack found himself questioning whether the existing categories are adequate: "It is for us to embrace the reality of the phenomenon and to take a step toward appreciating that we live in a universe different from the one which we been taught to believe."[45] Mack considered this step pivotal to breaking the abductions impasse.

His biographer Ralph Blumenthal felt Mack would have had trouble with *The Believer* as the title of his book, for Mack insisted that he was not what most people called a believer. "Yet I believe he believed," Blumenthal writes. "He believed in taking risks and breaking boundaries to boldly explore the deeper secrets of existence. . . . John Mack set forth, journeyed far, had many adventures, and returned to tell the tale around the digital firelight, for humanity's sake. It's what heroes do. It's what human beings do."[46]

8

Who Do We Think We Are?

After the M.I.T. abductions conference, I spent a lot of time reading many of the papers that would eventually be published in a large volume of the proceedings.[1] A horde of different opinions with a common pattern: practically any hypothesis could be "proven" by marshaling instances on its behalf. This eye-glazing exercise convinced me I needed not more information but *perspective*, and I couldn't think of a better source than Courtlandt Bryan, the insightful journalist who had begun drafting a comprehensive book that would be published three years later under the title *Close Encounters of the Fourth Kind*.

Bryan said the one case that stood out for him was that of Linda Cortile. According to Budd Hopkins, at 3:15 in the morning in late November 1989, Cortile was floated out the window of her twelfth-story apartment on the East River, New York City, into a hovering UFO before two cars of witnesses who subsequently confirmed her account. Bryan tracked down many of the witnesses, who provided a level of detail that he thought would be considered persuasive in a normal crime scene investigation. "Just sticking with the observations as reported, it's hard to avoid basic questions starting with what and how," Bryan told me. "What's the nature of reality, for such a thing to even be possible? If it happened, how the hell did it happen?"[2]

Great questions. Had Bryan put them to Hopkins? "Not yet," he said. I said I had a phone interview scheduled with Hopkins, and I would ask him myself and let Bryan know what I found out. Confederacy of journalists on the lonely levitation beat.

When I spoke with Hopkins, I asked him to characterize what was going on with levitation of bodies through solid substances in abduction cases—how exactly it happens. He said aliens obviously possess advanced technology that uses light beams to dematerialize and rematerialize bodies over short periods. He placed great emphasis on "obviously." Then I asked how he made sense of the paranormal dimensions of abductions phenomena such as synchronicity, which is the joining of conscious and unconscious intentions that points to intentionality beyond ordinary volition. Hopkins responded with disdain: "Oh, I don't find that stuff relevant. Evidence for the so-called paranormal is speculative and it's just not helpful to mix up abductions with *all that*."[3]

When I finished lifting my jaw off the floor, I wondered if it was actually possible that a leading researcher of an anomaly such as alien abductions might not be aware that experimental studies of paranormal phenomena have been presented in credible journals for more than 50 years. Or that evidence for paranormal events is supported by its obvious correspondence with reports about telepathic, clairvoyant, and psychokinetic events in the shamanic and religious tradition, as well as in everyday life. Or that in surveys during recent decades, large percentages of diverse subject groups have reported spontaneous experiences of extrasensory perception. Frederick Myers and other founders of the (British) Society for Psychical Research publicly distanced themselves from groundless claims, fuzzy thinking, and outright deception prevalent among mediums and occultists.*

---

*Hopkins deemed evidence for the paranormal merely speculative, yet considered evidence for alien abductions solid by comparison. This put Occam's razor in a new light for me. The principle of parsimony, though wise and pragmatically useful, is far from an absolute dispute-settling tool. The legendary blade cuts differently for different observers—and confirmation bias must be factored in.

Simply stated, there's considerable evidence for paranormal phenomena. Those who wave the evidence away in the name of science—the ever-present debunkers—invariably do so, quite unscientifically, on grounds that such phenomena violate "known laws of nature," even though the alleged laws turn out to be faith-based beliefs that rule the very possibility of paranormal phenomena out of bounds categorically in advance.

I decided to put this question to Hopkins: Could the reports of seemingly "impossible" phenomena be taken to indicate reality might have more dimensions than our present science knows about? The ferocity of Hopkins's response actually startled me.

"I'm sick to death of that question! Reality has all the dimensions it needs right now! This business of introducing fairy lore and anecdotes from shamanism and paranormal studies and the like, what that does is bring in extraneous stuff that just confuses the issues. I call it stewpot thinking because it stirs into the pot ideas that don't have any bearing."[4] Hopkins insisted abductions are indisputably real (event-level, five senses) happenings.

I couldn't quite put my finger on it, but I sensed that we might be saying similar things while meaning different things. Hopkins was dead certain we don't need more dimensions than we've already got. No disagreement from me; nature does what it does, with what nature has, as nature is comprised. UFO phenomena (including of course their paranormal features) are happening in reality *as it is*; the same was true of meteors before they were named and thereby officially "discovered."

But let's be sure we understand what the "happening" of UFO phenomena includes and what it suggests about our current maps of nature.

Philosopher Michael Grosso has commented on "the tantalizing mixture [which UFOs] present of objective materiality and subjective elusiveness." He accurately notes that UFOs are found to "affect radar, cause burns, leave traces in the ground, and at the same time pass through walls, appear and disappear like ghosts, defy gravity, assume variable and symbolic shapes, and strike deep chords of psychic, mystic, or prophetic sentiment."[5] A key objection of materialist faith is that phenomena with this profile don't conform to our maps of space-time, and thus, by implication, such phenomena *can't* be real. In any area of science, when the territory consistently doesn't match the maps, and when the territory refuses to disappear in order to fit the maps, at some point simple prudence suggests another course. Maybe the maps aren't up to date. Has anybody checked the maps lately?

Hopkins, the acknowledged dean of alien abductions research, had no difficulty wrapping his mind around the possibility that aliens possess the power to dematerialize our physical bodies and move them through solid structures, and then rematerialize our bodies on the other side. This is entirely consistent with his view of the visitors as *intruders* who come to us and do things to us that bespeak unimaginable technological prowess and consistent too with his general view of humans as helpless to fend off the incursions.

Let's think this through. If human bodies can be radically alchemized on the spot with alien "light beams," does it not follow that there might be more to embodiment than our materialist philosophies have considered? Phenomenology calls for "making a cut" between appearances as reported and what may or may not lie beyond them. Taking experiential claims of levitation on their own terms, yet as certainly speculative, it's difficult to avoid the implication that human flesh must have inherent plasticity that makes it susceptible to dramatic transmutation, even if alien fingers are working the metaphoric trigger.

It happens that testimonies to subtle bodies and subtle matter exist in virtually every sacred tradition. The *ka* of Egyptian religious lore; the *jism* or astral body of Neoplatonism and Sufism; and the spirit-body of Taoist yogic alchemy are said to be made of spirit-matter that can materialize and dematerialize, pass through physical barriers, and change shape or size. Moreover, hyperdimensional models of the universe currently proliferating among physicists and mathematicians have resonance with such accounts. Phenomena that might be described as "extraspatial" (more spatial dimensions than our accepted three) and as "hypersomatic" (involving subtle forms related to and extending our normal sense of being embodied) need not be automatically excluded simply because they don't fit contemporary maps and models taken by some to be true. In fact, data that "don't fit" *must not* be automatically excluded.

But I'm getting ahead of myself. Here's the question that interests me at this point: Are these extraordinary Others indeed *coming to us* and *happening to us*, as from one perspective they seem to be, or are we in fact unknowingly *meeting* on middle or shared ground, owing to our own "tantalizing mixture . . . of objective materiality and subjective elusiveness" as human beings? My hypothesis is *both*. This idea starts with recognition of a fascinating and unresolved polarity within the community devoted to tracking the UFO phenomenon.

On the one hand, the visitors are "alien" to us and our ways; they represent irreducible *otherness*. Yet, at the same time, there's no avoiding that in the nearly 80 years since Kenneth Arnold's fateful flight, it has come to seem natural to imagine aliens in human terms and to draw them close through our metaphors. They come to "our world." The procedures they perform on abductees are "medical," with procedures we recognize. They are interested in "our genetic material." They seek to "crossbreed with us." Notice that at the heart of this distinction between "them" and "us," there's clearly a "we" in the equation. The very fact that encounters between humankind and otherkind even register as phenomenal experiences indicates there must be fundamental continuities between their nature and ours. This is to say, we already inhabit with them a ground of shared forms; humans may already be involved in and share significantly in their realm, and they in ours. We show up in the same space. What is this shared realm, this common ground?

Fortunately, we can explore this question with the same broad-based empirical spirit that has brought us this far. In that pragmatic vein, I want to give Budd Hopkins's conjectures their due. It must be conceded that if the supernormal feats so widely reported in the literature of UFO encounters are real, and if comparable supernormal feats are not found in human arenas beyond these encounters, then simple logic dictates it is reasonable to follow Hopkins and attribute the former to some superior, advanced agency that is imposed in unprecedented fashion from beyond or outside the normal course of human affairs.

How would we proceed to find out whether such features are unique to UFO encounters, as Hopkins suggests, such that when they appear, they do so solely as the effect of alien agency outside our own nature? Stick with phenomenology. We can simply bracket all UFO phenomena, temporarily removing it from the data sample. Then we can use the established tenet that any scientific hypothesis must be *falsifiable*. This means that for any hypothesis to have credence, it must be inherently disprovable before it can become accepted as a scientific hypothesis or theory. It must be possible to conceive of some kind of argument or evidence that would invalidate the claim. Falsifiability currently doesn't require arguments against a theory, only that it is possible to imagine some kind of argument that would invalidate it.

William James established this test: "If you wish to upset the law that all crows are black, you mustn't seek to show that no crows are; it is enough if you prove one single crow to be white."[6] Harvard psychology professor Ellen Langer offered her own version: "If I can make one dog yodel, then we can say yodeling is possible in dogs."[7] Accordingly, if supernormal capacities are found in any human sphere not connected with alien abduction claims, that suffices to falsify Hopkins's implication that the capacities emerge solely through UFO experiences.

The result is that UFO encounters are seen to be one venue for such capacities, a special case or limited instance of the expression of a larger set of possibilities, as opposed to high-tech-wielding aliens as the unique source of extraordinary states and realities.

Importantly, the case for a larger evidentiary context for human transformative capacity makes a larger claim about the nature of reality, of the kind Courtlandt Bryan had in mind when he asked: What's the nature of reality, for such a [phenomenon as levitation] to be possible? Hamlet's answer comes to mind: "There are more things in heaven and earth, Horatio, than are dreamt of in your philosophy." Is there evidence of exceptional functioning or supernormal capacities (all it takes is one pale crow or one yodeling dog) in non-UFO realms of human experience? Yes. Across the board. A lot of evidence. The only questions are where to begin and how not to allow the sheer volume of data to trick us into attempting an exhaustive encyclopedia. There are two basic reasons evidence of inherent human transformative capacity goes largely unnoticed.

"Discoveries about our developmental possibilities are scattered across the intellectual landscape, isolated from one another in separate fields of inquiry," hidden in effect by "professional specialization and divergent belief systems, along with the information explosion."[8] So says Michael Murphy, one of the world's foremost investigators and theoreticians of exceptional and supernormal human capacities. Human potentials aren't more widely recognized because, paradoxically, they are so pervasive in our midst as to be effectively hidden in plain view.* Beliefs about what's possible play a powerful role in limiting open inquiry by distracting us from using the title of this chapter for direct inquiry. If the evolutionary process continues to unfold, what is our human role in this adventure? What are we being called to affirm and express? Who do we imagine ourselves to be?

---

*Fig. 6.1 "Extraordinary Capacities in Everyday Life" presents an overview on page 145.

◄○►

In 1950, Mike Murphy was an undergraduate at Stanford University on the day he took a seat for what he thought was a psychology class. In fact, the lecture hall was the site of a lecture about to be convened by Frederic Spiegelberg, a charismatic professor of comparative religions who had recently returned from world travels, where he had encountered the famous sage Ramana Maharshi, the philosopher Sri Aurobindo, and the renowned psychologist Carl Jung. As "mistakes" go, the class confusion was fortuitous. Spiegelberg's lecture would have a lasting effect on Murphy, stirring him to give up his premed courses and begin reading widely in philosophy, psychology, and religion, focusing on theories and visions of evolutionary development. Murphy also took up the practice of meditation.

In 1962, with Richard Price, a former Stanford classmate, Murphy started an educational institute on family-owned land on California's Big Sur coast. They named the institute after the Esselen Indians who had lived on the coast. In its first years, Esalen hosted seminars on Eastern thought and practice, Christian mysticism, shamanism, humanistic psychology, psychedelic drugs, new approaches to psychotherapy and a wide range of experimental body-based practices, and other subjects broadly clustered under the banner of "human potentialities and the education of the whole person." Program leaders included historian Arnold Toynbee, theologian Paul Tillich, psychologists Abraham Maslow, Carl Rogers, Rollo May, and B. F. Skinner, philosopher Alan Watts, comparative mythologist Joseph Campbell, and numerous pioneers in studies of creativity, experimental psychotherapies, and somatic education.

As time passed, the program emphasis shifted from a primarily cognitive approach based on lecture and discussion to meditative, emotional, and somatic work, an experiential context that writer Aldous Huxley would call the "non-verbal humanities." A signature idea seldom articulated directly in Esalen's printed course program was that both modern psychology and philosophy had gotten off course. Psychology was in the grip of deterministic assumptions that humans are nothing but stimulus-response machines (behaviorism) and that nothing but one's early life experiences shape our behavior (Freudianism). Philosophy had largely opted to replace the traditional metaphysical quest for meaning with what humanists saw as an obsession with language analysis games, grounded in nihilist assumptions shaped by postwar despair.

Though Esalen's teachers were of different minds on a good many topics (this was 1960s America, after all), the institute's programs were concerned with the fullest growth of the individual in the areas of love, fulfillment, self-worth, autonomy, intellectual curiosity, and metaphysical imagination. Science and religion, rather than being cast as irreconcilable enemies, were viewed as complementary ways of knowing and exploring various facets of existence.

In 1972, Murphy published *Golf in the Kingdom*, a novel about his encounter with a mystical Scottish golf pro named Shivas Irons, who made the game a transformative practice. Murphy began receiving letters from readers describing their own illuminations in sport, including perceptions marked by supernormal clarity, sensations of merging with the environment, uncanny feelings of physical suspension, empathy with others that seemed telepathic, and moments of unexplainable joy. Struck by such experiences and the ongoing response to his books, Murphy began assembling an archive dealing with exceptional and supernormal human experiences, inspired by Frederick Myers, a primary founder of psychical research, William James and his *The Varieties of Religious Experience,* and Abraham Maslow, who pioneered the study of peak experience.

The Esalen archive contained scientific studies of meditation, hypnosis and biofeedback; mental imagery and spiritual healing; contemplative practice; fitness training, martial arts and somatic education;

and other potentially transformative activities, including psychosomatic changes that happen in disorders involving dissociated identity and hysterical stigmata. Across these diverse fields, Murphy identified evidence that human beings have an extraordinary capacity for change that operates both creatively and destructively, consciously and unconsciously, and can occur as "side effects" of athletic or contemplative practice, as well as in the course of everyday life. The following section explores a cross section of examples.

- In the process of being treated for sleepwalking, an army officer exhibits deep indentations resembling rope marks on his arms. These appear as he painfully relives an earlier episode during which he is roped to his bed to inhibit his somnambulism.
- Diagnosed as schizophrenic, a man who expresses a great desire to give birth begins feeling something moving in his stomach— "like a baby," he says. During the next three weeks, his abdomen becomes more and more distended and he gains sixteen pounds without altering his diet. Repeated medical tests find no pathology to account for the growth.
- A group of experimental subjects, told what to expect from a certain drug, is able to produce not only that exact effect when given a dummy pill but also the side effects of the drugs they think they are taking.
- A woman, skilled at modifying physiological functions once considered inaccessible to conscious will, demonstrates a capacity to vary the firing patterns of single designated nerve cells and the muscle to which they are attached.
- A man diagnosed with dissociative identity disorder is found to be allergic to citrus juices in all but one of his personalities. He remains free of rashes and other symptoms so long as that one personality retains executive control.

Each of these instances has been described in prestigious medical journals or in books by respected scientific researchers. Connections between these cases, at face value, aren't immediately obvious. Yet, looking more closely, patterns begin to emerge.

Mind-generated bodily marks, including hysterical stigmata, sometimes appear spontaneously in response to trauma and catharsis. They suggest the body's plasticity and its precise responsiveness to mental imagery. During a cathartic recall of a beating by her father, for example, a female patient of the British psychiatrist Robert Moody developed a bruise on her hand closely resembling the imprint of an elaborately carved stick.

False pregnancy (pseudocyesis) likewise reveals the body's extraordinary responsiveness to images and passionate desire. This syndrome occurs in more females than males, not surprisingly.

The facile appearance and disappearance of allergies in individuals diagnosed with dissociative identity disorder offers additional evidence of the body's malleability—and of the intricate linkage of personality and physiology.

The placebo effect offers yet another window on the close relationship between mental and physical change. In a study to discover whether occlusion of the mammary artery would relieve the pain caused by angina pectoris, 100 percent of the subjects who received mock incisions while under general anesthesia showed improvement compared to 76 percent of the subjects whose arteries were actually tied.

The woman who was able to vary the firing patterns of single designated nerve cells and attached muscles is not alone in her talent. Among biofeedback researchers there is now a strong consensus that any physical process that can be brought to awareness through biofeedback can be voluntarily modified.

From these and other related examples of exceptional human functioning, an intriguing hypothesis can be put forward: that latent within the human personality are powers and potentialities that, when ignored or denied, either stagnate within us or take expression in the form of spontaneous, extraordinary, and sometimes bizarre psychophysical phenomena (such as false pregnancy symptoms in a male). Conversely, could it be that these dormant mind-body capacities—some seemingly ordinary, others apparently exceptional or even supernormal—might be susceptible to conscious direction through various specific actions, practices, and disciplines?

There's good reason to answer in the affirmative, as we will shortly see. Moreover, such phenomena might offer important clues to the nature of certain kinds of UFO encounters, especially those that transgress the dividing line between matter and mind, objectivity and subjectivity, form and consciousness. With this possibility in sight, we can continue examining data from a variety of experiential domains.

Medical research has shown that the achievement of physical fitness produces a great number of beneficial changes in cardiorespiratory capacity, muscle tone, bone elasticity and mass, hormonal balance, skin composition, immune response, vitality, mood, and appearance. There is little doubt about the basic plasticity of the human form through regular exercise. And this falls well within normal on the spectrum of human capacity.

There are also numerous instances of sudden and complete cures triggered by religious figures, faith healers, or shrines. None is more striking than the case of Delizia Cirolli, a Sicilian girl whose metastatic bone cancer of the knee was so far advanced that her parents made plans for her funeral. The plans were canceled when, after she drank water from Lourdes, the cancer went into remission and she was declared permanently and completely cured.

In the increasingly impressive field of mental imagery research, numerous clinical and experimental studies have shown that imagery-based therapies can facilitate relief from depression, insomnia, obesity, chronic pain, phobias, anxieties, cancer, and other afflictions.

The area of religious practice offers many compelling instances of extraordinary mind-body interactions. For instance, without any noticeable physical manipulation, the Indian yogi Swami Rama produced a 13-degree Fahrenheit difference in temperature between two sides of his hands. Tibetan lamas have demonstrated the ability to raise the temperature of their feet by as much as 15 degrees, a practice known as *tumo*.

In another Tibetan religious tradition, the ecstatic transcendence of gravity is evident in the long-distance walking of Tibetan ascetics trained in *lung-gom-pa*, a form of yogic walking during which enormous distances are traversed in a waking trance.

There have been more than 100 well-documented instances of Catholic religious figures who developed visible marks on their hands and feet—stigmata—symbolizing the wounds of Christ's crucifixion. Such physical signs typically emerge in states of great mental and spiritual focus, as in the case of a stigmatic named Marie-Julie Jahenny, a French peasant girl who correctly predicted the day she would receive a new stigmatization on her breast consisting of a cross, a flower, and the words *O Crux ave*. In clinical studies, certain hypnotized subjects have exhibited "skin writing," sometimes at the precise moment specified by their hypnotist.

Saint Teresa of Avila, the celebrated Spanish mystic and founder of the Discalced Carmelites, was said to have levitated during her intense contemplative raptures. During her canonization proceedings, 10 observers reported under oath that they had seen her rise from the ground while in ecstasy. Saint Joseph of Cupertino, a seventeenth-century Franciscan monk, was said to have been observed on more than 100 occasions while elevated from the ground in mystical rapture.

Such reports do not by any means confirm the reality of levitation for Saint Teresa of Avila, Saint Joseph of Cupertino, or alien abductee Linda Cortile of Manhattan. Still, it is important to bear in mind that it is a mortal sin to lie under oath during such proceedings and that those who testify in such proceedings typically are devoutly religious people. Father Herbert Thurston, author of *The Physical Phenomena of*

Mysticism, writes: "There can be little doubt that [Pope] Benedict XIV, a critically minded man who knew the value of evidence and who studied the original depositions as probably no one else had studied them, believed that the witnesses of Saint Joseph's levitations had really seen what they professed to have seen."[9]

Professional and amateur sportspeople frequently report paranormal or quasi-mystical experiences, indicating that athletic and religious practice share common features. These experiences include startling images of organs and cells, altered sense of time, supernormal energy, exceptional awareness of the playing field or general environment, telepathy, clairvoyance, out-of-body sensations, apparent weightlessness (and even the impression of momentary transcendence of gravity, or levitation), and instances of profound, all-encompassing peace.

To use anthropologist Gregory Bateson's phrase, is there a "pattern which connects" this wide range of human activity? Based on the preceding empirical evidence, Michael Murphy suspects the answer is yes; such phenomena "may constitute a vast experiment of nature, by which, conceivably, the human race is learning how to effect its transition to new levels of functioning, even to a new kind of evolution."[10] As fantastic as this idea may seem, evolutionary theorists Theodosius Dobzhansky and Francisco Ayala have argued that evolution has already "transcended itself" on two momentous occasions—the first being when inorganic elements produced living species and the second when animals gave rise to humans and our psychosocial realm. Each of these radical developmental pivots subsumed the structures and functions of the prior level(s), while also introducing novel elements that could not be predicted from those earlier levels.

In his book *The Future of the Body,* Murphy cites progressive continuities across separate realms; for instance, continuities between ordinary animal perception (ear, eye, nose), ordinary human functioning (the same senses but refined and cultivated through practice), and supernormal perception (clairvoyance, apprehensive of phantom figures,

auras, and similar non-ordinary luminosity). When the same continuities are identified for attributes such as communication skills, vitality,
movement ability, capacity to influence the environment directly, cognition, and love, Murphy finds the same progressive development from
ordinary animal and human functioning, to extraordinary and supernormal human capacities. And he argues that the types of exceptional
and supernormal development he chronicles may herald a "third evolutionary transcendence,"[11] a new human habitat where today's anomalies
prefigure tomorrow's norms.

Are there implications in Murphy's findings for our understanding
of UFO encounters? Let's explore. In light of recurring patterns in
close encounter reports, both humans and aliens become—in a very
real sense—species with indeterminate boundaries. Time after time
in the preceding pages we have seen examples of alien-human interactions that led to no small uncertainty about where to place the dividing line—or the buffer zone—between mind and matter. Jung stated
that the deepest "layers" of psyche become increasingly collective as they
descend into physical matter, becoming simply "world." A vast variety
of numinous beings have been depicted throughout history as holding
terra intermedia, middle ground, a status also ascribed to the beings
encountered in fairyland and shamanic upper and lower realms and to
luminous presences keeping watch at the threshold of death.

Fig. 8.1. (opposite) "Extraordinary experiences—intense,
overwhelming, indescribable—are recorded at every time in history
and in every place on the globe. . . . Most of the 'ecstatic interludes'
about which we have accounts seem to be purely spontaneous—
a man casually walking by a tennis court is suddenly caught up
in a wave of peace and joy 'as time stands still.'"
Andrew Greeley and William McCready, "Are we a nation of mystics?" *The
New York Times Magazine*, January 26, 1975.

Extraordinary Capacities in Everyday Life

Perception of External Events	Feeling that someone is watching you, after which you turn to meet his or her gaze.	Correctly sensing the location of water or other substances or lost objects without sensory cues.	Spontaneously, directly, and vividly apprehending the presence of someone physically distant or dead.
Somatic Awareness and Self-regulation	Direct and immediate feeling of bodily processes and structures such as cells, molecules, and atomic patterns within the body via what seems internal clairvoyance.	Picturing what appear to be chakras or other entities as depicted in esoteric teachings.	Hearing melodies that seem to reflect your physical condition, for which no physical sources are apparent.
Communication Abilities	Correctly sensing who is calling you on the telephone, even though the caller hasn't communicated for a long time, or thinking about someone who then calls you.	Feeling the pains of a distant friend, then discovering he or she is ill or injured. Accurately sensing someone's prayers or intentions in your behalf.	Feeling or otherwise directly knowing what someone else is thinking or experiencing. Having the same dream as a friend. Sensing the mood or intention of a pet or other animal.
Vitality	Experiencing immense energy, sometimes frightening in its intensity, for which there is no apparent cause.	Sensing a rush of electricity up the spine, or radiating out from the abdomen, accompanied by mental illumination or great strength.	Remaining free of infection in the midst of contagious diseases. Going without normal amounts of sleep for extended periods without loss of clarity, vitality, or physical strength.
Movement Abilities	Executing moves in sports beyond your normal ability while sensing a new power or "self."	Out-of-body experience (during which you may see your own body) after which you report events that could not be known to you in ordinary circumstances.	Sensing physical levitation during strenuous physical exercise, prayer or contemplation, or lovemaking.
Abilities to Alter the Environment Directly	Appearing to alter another's mood at a distance, as if by extrasensory influence. Feeling that you have invisible hands that touch another person, after which that person responds as if he or she had been touched.	Appearing to cause or correct a machine's malfunction by mental intention alone. Experiencing a powerful mood while taking a photo, then finding an unexplainable object or light on the picture you have taken.	Appearing to alter the flight of a ball by mental intention. Promoting a strong mood—whether loving or hateful, serene or agitated—in an empty room. Promoting or inhibiting plant growth in extraordinary fashion, as if by some sort of "green thumb."
Pain and Pleasure	Eliminating pain simply by willing it away.	Feeling inexplicable pleasure, or a stream of vitality, that seems localized in the spine, the solar plexus, or some other body part.	Experiencing profound joy during a routine task or in the midst of pain or discomfort, that seems to express the "joy of living," and may have a contagious effect on others.
Cognition	Correctly sensing unexpected danger.	Correctly anticipating a melody before it comes on the radio, or a dramatic event before it occurs, or words before a companion speaks them.	Correctly determining historical events connected with a particular location or object, as if by some sort of clairvoyance.
Volition	Accomplishing some deed requiring strength or endurance beyond your usual capacity, in crisis perhaps, during a sports competition, or to inflict punishment upon others.	Spontaneously throwing off the effects of injury or disease, or (on the darker side) psychokinetically triggering some affliction in others.	Spontaneously exerting subliminal influence upon others in such ways as harmonizing conflicting parties, bringing peace to violent situations, or causing discord or suffering.
Individuation and Sense of Self	Awakening to a witness self that is fundamentally distinct from particular thoughts, impulses, feelings, or sensations.	Momentarily apprehending all objects of perception as if they are contained within you.	Experiencing an identity that self-evidently existed before your birth and that will outlast your body's death.
Love	Experiencing love that allows you to feel a friend's suffering, deep intentions, or personal conflicts.	Experiencing a love for someone who is physically distant that appears to elevate that person's self-esteem and sense of well-being.	Experiencing rapport and affinity that removes all sense of boundaries between you and others, as if you and they were a single person or body.
Bodily Structures, States, and Processes	Pleasurable streaming sensations that envelop the body and seem to involve a significant enhancement of health.	A subtle effervescence from head to toes during sleep, through which you sense that your bodily processes are being altered.	Sensing an opening in the body—located perhaps between eyes, around the heart, near the navel, or at base of spine, through which energy is flowing.

Adapted from *The Future of the Body: Explorations into the Further Evolution of Human Nature* by Michael Murphy (Jeremy P. Tarcher, Inc., 1992)

Such phenomena are an invitation, at times approaching a knock on the head aimed to concentrate attention, for humans to revisit and reenter the ancient imagination of "body" as multiple, diverse, and intrinsically dynamic.

The Taittiriya Upanishad, one of the great sacred texts of ancient India, speaks of human nature as comprising five interdependent *sariras*, or soul sheaths, whose ruling principles are *anna* (matter), *prana* (life-force), *manas* (mind), *vijana* (supramental consciousness), and *ananda* (delight in the fact of being, or self-existent delight). The first four entities, or "bodies," are grounded in different levels of the manifest world, the fifth in Brahman, the Absolute, although each responds to all the others in a coherent, self-organizing way.

Eminent Greek philosophers of antiquity described various *ochemata*, soul sheaths or "vehicles" connected to the visible body. The Neoplatonic philosopher Damascius believed the soul possesses a certain shining (*augoeides*) vehicle (*ochema*) also called starlike (*asteroides*) and is eternal. The Islamic Shiite philosopher Sheikh Ahmad Ahsa'i proposed a four-fold partition of the soul, distinguishing two *jasad(s)*, "living organisms," and two *jism(s)*, "body masses" or "body volumes." The first *jasad* is the ephemeral material body; the second *jasad* consists of subtle archetypal forms. The first *jism* is a thing of the intermediary world, a kind of astral body; the second *jism* is the essential subtle body, thought to be the imperishable, eternal, transcendental individuality and the "light body."

Ancient Egyptians believed in a system of interlocking subtle bodies, among them the *ka* and the *ba*, in which life was embedded. All of these formulations had roots in far older shamanistic traditions where travel between three worlds—upper, middle, and lower—and interaction with non-ordinary entities in each realm was assumed. The idea was widespread that particular powers and states were associated with these separable yet interconnected vehicles. Although differing on particulars, these traditions largely regarded our physical form to be only part of a fuller personhood amenable to introspection and inspired sight. These images of multiple bodies prefigure the modern idea that we exist on many levels at once, knowingly or not, each level or realm having its own structures and processes.

Citing these images of human identity as being intrinsically multiple and extending along a continuum of subtle mental and physical states, Murphy draws from his study of numerous disciplines to observe that the human organism is radically plastic, capable of moving *as a body* into strange inner realms during near-death experience, deep meditation, sensory deprivation, or other activities. Something in our mind-body complex, it seems, can carry the observing self to other worlds with extensions in space and chains of events that give a sense of passing time. These images resonate with descriptions of many types of UFO phenomena.

Through training of awareness and concentration, as in sport and religious practice, and sometimes apparently spontaneously, individuals may find themselves apprehending forms, colors, sounds, touches that suggest that *other* worlds are embedded in *this* world. Yogis, shamans, religious adepts, and ordinary people have offered vivid accounts of interactions with benign and malevolent figures, angelic figures, departed relatives, and entities that seemed to know what was happening. British climbers Doug Scott and Nick Estcourt, explorer Ernest Shackleton, seafarer Joshua Slocum, and aviator Charles Lindbergh all described disembodied entities that tried to communicate with them and that persisted for hours or days. Because human perception is shaped by habitual mindsets and also because interpretive cultural filters are remarkably diverse, it is reasonable to consider that such entities— if they do exist—might shape themselves to fit the expectations and mental habits of different observers in various contexts. Various disembodied or subtle-bodied entities might be perceived as the angels, devas, elves, fairies, jinn, or (in our time) UFO aliens of the subject's culture. This is the essence of a *comparative* approach that refuses to privilege the phenomena of any specific framework.

In all this experience, from the slightest modifications of awareness to three-dimensional visions, subjects typically feel as if they are comprehending something beyond this world, something with its own inherent reality. This leads Murphy to ask:

> Are those "somethings" aspects of a greater existence, distorted perhaps by the subject's perceptual filters? Are they first glimpses of a "larger earth"? To a frog with its simple eye, the world is a dim array of greys and blacks. Are we like frogs in our limited sensorium, apprehending just part of the universe we inhabit? Are we as a species now awakening to the reality of multidimensional worlds in which matter undergoes subtle reorganizations in some sort of hyperspace? Is visionary experience analogous to the first breathings of early amphibians? Are we ourselves coming ashore to a "larger earth"?[12]

The English essayist Thomas Browne, in a much-quoted passage from his *Religio Medici*, characterized the human being as "that great and true Amphibian whose nature is to live, not only like other creatures in diverse elements, but in divided and distinguished worlds."[13] If there is a "teaching" of the UFO phenomenon, perhaps it is to remind us of the multiple worlds we inhabit, a reality with which most of humanity has lived for centuries and that has been forgotten in order to be discovered, or remembered.

Ancient Vedic texts refer to 400,000 humanlike races of beings living on various planets. Out of this plethora, human beings are said to be among the least powerful, which ties in with the picture that emerges from UFO encounters, the abductions in particular. Many of the humanlike races are said to naturally possess certain powers called *siddhis* (pronounced *sid-hees*). This Sanskrit term is roughly synonymous with the Roman Catholic term *charism*, referring to extraordinary human capacities that typically arise as byproducts of meditation and related contemplative practices, though they also occur spontaneously outside the context of formal discipline. Among such capacities are mystical cognitions, clairvoyance and telepathy, and extraordinary physical abilities, including psychokinesis. It is acknowledged that humans can also potentially acquire these powers, and some people have greater abilities in this regard than others.

Historically, contemplatives have viewed such manifestations as potential distractions from enlightenment. In that context, siddhis are hindrances to life's greater good when they stimulate egocentricity and other kinds of destructive activity. When the great wisdom traditions of the East emerged, their authors didn't have our modern knowledge of cosmic and biological development. The founders of most mystical traditions viewed the world not as an arena for conscious embodiment but as a place marked by suffering and death. The common goal of contemplative practice was to get off the grinding wheel of death and rebirth. "No more birthdays," as a world-weary Buddhist refrain put it.

But from an evolutionary standpoint, these faculties can be seen in another way—as facets of emergent human development, as capacities inherent to the richer life that is available to us. If these capacities are latent to our nature—if they point to surplus potential of the cosmos that is bound to manifest as sideways contortions like false pregnancy and stigmata—perhaps the time is right to give serious consideration to developing these faculties as organs and limbs of our future nature? What might be expected, for instance, if more abductees took up various martial arts, developing their *ki* and *chi*, their subtle energy bodies? Would they find themselves more able to navigate the "unearthly" elements in which they suddenly find themselves? If Hopkins is right about recurring abductions, suppose first-time abductees later began practicing meditation and rudimentary sensory awareness exercises, training their attention to return to the present moment each time it fades or gets carried off by trains of thought. By practicing the shamanic art of remaining lucid in dream states, might they find it easier by the next abduction attempt to stabilize their attention more fully at subtle bodily levels, keep better track of external stimuli and internal responses, and engage the presence more fully?

Would these individuals have an advantage over others—for instance, in remaining conscious during the transition between the mundane world in which they are picked up and the fantastic realm into which they are floated or carried? *Doorway amnesia* is the term given by UFO researchers to the characteristic absence of recall at this crucial threshold. In Greek mythology, doorways, thresholds, and passages belong to the province of a familiar god. Named Hermes.

And so, the implications of supernormal capacities may shed new light on UFO encounters, yet ultimately the implications go further. No doubt there was wisdom in the world's early sages urging spiritual practitioners to place *moksha* (liberation) above *siddhis* (powers). It will be argued that even if "superpowers" are real, humans aren't ready, are not mature enough to take them on. Meanwhile, left unattended, these latent faculties have a way of taking on humans and manifesting in strange and often counterproductive ways. And today we know things about the course of our universe's development that the sages of earlier eons had no clue of, starting with the fact that the world we inhabit is neither static nor cyclical. Based on graduation after graduation of species for several hundred million years, it's conceivable that uncharted human potentials may correlate with the dynamism of the evolutionary adventure itself.

When I started trailing this phenomenon in primary school, it didn't occur to me that investigating UFO reports might raise questions about untapped human potential. Through my own eventual encounters with the exceptional, I came to believe the human side of the equation wasn't a settled base camp for exploration, with guarantees of getting back before dark. When John Mack and I first spoke, we agreed UFO events are real because they happen, like the phenomena this chapter brings to view. As to the nature of a world in which such realities are possible, this question remains. In the coming chapter, the question opens to a historic effort to expand the purview of UFO research to include all the known data.

9

The Bigelow Factor

Expectations of imminent breakthrough have been a thematic mainstay in the UFO conversation going back to Kenneth Arnold's Mount Rainier sighting. In early 1990, longtime UFO researcher and historian Jerome Clark predicted the '90s would be "The Last Decade" of the UFO mystery.

> Among some close observers of the UFO scene there is a growing sense that the UFO controversy as we have known it since 1947 may not survive the coming decade. The Roswell and Gulf Breeze cases were breaking long patterns of secrecy, and there were clear signs of accelerating openness. The day is coming, we may be sure, when the scientific community abandons its near criminal negligence and concedes its shameful failure to address the most important scientific question of the 20th century. When that happens—when we ufologists are proven to have been right all along—we will be lucky to enjoy half an hour's worth of vindication before we get trampled to death in the stampede.[1]

Countless such predictions have come and gone. Most tend to be well-worn variations on the theme of impending disclosure: "Any day now, the lid on the government cover-up is gonna blow sky-high." When the '90s left town, UFO researchers had survived another stampede that didn't occur. Still, Clark seemed to be on to something. An end was coming, but an end to what? Not to the search as a whole or the revelation of final answers as Clark supposed. In hindsight, there were signs of an end to a particular approach to resolving the phenomenon that had dominated the field for decades. An approach based on an assumption that weekend UFO researchers would finally, and soon ("soon" is the watchword of the Imminent Disclosure mythos), reach the magic number of credible sighting cases that would lead to the kind of certainty Clark envisioned.

A growing number of researchers believed this approach had become actively unproductive and a sharp course correction was necessary. Groundwork was being laid for a breakthrough of a different type that would take shape over the next two decades. The people laying the foundations had no idea themselves where their tentative efforts might lead. They were "making a path by walking," in the poet Antonio Machado's phrase.

And they had taken only the first steps. At the time of Clark's writing, a series of low-key discussions and activities had begun in Las Vegas about revamping the framework of UFO research. It was a conversation about the need for the UFO story to include—more exactly, to stop excluding—aspects of the phenomenon that nuts and bolts researchers had never known what to make of and had shunned for decades.

The paranormal stuff. The anomalies of mind-matter interaction that shouldn't be taking place if reality is made up of nothing but inert chunks of matter flying around by mathematical formulas. Telepathic communication between humans and aliens. Teleportation of human witnesses into what seemed to be solid-state craft, which often simply disappeared on the spot after placing witnesses back at the beginning, as famously reported by Hickson and Parker in Pascagoula. People who see a UFO and then develop supernormal capacities such as precognition and causing lights and electronic equipment to malfunction just by being around them. Visitors to a surreal ranch in rural Utah making contact with a paranormal force and "taking it back home with them" to suburbs on the East Coast.

These things are officially impossible. Yet these things routinely "co-occur" with UFO events. In the same year as Clark's article, actor Charles Grodin published a memoir with the sardonic title, *It Would Be So Nice If You Weren't Here.* Many conventional UFO researchers wished the same about the weird stuff that goes bump in the night. A landing on the White House lawn would so nicely seal the deal, as Hollywood had predicted for decades. But simply telling the high-strangeness factors to be gone hadn't worked out; the phenomenon invariably responded by taking wilder forms. To a growing number of thinkers, the high strangeness factor was now seen as intrinsic to the phenomenon. It was time, in John Mack's phrase, to stop shrinking and start expanding.

This was an informal group of creative researchers with longstanding credibility and skin in the game. Their organizing premise was simple: the full UFO story needs to encompass the totality of manifestations observed—an obvious premise in ordinary science. It was getting clearer that the established practice of categorically ruling the paranormal features off the table was really no different from debunkers who take the same approach to the entire phenomenon. But to take all aspects of UFO evidence at face value was also an error. "In my view, the widespread belief among researchers of the field in the literal truth of the 'abductions' is only a very crude approximation of a much more complex tapestry," wrote Jacques Vallée around this time. "Another reality is involved here."[2]

These two habits—reflexive debunking and knee-jerk belief—are the same impasse reached from opposite directions. The view from Vegas was that progress had stopped. It was time for a more proactive approach. *Something different.* There was uncertainty about what that might look and feel like. There was also determination to find out. Some talked about the need to start meeting the phenomenon on its own ground, whatever that might mean. A few suggested the human-UFO equation already involved common ground; it was time to lean into that, maybe *dig in,* even if specific action steps weren't yet apparent.

Excitement was in the air, along with mindfulness that big ventures carry big risks. Memories of the field's past grandiose expectations hung like Marley's ghost. The embryonic discussions included individuals who would go on to be key players in events that would change the face of the phenomenon, including its eventual public face. But that was still years off. For now, a "breakthrough" quite unlike what Clark envisioned was quietly forming, appropriately enough, in the fabled City of Second Chances.

By the norms of Central Casting, Robert Thomas Bigelow doesn't fit the bill of a pivotal figure in UFO research. But really who does, in the Wonderland where this phenomenon holds sway?

J. Allen Hynek, perhaps? Starting out as a consultant to the air force, Hynek was considered competent to explain away all UFO sightings without wrecking his credibility in the process. The assignment was unspoken; his superiors knew they couldn't get away with telling a man of science who valued his integrity to knowingly deceive the public. The tacit hope was that Hynek would deceive *unknowingly,* starting with himself. They banked on a respected astronomer preferring the approval of his scientific fellows over being thought gullible for giving credence to "ridiculous" UFO details that appeared to contradict basic physics.

Hynek had taken the assignment thinking most if not all UFOs might have prosaic explanations. This is worlds apart from the debunker's ideological passion for ridiculing witnesses in the name of protecting reality from dangerous superstition. He started as empiricist on speaking terms with both open-mindedness and skepticism, remaining true to that cause. Hynek didn't change his mind; the growing evidence did that for him. If I could go back to my phone interview with Hynek, I would ask how he had coped with his early doubts. As the plausibility of denial disintegrated steadily, how long had he kept his misgivings to himself? I suspect Hynek began keeping quiet company with fellow outsiders from the caustic culture of debunking that pretends neutrality. At some point, a threshold was reached for Hynek, and light bulbs went off, for once in his own head rather than from camera flashes at contentious news conferences. Hynek was out the door and ready to chart a new path bearing credible witness to an astonishing yet consistent body of anomalous observations.

In plot development, that's a powerful second act—*conflict and complication*—opening to a compelling third act—*resolution and fulfillment*. Hynek must have been amused at the perception that his transformation on the metaphoric road to Damascus led him to "become" a truth teller, although there may have been a period in which he said things he no longer believed. Maybe there was a single moment when telling the truth as he was given to understand it was like coming home. Hynek mistakenly thought that's what the air force brought him on board to do; this is what lends his character credibility, and sympathy. He hadn't grown up assuming military officials who take oaths of allegiance to duty and honor would deliberately mislead the public about odd sightings in the sky, especially when the reason was to avoid admitting they didn't have a clue what they were dealing with.

Some say it took too long for Hynek to come to his senses, but again, who's making the calls? Character emerges as events in a narrative dictate time and place, along with hidden contingencies understood by the ancients as Fate (forces sometimes appearing as personified characters in the works of Shakespeare). In the Bible, Saul became Paul nearing Damascus when the time was right—and more likely, it was a moment *out of time*. This was also true for Hynek, who never looked back.

How does any of this pertain to Robert Bigelow? As a young boy, he heard his grandparents talking matter-of-factly about a flying saucer that buzzed their car as they drove along a country road just outside of Vegas. The craft had shot off at a sharp angle before they were able to get a clear look at it. This left them speechless and confused. The wonder of the story never left Bigelow, who developed interests in philosophy and leading-edge science even as he went on to achieve financial success as the founder of Budget Suites of America, a chain of extended-stay hotels, with considerable success later as an aerospace entrepreneur.

Are we alone in the universe and what happens when we die? Bigelow has made no secret of his passion for this question. His well-earned billionaire standing afforded him the capacity to fund research in these areas. By the early 1990s, Bigelow had begun underwriting a series of trailblazing science projects at the University of Nevada at Las Vegas. The programs were designed to bring top-level intellectual inquiry to subjects including altered states of consciousness, near-death experiences, unidentified flying objects, and extrasensory perception. Bigelow viewed these areas not as "fringe science" but as phenomena currently at the edges of appropriate inquiry. He sided with Saint Augustine: "Miracles do not happen in contradiction to nature, but only in contradiction to that which is known to us of nature."

Bigelow had also started funding researchers promising approaches aiming to better understand these subjects. As time passed, he got frustrated with the lack of results from investigators who had accepted his backing. Just as J. Allen Hynek changed jobs to stay on course with his commitment to real science, Bob Bigelow decided it was time to revise his strategy of funding scattershot research projects. He was ready to increase his commitment to match the scale of the opportunity.

Through a modern psychological lens, such decisions typically get cast as moments of "self-discovery." The Greek term *daimon* (*genius* in Latin) resonates with modern translations into terms such as *angel, soul, inner twin, life companion*, and *heart calling*. The ancients believed fate attaches to a person like a particular accompanying guide. Translators never call *daimon* a "self," a term that blinds the modern eye to what the ancients called "the invisibles." The Great Men and Women theory of history isn't required for thinking this way about something that sooner or later calls anyone—*everyone*—onto a particular path; that sense of "this is what I must do, this is who I am." In this myth, who we are is given all at once, yet paradoxically this condition is slowly revealed in the street life of ordinary quandaries, tight spots, fixes—much as an acorn contains the oak that emerges over time. Character is given as uniqueness that asks to be lived; a gift, as the ancients said, from the guardians at the moment of birth. The sense of a calling *to* life, the mystery at the heart of every human life, that there's a reason I am here.

Bigelow well understood that modern science had achieved remarkable results through empirical methods that explored the material world. It was time for a more organized and focused approach to queries that had been left to faith and superstition for centuries. What is consciousness and does it have causal power to influence material reality? Given the fact that immediate experience is the sole carrier of reality as far as anyone can ever know, what if consciousness is primary and foundational and gives rise to physical reality, rather than the other way around?

What exactly is matter, and does it have grades ranging from gross (dense) to subtle? Bigelow knew these questions opened to others beyond the direct scope of everyday science: Who are we? Where did we come from? What is the part of a human individual in the play of existence? He wasn't shy about raising these questions as essential human concerns.

Bigelow decided to set up an institute. Step one: place an ad in a leading science publication to find a qualified scientist to put in charge of daily operations. He had no idea this act would initiate a sequence of events that would shape a genuinely comprehensive approach to the UFO phenomenon. A full-spectrum approach empowering scientists from various fields to investigate all of its facets and dimensions, allied with philosophers and scholars of the sacred and other humanities willing to ask questions of sufficient scope and depth to be meaningful. Crucial to this integral methodology: prioritizing witness reports and human effects.

It all started with Bigelow's ad.

Colm Kelleher was a biochemist doing research on immunology and respiratory medicine in Denver when he saw the unusual job placement ad in the journal *Science*. He had no idea how much his life was about to change.

In the middle of listings for postdoctoral fellows in immunology and biotechnology, Kelleher spotted Bigelow's half-page notice talking about the origin and evolution of human consciousness in the universe. He read it more than once to be sure the words meant what they seemed to say. Bigelow was calling his organization the National Institute for Discovery Science (NIDS) and looking for key staff. Kelleher picked up the phone, called the number, and eventually got through to Bigelow, who invited Kelleher out to Vegas for a face-to-face interview. Bigelow had a lot of questions about how science could be applied to anomalies research. They talked about crop circles, cattle mutilations, and the various facets of UFO sightings, Kelleher recalls. "I answered all his questions and he hired me to start work there very quickly."[3] A few weeks later he was on a plane to take up his new role as deputy administrator of NIDS.

In answering the ad, Kelleher remembered the words of one of his postdoctoral mentors: "If you want to catch a big fish, the best way is to fish in waters that are unpopulated by other fishermen."[4] With his extensive training and experience in biology, cell biology, virology, and biochemistry, along with well-honed project management skills, Kelleher jumped at the chance to do groundbreaking science in an area where few scientists had ventured. "NIDS wanted to bring as broad a range of expertise and technology as possible to bear on UFOs and other problems that mainstream science had thus far ignored,"[5] Kelleher says.

An organizational meeting in January 1996 brought together most of the NIDS board for the first time in the same room: Hal Puthoff, who had directed a legendary program at SRI International to investigate paranormal abilities; Harrison Schmitt, a former astronaut and U.S. senator; John Alexander, former U.S. Army Intelligence officer and a leading advocate for military applications of the paranormal; Jacques Vallée, astronomer and renowned UFO researcher who had pioneered in developing ARPANET, a precursor to the modern Internet; John Mack, Harvard psychiatrist and investigator of claims of human abduction by aliens; and George Knapp, award-winning Nevada journalist who presented to the board about UFO files he'd obtained during a trip to Moscow.

When the late U.S. senator Harry Reid of Nevada attended a NIDS board session later that year, he was captivated by their approach to UFOs and related phenomena. "The meeting was held in a large conference room filled with prestigious academics, former U.S. senators, interested members of the public, and a few oddballs," Reid recalled years later. "Speaking about NIDS, Dr. Kelleher has aptly said, 'We don't study aliens, we study anomalies. They're the same thing in people's minds, but not our minds.' That's how I feel about UAPs."[6]

After Kelleher had hired his core NIDS staff, Bigelow heard about a 500-acre ranch in northeastern Utah owned by a Mormon couple, Terry and Gwen Sherman, who had bought the place with a desire to get back to the land. They had no idea that site would come with "too-large-thrice-over wolves that refused to die by bullet, cattle with their reproductive organs sucked clean out, and a multitude of UFOs," as the couple had told the *Deseret News* in 1996.[7] Bigelow recognized an ideal opportunity to bring all NIDS resources to bear to study numerous anomalies, including poltergeist activity, cattle mutilations, unusual flying objects, and varied paranormal activity.

Within a month of purchasing the property, NIDS deployed an array of sensors including surveillance cameras (visible and near-IR), electromagnetic detectors, custom-built optical communications equipment, portable ionizing-radiation detectors, portable spectrometers, and more. The team also consistently patrolled the ranch with dogs as biosensors. "For the next couple of years I spent more than 300 days at Skinwalker Ranch," Kelleher recalls. "And soon after deploying on the property, I had the first of several in-your-face experiences that defied my best attempts to explain them in conventional terms."[8] He was standing outside the main command and control center, when a low-flying object moved rapidly and completely silently over Skinwalker Ridge right above his head. Kelleher continues:

> It was moving at the same acceleration of an F-18 jet, but it did a perfect U-turn above my head. It was almost spooky how solid it was, and the turn it made was pretty well impossible for an F-18 to make. There was another scientist standing right next to me, and then it just exited straight over Skinwalker Ridge on the same path that it had come in on. It was gone within 30 seconds. And that was my basic introduction to life on Skinwalker Ranch.[9]

NIDS continued studying the ranch via high-tech sensors and human eyes and ears. Scores of independent visitors to the ranch observed flying orbs of various colors, metallic UFOs, otherworld creatures, discarnate voices, poltergeist phenomena, electronic anomalies, and orange "portals" in the sky. The organization pioneered new methodologies to investigate the cattle mutilation phenomenon in cases throughout the northwestern and southwestern United States. Kelleher's team had questions. In the strangest cases, where were the tracks, the human footprints or tire marks that would be expected? Ranchers would leave cattle, only to return in thirty minutes to find surgically precise massacres with no signs of blood or predators, human or animal. And not every case was recent. A farmer told of walking into his field and seeing a cigar-shaped craft floating about 40 feet off the ground. One of his cows dangled from a thick cord. The craft got away, but the cow was found the following day across the street, dead and badly cut and burned. The year was 1810.

NIDS also devoted thousands of hours to investigating the so-called "black triangle" UFO phenomenon. Kelleher's team personally investigated over 100 cases of large (300 feet), silent, triangular craft that floated at extremely low altitudes over densely populated areas or down interstate highways. Over nine years, the organization accumulated a detailed database of approximately 1,600 UFO cases. But the event that would break new ground had nothing to do with an anomalous sighting. Ironically enough, it took place after Bigelow decided to shutter NIDS in 2006 so he could continue his efforts in different venues. The following year, Bigelow got an unexpected letter that would be as pivotal as the ad he had placed a little over a decade before.

Written on an official Defense Intelligence Agency (DIA) letterhead and dated June 19, 2007, the letter was from James T. Lacatski, a nuclear physicist with expertise in fusion plasmas and directed energy weapons. "It's not exactly rocket science" is an overused phrase, but here it applies. Lacatski was *exactly* a rocket scientist with a sterling reputation for national service. He had finished reading *Hunt for the Skinwalker*, the book by Colm Kelleher and George Knapp detailing the full range of anomalies on display at the remote Utah ranch. Lacatski wrote Bigelow to ask to visit Skinwalker for the purpose of "developing a strategy on how my office (DWO) can characterize the potential threat aspects of the phenomena encountered in your research efforts."[10]

Bigelow got in touch with his friend Senator Harry Reid and described the letter. Reid agreed to meet with Lacatski at Reid's home outside Washington, where Lacatski said he couldn't understand why UFOs were of so little interest to the scientific community. A month later, Lacatski and Bigelow flew to Utah and drove to Skinwalker Ranch. After a tour of the property on a beautiful and hot July afternoon, the two headed for the nearest building, a picturesque dwelling known as Homestead 1. During the conversation that followed, Lacatski became engrossed in something that appeared behind Bigelow:

> [A]n unearthly technological device had suddenly and silently appeared out of nowhere in the adjacent kitchen. It looked to be a complex semi-opaque, yellowish, tubular structure. Lacatski said nothing but stared at the object, which was hovering silently. He looked away, looked back, and there it still was. It remained visible to Lacatski for more than 30 seconds before vanishing from the spot.[11]

Lacatski later said that prior to the stunning display, he had never seen anything unusual in his life. He had been on the property for about an hour and seen in clear daylight a floating technological device within a few feet of where he stood. It wasn't lost on Lacatski that of the four people in the room, he alone had seen whatever it was. He found it difficult to take the sighting as entirely random. The personal nature of the event motivated him to follow up with his superiors at the DIA about the potential of unknown aerial activity in U.S. airspace.

Things began moving quickly. Returning to Washington, Lacatski met with Senator Reid, who introduced him to two fellow senators, Democrat Daniel Inouye of Hawaii and Republican Ted Stevens of Alaska. The three senators went to work lobbying the leadership of the Senate Appropriations Committee to create the language to appropriate $22 million for a program to research the threat potential of UFOs. The Defense Warning Office of the DIA was designated as the architect of a program that was named the Advanced Aerospace Weapon System Applications Program (AAWSAP).

The creation of AAWSAP was an unprecedented step forward in the history of the ambivalent, awkward, and sometimes adversarial relationship between the U.S. government and the UFO phenomenon. When the DIA put out a formal request for proposals in 2008 inviting aerospace companies to publically compete for a five-year funding contract to study advanced aerospace threats, the contract might have gone to Lockheed Martin, Honeywell, Raytheon, Rockwell, or Northrop Grumman. None of these companies submitted proposals. Only one company did: Bigelow Aerospace Advanced Space Studies. The contract went to BAASS.

Designated as program manager, Jim Lacatski brought Colm Kelleher on board as deputy administrator. Kelleher began a round of staffing interviews for the new outfit. In December 2008, a retired marine lieutenant colonel, Doug Kurth, appeared for an interview with an impressive resume and a soft-spoken yet confident manner. Within 10 minutes of starting the interview, Kelleher knew he had BAASS's second hire. Then came an *oh, by the way* moment near the end of the conversation. Kurth mentioned that in his previous career he had been the commander of the Red Devils, a marine corps F/A-18C squadron that had been part of the USS Strike Group Nimitz southwest of San Diego in November–December 2004.

Kelleher sat up. Kurth went on to describe his participation in what has become known as the Tic Tac event, one of the most famous UFO cases in the world. Kurth calmly described getting a radio call asking him to investigate an unidentified airborne contact. Approaching from about 15 nautical miles from the reference point, Kurth descended through 15,000 feet and saw "a rather large disturbance in the ocean surface." He stressed that "the seas were surprising calm that day with rolling swell but no surface waves."[12]

It was during this event that U.S. Navy commander David Fravor had famously seen and engaged with the unidentified thing that was later given the Tic Tac moniker. Kelleher immediately recognized this could be an important case for the nascent organization to investigate as part of the AAWSAP contract. At Kelleher's request, Kurth wrote up his recollection and generated an exhaustive list of eyewitnesses to interview, which Kelleher sent on to Lacatski at DIA.

Within less than six months, Kelleher and his core team had recruited a team of some 50 scientists, engineers, database analysts, and retired law enforcement officers as investigators, among other positions. When AAWSAP uncovered and broke the Tic Tac case in 2009, personnel were dispatched to interview pilots and radar operators on the USS Princeton. By the end of 2010, BAASS-AAWSAP had delivered over 100 separate reports on UFOs to the DIA. The reports ranged from computational fluid dynamic analysis of Tic Tac performance to the so-called hitchhiker effect, in which people who visited Skinwalker Ranch appeared to "bring something home with them." AAWSAP hypothesized an infectious agent model for the "transmission" of anomalies from place to person and, sometimes person to person.

After decades of public and private antipathy toward witnesses and researchers of a phenomenon that did not officially exist, the emergence of AAWSAP as an official government body was widely recognized for its comprehensive breadth and range. Between 2008 and December 2010, a seasoned team investigated not only the technology of UFOs but also their medical, paranormal, and psychic correlates. No comparable effort anywhere in the world was being made to do this. No aerospace company other than Bigelow's group even submitted a bid for the AAWSAP contract, largely because no other such organization had the experience, aptitude, or sheer moxie.

Four decades earlier, journalist and anomalies researcher John Keel had issued a rallying cry to the research field and the public at large. No approach to the phenomenon that is not cross-disciplinary and inclusive of all realms of evidence, he insisted, stood a chance of yielding insight that could match the depth and scope of the phenomenon. Keel intuited that "it" knows more than we do and has access to more of reality than we do. Nobody in the UFO field disagreed with exploring the whole phenomenon; the long-term sticking point had been a lack of consensus about how to define that.

"There is a natural tendency to concentrate on only those facets that seem most interesting, or which seem to provide the best evidence," Keel noted. "The phenomenon of unidentified flying objects is a gigantic iceberg, and the truly important aspects are hidden beneath the surface."[13] He grew impatient with the UFO establishment's bias toward what he considered trivia, random sightings irrelevant to the whole, and side issues of government policy, analysis of personalities, and conflicts between the various factions of the UFO movement.

Keel was convinced the answer was to "study the people who have experienced these things. . . . You study the medical and psychological effects of their experiences. This cannot be done by teenagers with telescopes and housewives with tape recorders. It must be done by trained professionals. . . . We need to know much more about the human mind and how it is linked up to the greater source."[14]

He had left the field before Bigelow arrived suited up for a new season of inquiry into what's going on. Whether or not Bigelow knew Keel's books, the men were on the same page. Bigelow was equally weary of the field's inability to see beyond the limits of any single frame of reference, not to mention the popular beliefs and speculations largely founded on biased reporting and gross misinterpretations. Aligning mouth with money, Bigelow helped bring into a play a comprehensive research mission committed to a broader course.

Much of the logic behind AAWSAP is made explicit in an important paper on UFOs and "the physics of high-strangeness," coauthored by Jacques Vallée, who served on the NIDS science advisory board, and physicist Eric Davis, a former NIDS staffer who tracked Skinwalker phenomena on site. The paper takes both debunkers and believers of IETV (the hypothesis of intelligent extraterrestrial visitors) to task for their anthropocentric (human-centered) biases. Debunkers are challenged for assuming visitors would not perform the absurd behaviors of ufonauts. Believers are criticized for ignoring or minimizing reports from cultural sources that don't match their IETV filters.* Vallée and Davis were confident that:

> [A] bridge could be formed between the disparate . . . communities if both would only recognize a simple fact: *No experiment can distinguish between phenomena manifested by visiting interstellar (arbitrarily advanced) ETI and intelligent entities that may exist near Earth within a parallel universe or in different dimensions, or who are (terrestrial) time travelers.*[15]

Vallée and Davis added this note: "Current hypotheses are not strange enough to explain the facts of the phenomenon. . . . We must

---

*A recurring theme in Vallée's opus is a criticism of the adamant refusal of some abduction researchers to account for historical parallels to "abductions" in cultures predating the contemporary UFO phenomenon. Vallée writes in his book *Dimensions*: "If these objects have been seen from time immemorial, as I will show, and if their occupants have always performed similar actions along similar lines of behavior, then it is not reasonable to assume that they are 'simply' extraterrestrial visitors. They must be something more."

propose new theories and experiments in order to explore these undiscovered facets. This is why continuing study of reported UAP events is important: It may provide us with an existence theorem for new models of physical reality."[16]

What Vallée and Davis are saying deserves some unpacking because it covers important ground. On an experimental basis, there's no means to distinguish interstellar visitors from intelligent entities that may exist near Earth within a parallel universe or in different dimensions, including terrestrial time travelers. Our theories about the phenomenon aren't strange enough to match what the phenomenon has been presenting. New theories are needed, along with new experiments, new ways of engaging. This could lead to a new explanatory framework ("an existence theorem") accounting for more of the phenomenon's features. We could end up with "new models of physical reality."

The evidentiary case of Vallée and Davis suggests we need not only new models of *physical* reality but new ways of thinking about the relationship between matter and mind in light of UFO behaviors and characteristics. The authors cite physical characteristics that, despite unknown origins, don't appear to challenge conventional physics— for instance, objects that occupy a position in space (consistent with geometry), interact with the environment through thermal effects, produce turbulence, and when landed leave indentations and burn marks. The game changes, however, when what the authors call "antiphysical" effects enter the picture:

> Objects sinking into the ground, shrinking in size, growing larger
> or smaller, or changing shape or becoming fuzzy and transparent
> on the spot. Objects dividing into two or more craft, or multiple
> objects merging into one object at slow speed, or disappearing
> at one point in space and appearing elsewhere instantaneously,

or remaining observable visually while not detected by radar, or appearing as balls of colored, intensely bright light under intelligent control. More remarkably: objects generating missing time or time dilation in witnesses, or producing dilation of space such that witnesses report observing an interior many times larger than the exterior size.[17]

Such phenomena are so remarkably unlike anything resembling physicality that the authors' choice to describe the effects by negation, "anti-physical," makes pragmatic sense. But in the final analysis, this isn't much different from describing wet as antidry, bold as anticautious, going as antistopping. At some point, it makes more sense to speak of *degrees* of physicality or degrees of consciousness: matter as the densest form of spirit and spirit as the subtlest form of matter. But such an apparently reasonable compromise can't be undertaken without spelling trouble for physicality and materiality as physicalists and materialists define nature.

The predominant scientific worldview holds reality to be made up of tiny pieces of undetermined dead stuff labeled "matter" spinning around in fields of force in accord with mathematical laws. This ideology of science—*scientism*—declares nature completely devoid of purpose, meaning, intention. And yet, through random cosmological processes nobody can explain (as if by magic), some of the dead stuff manages to become not only alive (blooming, buzzing, swarming, breathing, jumping, eating, procreating) but also aware of itself and its surroundings, capable of asking the same questions as Bigelow, all of which pretty much reduce to a single query: *What's going on here?* In the experiment known as *Homo sapiens sapiens,* the animal that knows that it knows, nature reaches a point where it is capable of asking what it is, capable of beholding the astonishing fact of being anything *at all.*

◄o►

December 16, 2017, was the day the world learned through an article in the *New York Times* about $22 million spent by "The Pentagon's Mysterious U.F.O. Program."[18] The front page article, written by veteran journalists Leslie Kean, Ralph Blumenthal, and Helene Cooper, featured this passage:

> Working with Mr. Bigelow's Las Vegas-based company, the program produced documents that describe sightings of aircraft that seemed to move at very high velocities with no visible signs of propulsion, or that hovered with no apparent means of lift.[19]

Just over four years later, on June 24, 2021, the Office of the Director of National Intelligence (ODNI) issued an intelligence assessment of the threat posed by the UFO phenomenon (now officially rechristened unidentified aerial phenomena or UAP). In the report, the ODNI bluntly reported that "UAP clearly pose a safety of flight issue and may pose a challenge to national security."[20]

The report marked a radical turnabout for the United States government to acknowledge the existence not only of UFOs but of a partially classified program to investigate them. The ODNI report got plenty of fanfare, but it didn't lead to the stampede that longtime UFO researcher Jerome Clark had predicted in 1990. In his legendary book *The Structure of Scientific Revolutions*, the philosopher of science Thomas Kuhn described how awareness of anomaly leads scientists to extended exploration of the anomaly. Primal battles ("paradigm wars") take place about whether a phenomenon represents a genuine discrepancy. Inquiry closes "only when the paradigm theory has been adjusted so that the anomalous has become the expected."[21]

That day hasn't come with the UFO, but it is closer today than when Clark predicted full disclosure by the end of the '90s. It is closer due to decades of efforts that began with Bigelow-sponsored symposia on new science at the University of Nevada and continued in substantive projects with a through line of acronyms: from NIDS to BAASS to AAWSAP over nearly three decades. In 2020, Bigelow added a new acronym to his collection by starting up the Bigelow Institute of Consciousness Studies (BICS). This initiative aims to continue his longstanding interest in forging research on survival of human consciousness following death.

Allen Hynek and Bob Bigelow came to the UFO phenomenon with different backgrounds—Hynek as astronomer, Bigelow as entrepreneur—but in their passion for discovery they could be brothers from different mothers. Hynek reclaimed his autonomy by saying good-bye to the gig of explaining UFOs for the air force. Bigelow's independence has never been in doubt. By all appearances he remains, to paraphrase Joni Mitchell, *a free man in Vegas, unfettered and alive.* Every now and then, Bigelow can be found enjoying reporters' efforts to get him to hedge his bets. In 2017, he sat down with *60 Minutes* reporter Lara Logan:

Lara Logan: Is it risky for you to say in public that you believe in UFOs and aliens?

Robert Bigelow: I don't give a damn. I don't care.

Lara Logan: You don't worry that some people will say, "Did you hear that guy, he sounds like he's crazy?"

Robert Bigelow: I don't care.

Lara Logan: Why not?

Robert Bigelow: It's not gonna make a difference. It's not going to change reality, of what I know.

Lara Logan: Do you imagine that in our space travels that we will encounter other forms of intelligent life?

Robert Bigelow: You don't have to go anywhere.

Lara Logan: You can find it here?

Robert Bigelow: Yeah.

Lara Logan: Where exactly?

Robert Bigelow: It's just like right under people's noses.[22]

10

Musing on the Future of Reality

A recurring implication of the phenomena described in these pages is that the objective world of matter may be closer to the subjective world than most of us have dared imagine, certainly closer than envisioned by either establishment science or institutional religion. As Jeffrey Kripal said at the outset:

> One begins to suspect that what we call "science" and "religion" are just two cultural frameworks that we have invented for our own all-too human purposes, and that neither of them really work very well in this ufological realm. Whatever is going on with the UFO ain't science and ain't religion. What it is one no longer quite knows. All one knows is what it ain't. Well, it ain't simply objective. And it ain't simply subjective.[1]

From that premise, UFO encounters and evidence for supernormal nature traverse an expansive human field. Aligning the experiences described on page 145 ("Extraordinary Capacities in Everyday Life") with phenomena specific to the UFO framework, we're confronted with resounding contradictions in our culture's contemporary world-view defining the nature of reality. As the dichotomy between subjectivity and objectivity appears more like a bridge of connection than a wall of separation, even the distinction between depth psychology and physics comes into question. Was the reality of this divide always in name only?

And then another presumed dichotomy pops into view—the one between science and politics. To illustrate the interchange between these two domains, let me propose the simplest way I can conceive of to include anomalous phenomena in our official accounts of reality: Just do it. Acknowledge that nature has already voted on its own contents, and get to work on new maps that include the anomalies in a larger territory. Larger, not because reality has suddenly come up with something new but because facets of reality were previously overlooked or mistaken for something else, or noticed but considered unimportant, or overtly refused by particular arbiters of reality based on ideological rather than empirical considerations.

But simply adding in the anomalies turns out not to be so simple, thanks especially to ideological factors. In his 1962 book *The Structure of Scientific Revolutions*,[2] the philosopher of science Thomas Kuhn created a masterwork describing the complex and often arduous process by which large changes happen in scientific thinking and societal understanding. Kuhn alerted us to the idea of a "paradigm" as a lens or filter through which we comprehend reality. Though such frameworks are essential to focus observation, the problem comes when we lose sight of their unavoidable distorting effects, the subtle ways they shape not only what will be accepted but what in a real sense can be seen and is allowed to be. Anything not adapted to the paradigm's filtering effects doesn't show up, or if noticed, it is easily dismissed. This applies in spades to non-ordinary phenomena that conjure implicit polarities of language such as exists/does not exist, real/unreal, objective/subjective, happened/did not happen.

Kuhn noted that these dynamics tend not to be in play during long periods of what he called "normal science." This is when most scientists do their daily work based on the assumption that the scientific community of which they are part knows what the world is like. Novel or unexpected observations that arise during periods of normal science are easily set inside as hiccups, glitches, trivia. For a while, the novelties are tolerated and don't cause doubts about an accepted theory, as scientists are confident these anomalies will be explained over time. If every unexpected observation provoked scientists to question the foundation of their theories, no detailed work would ever get done. Normal science is stable science.

Then, during periods of what Kuhn called "model drift," discrepancies become more plentiful and appear more frequently, causing everyday scientists to spend more of their time battling the anomalies. They may or may not know or acknowledge this because the effort often seems to be minor problem-solving, sincere efforts to explain inconsistencies as "noise in the system." It's when anomalies become serious, when they become too numerous and too significant to sweep away, that more everyday scientists realize the anomalies undermine the core assumptions of the prevailing scientific paradigm. Kuhn called this the "crisis" for the embattled paradigm.

Other scientists during this period dig in their heels and fight for the existing worldview. A period of protracted battle called a paradigm war kicks in. Kuhn observed that under such circumstances, the rules for applying the existing paradigm eventually become relaxed, as ideas that challenged the existing paradigm are gradually accepted by a new generation of scientists not wedded to the assumptions that have come to be revealed as flawed. The physicist Max Planck is credited with this observation: "Science advances one funeral at a time." What Kuhn called a "paradigm shift" takes place not as some decisive event marked by ribbon-cutting ceremonies marking a formally revised reality but instead as a gradual and tacit process that doesn't even recognize explicit competition between "old" and "new" paradigms. A new generation gets to work doing normal science within a paradigm that better explains observations that triggered the original crisis.

Ironically, the very disagreements that triggered the paradigm crisis, typically argued with scorched-earth intensity, tend to be downplayed later by historians who emphasize that the scientific method is defined by gradual, uninterrupted growth of piecemeal knowledge. This is a remarkable narrative feat, for indeed a revolution has taken place that changes a domain, along with the language about some aspect of nature considered important enough for pitched battles to be fought over and the cracks eventually papered over after the dust has settled. A triumphant scientific revolution succeeds in redirecting scientific resources and bringing into view a new portion of reality to study. The behavior that changes is not that of nature at large but of human observers with greater acuity and intellectual integrity toward nature. And still, no big fanfare. A classic and often-cited paradigm shift is that in which Lamarckian evolution (based on the inheritance of acquired characteristics) was replaced with Darwin's theory of evolution by natural selection.

At first glance, Kuhn's model seems apropos to the UFO debate. For example, there's definitely a sense in which the phenomenon's signature characteristics, especially the paranormal features, subvert accepted norms of reality. This can be likened to Kuhn's phase of normal science in which anomalies begin showing up. Some proponents of UFO reality might go so far as to argue that the widely trumpeted Pentagon report of June 2021 acknowledging some UFOs as officially "unexplained" constitutes the long-awaited definitive paradigm shift often referred to as "Disclosure."

But the celebration would be premature, as there's a crucial stage in Kuhn's account of paradigm change that comes before the phases described so far. The stage Kuhn called "pre-science" is known for constant bickering over fundamentals, disorganized and unfocused activity, and the lack of a commonly agreed observational basis (many conflicting theories composed of their own set of theory-dependent observations that aren't accepted or even recognized by other theorists). These dynamics were in play at the M.I.T. abductions conference and are characteristic of UFO conferences going back to the Ken Arnold era.

Debunkers are quick to say the commotion among UFO researchers means the alleged phenomenon isn't ready for science. But in many respects, it's just as accurate to say the science establishment isn't ready for UFOs, as evidenced by its unwillingness to acknowledge that there's even a "there" there—actual data worthy of engaging. The parapsychology research community went through a similar "sheer contempt for the very idea" phase many decades earlier. In the final analysis, claims for the reality of supernormal experience across the board are routinely denied a fair hearing by the science establishment, not because the claims lack merit or aren't amenable to empirical inquiry but rather because reasoned arguments for their relevance would require a revision of the cherished materialist worldview. Paradigm wars about the nature of reality aren't immune to scorched-earth battle tactics. As the character Mr. Dooley said in a nineteenth-century American novel, "Politics ain't beanbag."[3]

Scientific materialism is sometimes referred to as physicalism, and while there are subtle differences, the terms can be used interchangeably without sacrificing coherence. The most basic assertion of materialism/physicalism is that reality is exclusively material/physical. Materialism declares that reality exists outside of consciousness, completely independent of anyone's subjective perception of it. There's nothing more to a human being than an assemblage of stand-alone, inanimate (dead) material particles occupying the framework of space-time. And as for those subjective perceptions, they are mere side effects ("epiphenomena") of matter. Consciousness (including subjectivity, the capacity for first-person experience) is held to be nothing but a consequence of these complex arrangements of random, minuscule "building blocks" of spinning matter as emergent phenomena of brain activity.

Left unanswered: How do we get consciousness simply by stringing together dead subatomic particles? Can we ever know anything but that which appears in our own mind? This points to what is widely known as "the hard problem of consciousness," *hard* because, as philosopher Bernardo Kastrup observes:

> When it comes to consciousness, nothing allows us to deduce the properties of subjective experience—the redness of red, the bitterness of regret, the warmth of fire—from the mass, momentum, spin, charge, or any other property of subatomic particles bouncing around in the brain.[4]

Contrary to the materialist idea that all of reality ultimately reduces to material conditions, Kastrup says the more fundamental and necessary reduction is the one that recognizes consciousness as always already *prior*, as the very "space" in which all phenomena show up:

> Consciousness is the one unquestionable empirical fact of existence, the only carrier of reality anyone can ever know for sure. . . . After all, what can we really know that isn't experienced in some form, even if only through instrumentation or the reports of others? If something is fundamentally beyond all forms of experience, direct or indirect, it might as well not exist. Because all knowledge resides in consciousness, we cannot know what is supposedly outside consciousness; we can only infer it through our capacity for abstraction.[5]

With experience as the immediate empirical given of existence—in philosophical terms, the irreducible *ontological primitive*—it becomes clear that the materialist assumption of a reality external to experience, composed of a *separate substance* named matter with stand-alone status, is simply an abstraction, ironically produced by and appearing in consciousness. "I claim that we do not need more than consciousness to explain reality: *all things and phenomena can be made sense of as excitations of consciousness itself*,"[6] Kastrup writes. On this account, the foundation of all reality is a transpersonal flow of subjective experience that Kastrup metaphorically likens to a stream. Aldous Huxley termed this broader stream *Mind at Large*. Jung called it the *collective unconscious*. Our personal awareness is simply a localization of this flow, a whirlpool in the stream that leads to the persistent illusion of personal identity and separateness.

Kastrup points out that it is simpler and far more consistent with direct experience to infer that the boundaries of a *known* ontological category (personal consciousness) extend beyond face-value boundaries, than to infer through mere abstraction a whole new ontological category called matter, which when searched for at the quantum level smiles back elusively, Cheshire Cat–like, as mere probability fields. The fact that a realm seemingly external to the personal mind may "feel like" something *different* that can be given the name "physical" is itself a qualitative, experiential evaluation, appearing in (where else?) phenomenal consciousness. "We all share the same world because, like islands in an ocean, our personal minds are surrounded by one and the same mind-at-large."[7] As William James said, reality is made up of *experience*, which by definition is qualitative. Some experiences feel like mind, while other experiences feel like matter. The difference is in feeling, not in kind.

I readily acknowledge that these large ideas have the potential to take us far beyond the apparent scope of this book. Holding doctorates in philosophy (ontology, philosophy of mind) and computer engineering (reconfigurable computing, artificial intelligence), Kastrup is the author of 10 books in which he makes a sophisticated analytical case for a renaissance of metaphysical idealism, the notion that reality is experiential in essence. I'm happy to leave the heavy philosophical lifting to

Kastrup while highlighting his ideas challenging numerous materialist assertions made without even a nod to proof, the foremost being that the brain produces consciousness. This claim must be measured against voluminous veridical reports of near-death experiences, with complex perceptions, cognitions, emotions, and intuitions occurring during documented absences of brain activity. Moreover, a series of meta-analyses of large-scale parapsychology and anomalous cognition studies makes clear that nonlocal perceptions are indeed possible. By now it is clear as well that paranormal illuminations are part and parcel of the UFO mainstay.

Materialist and physical models have been roundly criticized for their inability to accommodate non-ordinary phenomena, but this should not be taken to imply that the models are adequate to accommodate the ordinary. They are not. Humans have no access to any purported reality that is not qualitative and experiential; to repeat, consciousness is the only carrier of reality we know and can know. There's no way even in principle that the qualities of experience can be deduced from matter as defined by those models. The conceptual incoherence now extends to leading materialist philosophers (Daniel Dennett, Owen Flanagan, and Patricia and Paul Churchland), who have gravitated self-assuredly to the astonishing position that consciousness as such is illusory. "How can any of us take seriously someone who stands up and pronounces that his or her own mind doesn't exist?"[8] asks Stephen Echard Musgrave. But this is the stultified state of play in moribund academic philosophy.

My use of the verb *musing* in this chapter's title is no accident. In the remainder of the chapter I will ponder, reflect upon, and extrapolate from Kastrup's thinking on "meaning in absurdity," the title of one his books. I'll improvise on his engagement with the thinking of Jung, whom Kastrup names as a major intellectual mentor. My aim is to invite you to imagine "cosmological individuation" through the territories Jung spoke of as the personal and collective unconscious. "The contents of the unconscious are not the most primitive or the most advanced," Kastrup observes. "They are merely closer to the origin of all things; to the core of who we are and what reality is."[9] Was Jung unknowingly chronicling the true physics of nature?

Over a century ago, Sir William Crookes had this to say of extraordinary phenomena he had witnessed: "I never said it was possible, I only said it was true."[10] In riffing on the ideas of Jung and Kastrup for a thought experiment on the future of reality, I embrace Crookes's remark, and for good measure happily reverse its terms: "I never said it was true, I only said it was possible."

In early February 1951, Jung wrote to a friend that he had not been able to determine whether UFOs were best considered rumors related to mass hallucination or "a downright fact." What remained unclear in his mind was "whether a primary perception was followed by a phantasm or whether, conversely, a primary fantasy originating in the unconscious invaded the conscious mind with illusions and visions."[11] In the first case, a physical process provided the basis for an accompanying myth; in the second case, a psychic process created a corresponding vision. Jung also considered a third possibility: UFOs could involve synchronicities, meaningful coincidences of events separated by time and/or space, happenings that suggest unseen links between consciousness and matter. This hypothesis reflected Jung's lifelong interest in paranormal phenomena and unusual states of consciousness.

In a short 1959 book entitled *Flying Saucers: A Modern Myth of Things Seen in the Sky*, Jung delved into the relationship between UFOs on the one hand and, on the other, parapsychology and psychokinesis—mental influence on inanimate objects. Perhaps UFOs might be "materialized psychisms"; that is, actual physical or paraphysical materializations formed out of the collective unconscious. His comment that this very idea "opens a bottomless void under our feet" indicated he appreciated the challenges such thinking posed to ordinary notions of reality. Still, the idea of a shifting rather than absolute dividing line between mind and matter, spirit and nature, was not new to Jung, who originated a doctrine about the fundamental structures of the psyche and ultimately all of nature, forms he called *archetypes*.

Jung's map of the human mind divides the psyche into three primary segments. The first, *ego consciousness*, corresponds to our everyday awareness of ourselves as singular agents functioning in the context of a wider world ostensibly separate from ourselves. Jung understood that we normally and erroneously identify solely as our egos. Through non-ordinary states of consciousness—for instance, dreams, meditative states, psychedelic trances—we can gain some awareness of deeper layers. The second and deeper segment, the *personal unconsciousness*, is composed of aspects of our personalities that were once in ego consciousness (thoughts, feelings, memories, emotions, drives, etc.) but have since been forgotten, rejected, or blocked through repression. These psychic contents never go away but remain active in a parallel life that we ordinary can't call up through introspection, yet which often surfaces in times of stress, challenge, or crisis. The psyche's third and largest layer, the *collective unconsciousness*, is the repository of the mental activity common not only to all humanity but all conscious beings. Though this unfathomably vast, creative, and dynamic realm is intrinsic to who we are, its contents tend to remain beyond the conscious reach of the ego, surfacing when individuals undergo an identity crisis involving drastic changes to their meaning system (unique goals, values, attitude and beliefs, sense of purpose), typically due to a spontaneous existential or spiritual experience—or a UFO encounter.

The collective unconscious embodies potentialities for experience structured according to what Jung called *archetypes*: primordial, a priori, self-existent templates of psychic activity. Jung describes the archetypes as:

[U]nconscious but nonetheless active-living dispositions, ideas in the Platonic sense, that perform and continually influence our thoughts and feelings and actions.[12]

These "ideas in the Platonic sense" have:

[E]ffects which have an *organizing* influence on the contents of consciousness.[13]

Although archetypes can't be known in themselves, Jung said we recognize archetypal experience whenever we are in the presence of that which speaks to us as deep, necessary, universal, basic, fundamental. Biological archetypes include Mother, Father, Brother, Sister. Good or Terrible Mother and Tyrant Father are psychological archetypes. Professional archetypes include Scientist, Healer, Dictator, and Capitalist. Archetypes "hold whole worlds together and yet can never be pointed to, accounted for, or even adequately circumscribed,"[14] writes psychologist James Hillman, who as a young man trained under Jung in Zurich. Jung held that archetypes span the boundary between instinct and spirit—the former in that they drive, steer, and mold thoughts, emotions, and behavior, the latter in that they may take "a distinctly numinous character which can only be described as 'spiritual.'"[15]

The Trickster archetype, pervasive in the UFO controversy, embodies logical contradictions and shape-shifting disregard for dichotomies like objective/subjective, real/unreal, happened/didn't happen. Kastrup writes:

For the most part, we have repressed Trickster's ambiguity and contradictoriness for the benefit of an obsessive search for explanation and closure. . . . Anything that transcends logic will appear illogical and absurd, like a prank or pun, from the point of view of logic. As such, perhaps the Trickster has a fundamental role to play in the expansion of our understanding of nature. Its exile in the deepest reaches of the unconscious is unfortunate.[16]

As much as ego consciousness seeks to keep the seeming chaos of the unconscious at bay, a crucial role of the archetypes (often through Trickster figures) is to exert formative influence on ego consciousness to compensate for the ego's lack of balance. Yet the ego also wishes to keep unruly psychic forces in their place, thereby reducing the greater freedom of the chaotic underworld; likewise, the unconscious may view the rational ego as an impediment, an obstacle to be overcome. Balance is a two-way street and, for society and individuals alike, is never static. This oscillation is apparent in the way UFO sightings juxtapose logical elements (the appearance of the Zimbabwe craft as consistent with an object moving through space) and absurd factors (the strange staccato-like movements of an alien seeming to run repeated stretches in slow motion, as if the scene were being rewound and replayed).

For decades, Jungian therapists and theorists have tended to interpret Jung's three-part model as if psyche were a reality located solely inside the individual, consistent with Descartes's division of mind as interior and matter as outward. Jung's study of synchronicities, however, led him to the revolutionary view that the greater part of the psyche lies outside the personal self. He began fleshing out an idea that had been implicit in his theories all along: that the collective unconscious underlies not only consciousness conceived as interior life but the physical world at large. A lifelong student of Jung's work, Kastrup recognizes this as a groundbreaking move, "as it means that physical events are orchestrated by the same a priori patterns that orchestrate events in consciousness."[17] Kastrup says Jung acknowledges this explicitly:

> [T]he archetypes are not found exclusively in the psychic sphere, but can occur just as much in circumstances that are not psychic (equivalence of outward physical process with a psychic one).[18]

To remove any doubt, Jung confirms the impulse of the unconscious to manifest beyond the psychic sphere:

> It is perfectly possible, psychologically, for the unconscious or an archetype to take complete possession of a man and to determine his fate down to the smallest detail. At the same time objective, non-psychic parallel phenomena can occur which also represent the archetype. *It not only seems so, it simply is so, that the archetype fulfills itself not only psychically in the individual, but objectively outside the individual.*[19]

In alliance with the Nobel Prize–winning quantum physicist Wolfgang Pauli, Jung proposed synchronicity should "be understood as an ordering system by means of which 'similar' things coincide, without there being any apparent 'cause.'"[20] Again, Kastrup emphasizes the significance of what Jung is up to:

> [H]e is extrapolating the natural basis for cognitive associations in the psyche to a universal basis for the organization of all events in nature. He seems to regard the whole universe as a supraordinate cosmic mind—a "greater and more comprehensive consciousness"—operating on the principle of association by similarity, just as the human psyche does.[21]

Jung's expanded framework opens the door to speculations about whether a "greater and more comprehensive mind" acting on a "principle of association by similarity" may be at play in UFO cases of many types; for instance, that of Charles Hickson and Calvin Parker, who prior to their encounter at Pascagoula had chosen a first site for fishing but spontaneously moved to a new one because the biting insects had gotten too intense. Or Dennis Sant, witness to the 1980s–90s sightings in the Hudson Valley, New York, who suggested something beyond mundane explanations: "From beginning to end, the nineteen to twenty minutes that I [had] viewed the craft was also a time of self-examination of myself and who I was."[22] Or the dramatic cinematic portrayal (based on real-life UFO cases) of geographically separate witnesses inexplicably drawn to Wyoming's Devils Tower rock formation in *Close Encounters of the Third Kind*. This list could be long. This principle of similarity is also found in everyday life: an individual possessing a telepathic empathy that no one else appreciates or hearing suprasensory music that he or she is hesitant to describe, or a "zoned" athlete experiencing extrasensory perception unrecognized by coaches.

By their very unpredictability and inability to be replicated in experimental trials, such happenings are often dismissed as mere coincidence. Given that the dichotomy between the inner reality of the psyche and the outer reality of the physical world is deeply ingrained, it will take more than synchronicity anecdotes and theory to make a convincing case for mind and matter as essentially continuous rather than intrinsically separate. If only a rigorous experiment could be designed to test whether minuscule building blocks of lifeless matter, considered by scientists of physicalist faith to be the sole substance of reality, might somehow be able to *communicate with* other such blocks of across vast distances. Surely even confident proponents of the physicalist view would welcome the opportunity to test a hypothesis so unlikely, bordering on the outlandish.

The experiment has not only been designed, it has been tested numerous times, with compelling outcomes. "It is somewhat of a mystery why society is not abuzz with commotion about the dumbfounding implications of it,"[23] Kastrup says of research with so-called entangled subatomic particles, photons to be precise.

Start off with a light emitter set up to generate two subatomic particles at the same moment. Send out the photons in opposite directions, one emitted toward the left, the other toward the right of the light source.

On both sides, at long distance from the source, place detectors that can measure specific properties of the two incoming photons.* The distance from the source located in the middle (see "The Demise of Realism" on page 187) is to ensure that the calculation performed on one side cannot influence the calculation performed on the other side. Because it takes time for each photon to arrive at its corresponding detector, wait until the photons are far enough away from one another that complete separation is assured. Once this condition is satisfied, use the two detectors to make separate measurements of each photon.

This is when things start getting strange. Quantum theory doesn't permit us to assume the reality of the photons' properties prior to computing them. This is contrary to classical physics, but it is the nature of quantum phenomena; thus, we must think of the photons taking on the property to be measured only at the moment of measurement, after the race has been run, not when the photons leave the emission device. Another important prediction of quantum theory: whatever property the first proton "chooses" to take on when calculated by the first detector, the property the second photon takes on when measured by the second detector will depend on the first photon's "choice."

This is exactly what's observed to take place. Despite the physical separation of the photons, independent assessments made by the two detectors confirm the two photons are strongly correlated. In quantum parlance, the two particles are said to be "entangled." It's as if the two photons separated by enormous distance are still connected after they leave the light source. But let's proceed with caution and consider alternative theories. Could it be that the measurement of connection was somehow not actually separate from the act of measurement? Many scientists familiar with the study assumed the answer must be yes; how else to explain what seemed like magic ("spooky action at a distance," in Albert Einstein's phrase)?

---

*Technically, the detectors are polarizers that gauge the polarization of the incoming photon along a predetermined course.

Yet further measurements confirm the experimental results. This led Einstein to declare the two entangled photons must have shared an identical hidden property from the instant they were created at the source, and this property was somehow preserved after the two particles were launched in opposite directions. This hypothetical hidden factor supposedly influenced computations on both sides and explained the connection between separate observations at the two detectors. Einstein did not spell out the hidden element or how it worked; he simply pointed out that it was feasible. Bernardo Kastrup brings context:

> Notice that Einstein's view was grounded in *realism*: the hypothetical hidden properties are seen as facts of the world "out there," completely independent of observation . . . Moreover, Einstein's view also

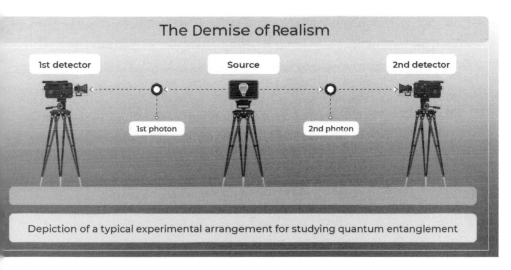

The Demise of Realism

1st detector · Source · 2nd detector

1st photon · 2nd photon

Depiction of a typical experimental arrangement for studying quantum entanglement

Fig. 10.1. When two particles, such as a pair of photons, become entangled, they remain connected even when separated by vast distances. Separate experiments by the Global Consciousness Project (started at Princeton University in the early 1990s) seem to indicate that mental states (the global outpouring of shock or grief accompanying major world events) and physical reality (the output of random number generators placed across the globe) are not separate.

assumes *locality*: the hidden property of each tangled photon resides solely in the respective photon and depends on nothing outside it, even if the hidden property happens to be the same in both photons of the pair. Because of these two characteristics, we say that these hidden variables of quantum entanglement entail *local realism*. More importantly, *local realism requires a hidden variables theory of quantum entanglement to hold true.* If not, local realism is fallacious. In this latter case, the question would then be: Which part of local realism has to be abandoned? Locality, realism, or both?[24]

The stakes are huge. Joining the fray, physicist John Bell performs a series of experiments and concludes that local-realist properties could not possibly explain away evidence of quantum entanglement. Physicist Alain Aspect and his team follow up with their own experiments increasing the distance between detection devices, but these further confirm quantum mechanical predictions of counterintuitive connection at great distances. Just when it appears that local realism is dead, skeptics come up with a new scenario: The two detectors could be exchanging (in advance of the photo emissions) some kind of hidden signal that might influence the measured correlations. It is even suggested that maybe the supposedly independent detectors were "tipping off" the source, which somehow "knew," in advance, the exact combination of properties the detectors were configured to measure. Again, no explanation is offered for how this might work.

Along comes a 2007 paper in the distinguished, peer-reviewed science periodical *Nature*,[25] describing experiments by a respected team of Austrian and Polish physicists who conclude that merely abandoning locality simply isn't adequate to explain quantum entanglement. Multiple, independent corroboration of the evidence makes it necessary to *discard realism itself,* or at least many of its most intuitive features. Kastrup agrees there's no other alternative consistent with the findings:

It is thus fair to say, within the current framework of scientific thought, that realism as we normally understand it must be abandoned. Remember, the inconceivably small subatomic particles these experiments are performed on are supposedly building blocks of the whole of nature. Therefore, the defeat of realism for subatomic particles entails that *there is no such a thing as a strongly-objective world* [fundamentally independent of conscious observation.[26]

Defenders of realism still weren't ready to throw in the towel. Many emphasized that brain science acknowledges clear correlations between brain states and first-person conscious experience. They were equally quick to imply, with zero evidence, that this means brains *produce* consciousness. Also, what about the fact that different people gathered in roughly the same location seem to agree on what the world "out there" looks like? Besides, since brains are clearly separate from one another, minds *must be* separate as well.

Notice how this deftly begs the question by assuming in advance as fact the very hypothesis it seeks to prove. The argument takes realism as a given by simply presuming separate brains are synonymous with separate minds. There is of course another possibility: that minds beyond brains are connected or even unitary. The notion that consciousness is confined to the body is simply an assumption. Personal psyches with a unique point of view can be understood as sharing a common root in a larger, transpersonal field of consciousness external to the perspective of personal psyches. This idea only entails extrapolating consciousness beyond its face-value personal boundaries. Which leads Kastrup in this remarkable direction:

For all we know, we may all be having a shared "dream."[27]

How could this be true except as metaphor and myth? Obviously, this interpretation assumes that myth is synonymous with fanciful or false. In this emerging context, myth and metaphor matter; they are *material.*

Our myth-making capacity may be nature's way of bringing images of potency and secrets from nature's own depths closer to the neat dwelling of daylight's conscious awareness. All very interesting—but if we lose realism as the benchmark for evaluating the ways of this world, what are we to do with longstanding axioms that seem self-evidently true? Axioms of the "every schoolboy knows" type, such as:

> Certain statements are considered true or false without need for explanation or substantiation.
> For instance: "An assertion is true, or its negation is true."
> If A = B and B = C, then it's self-evidently true that A = C.

In formal logic, this is Aristotle's "law of the excluded middle." By definition, this form of logic doesn't allow for degrees of truth. UFOs and supernormal phenomena that blur the boundaries between the inner reality of the psyche and the outer reality of the physical world violate this logic.

Realism is based (and depends) on the fundamental assumption that a real reality exists, and certain theories, ideologies, or personal convictions reflect it (match it) more correctly than others. We can make statements about nature, but nature has its own independent states beyond such statements. Nature is what it is, regardless of what we say or believe about it. "Facts don't care about your feelings," to quote political commentator Ben Shapiro. When John or Jane makes a statement about reality, the statement is true if it corresponds to objective facts about the world "out there." This is the "correspondence theory of reality," which rules false any statement lacking this essential correspondence with objective facts.

What is easily missed, overlooked, or simply ignored about these two convincing axioms is precisely that they *are* axioms. This is to say, they are deeply engrained assumptions easily taken as self-evidently true, as opposed to empirically established laws. Axioms are common sense, intuitive starting points that evolved through the pressures of natural selection to provide a conceptual framework for survival in a chaotic and threatening ecosystem where making snap, dichotomy-based judgments (fight or flight) about potential dangers provided survival advantages. Our logic, and the rest of our psyche, did not evolve to capture general truths about the nature of reality, especially truths suggested by questions about purpose, value, and ultimate meanings.

A fundamental effect (and for all we know a primary intention) of the UFO phenomenon has been to drive home the fact that at the bottom of what we consider unmistakably real lies a set of arbitrary axioms widely presumed by every schoolchild to be based in laws of logic. What if nature has many more degrees of freedom than are permitted by Aristotelian logic? Suppose nature follows a logic that has fewer or different axioms or perhaps doesn't follow logic at all, at least in forms we are accustomed to expect?

Joining three broad fields of inquiry—Jung's three-part model of the psyche (including his theory of synchronicity), the sobering implications of quantum entanglement, and the explanatory failures of physicalist assumptions about nature—Kastrup puts this hypothesis on the table:

> If, as depth psychology has discovered, the psyche is layered in "realms" ranging from ego-consciousness to the collective unconscious, then so is the world. . . . Crucially, the ultimate map of nature may be the map of the psyche as uncovered by depth psychology. As such, depth psychology may take precedence over physics [as conceived in materialist terms] as a description of the universe.[28]

Among the radical implications: Because our psyches comprise unconscious layers, there are unconscious (or *obfuscated*, Kastrup's chosen term) manifestations of reality to which we have access, with varying degrees of awareness, concurrently and constantly. In Kastrup's map of nature:

Our ordinary waking experiences [rational and ego-consciousness] may be merely islands betraying an unfathomable underwater mountain chain of world-instantiations [manifestations of phenomena]. As such, our ego-consciousness may be but one viewpoint in the many levels of unfolding storytelling . . . . The logical world of ego-consciousness is a consensus creation: logic is a coherence-enforcing, tacitly agreed set of constraints, driven by our innate need to find closure. We build a world where the story is linear, self-consistent, continuous, and where truth is seemingly literal; a world where the principle of bivalence [dichotomies galore: real/unreal, happened/did not happen] rules supreme. Classical logic is the veil of veils: a self-imposed filter on the stories; a straitjacket of thought we wear most of our waking lives and which prevents us from seeing the nature of being for what it really is. If only we could 'turn off' classical logic for a moment, we would be in awe of what would become clear to our cognition.[29]

These propositions approach the central thesis of this book. Extraordinary phenomena in the lives of real people that don't conform to the "rules" of restrictive yet arbitrary axioms rise up from the depths of reality. The phenomena make direct contact with rational-egoic structures of consciousness that can only consider the phenomena absurd. This triggers the reflex action of automatic dismissal by reality-reinforcement mechanisms at the rational-egoic surface. Emphatic assertions such as "Such reports aren't true because they can't be, as we know from the established laws of reality" enter the discourse. I have often been struck by the palpable frustration of debunkers when witnesses to UFOs and other extraordinary phenomena stand by their experiences. Reflexive debunkers have no noncircular argumentative recourse—their blanket dismissals, founded on axioms they take as self-evidently true, only go so far. This speaks to the frequency with which debunkers turn to

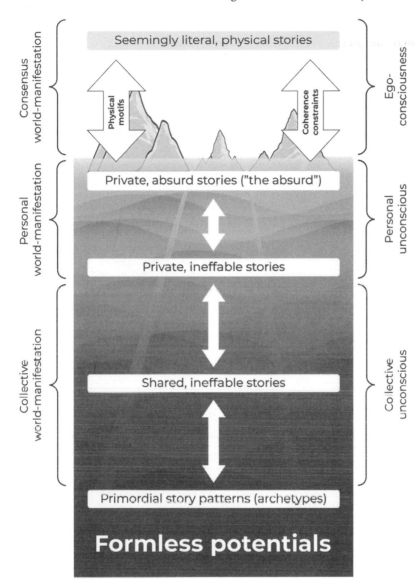

The cosmology of the absurd; and beyond

Fig. 10.2. Bernardo Kastrup's map of psyche as continuous with nature demonstrates that as we go deeper into unconscious, metaphor- and symbol-based layers of the psyche, longstanding constraints imposed by rational-egoic consciousness may begin to loosen, supporting and enabling the emergence of "absurd" phenomena not constrained by axioms wedded to binary logic and linear cognition.

character assassination—witnesses to the impossible must be liars, fools, con artists.

Yet the debunkers have a point. Without a framework based on the law of the excluded middle and correspondence theory of reality, how are we to distinguish fact from fiction? We do so the way we always have; namely, by *cultural consensus.* The surface or "island level" of the psyche represents the everyday realm of consciousness where distinctions such as real/unreal, matter/mind, fact/fiction hold sway by *consensus,* according to what Kastrup calls "coherence constraints." Stories about what is real meet other stories rising up from deeper, absurd levels of our collective matrix. This process descends to the very deepest levels the formless potential of archetypes hold forth. Kastrup continues:

> What appears to be different entities—separate mountain peaks, islands, individual egos—are actually protuberances, salient features of a single underlying matrix; mere viewpoints taken by a unified mind. The coherence constraints applied by each individual ego in the construction of our consensus world-instantiation may be shared through—perhaps even enforced by—this underlying unified matrix. The very choice of these constraints may be a choice of the matrix as a whole, simply expressed through the filters of individual egos with small, local variations and fluctuations.[30]

Here Kastrup masterfully links the individual psyche to collective consciousness, showing the enforcement power of the latter over the former, as a general rule. We begin to get a sense of how this worldview does not entail the anything-goes of relativism, the position that any view or opinion is as good as any other or that everybody is right regardless of how ridiculous their arguments and positions. Kastrup responds that ultimately, even in a world where consciousness is primary, common coherence constraints emerge naturally and unavoidably:

Think of the collective dream we talked about earlier, where no individual dreamer could change the dream on a whim, since the dream was an amalgamation of many inputs. Moreover, like the mass of an enormous crowd moving in unison, a collaborative world-instantiation on this scale would acquire unfathomable momentum and become seemingly autonomous; as if it had a will of its own, independent of the will of each person in the crowd.[31]

Think of collaboratively constructed ant colonies, where an apparently integrated and autonomous global behavior uncannily emerges from interactions between individual ants. Extrapolating from this analogy, Kastrup insists that as absurdities rise into the consensus reality of an expanded rational-ego sphere, it remains perfectly legitimate to articulate rules of evidence that hold sway within our consensus world-picture: rules that determine what conditions must be fulfilled for a statement to be declared true or false. Owing to the gradual relaxing of consensus constraints at the rational-egoic "island level," social reality comes to include absurd phenomena involving violations of causality, such as synchronicities and a wide range of paranormal UFO features. Over nearly eight decades, the surrealism of UFO phenomena has taken on new degrees of normalcy, just as rocks falling from the sky came to be accepted at another time. How easy to forget that any apparent anomaly in nature is relative to the extent that the anomaly violates not that natural order but expectations about the nature of that order. Gradual recognition of the reality of meteors changed human anticipations about what nature includes; very different from saying they changed nature, which is always fully itself.

The extent to which reality is in fact grounded in ever-evolving *consensus* is crucial in this larger perspective. Although discussions continue in philosophy about whether or not logical axioms are empirical, in fact they are largely arbitrary, functioning as adages, maxims, and proverbs to provide reassuring guardrails for a young species as it

navigates environments fraught with uncertainty. Can we say defini-
tively that the logical axioms taken as intuitively correct by the human-
primate mind (possessed of language skills for approximately 30,000
years) must encompass all the degrees of freedom of nature at large?
A strong case can be made that for all we know, nature in itself could
be essentially absurd, at least by the order-giving criteria of egoic rationalism. Through the apparatus of our novice species-cognition, it is we
who bring order to reality—to such an extent that we don't recognize
our role in the process. What Kastrup calls "coherence-constraints" get
imposed collectively and tacitly. In a very real sense, the professional
nay-saying debunker plays the "bouncer" role to enforce those constraints. This scenario recurs throughout the UFO controversy, ensur-
ing never a dull moment for merry Proteus.

Growing openness to UFO phenomena in the public sphere means
its reality is moving beyond former coherence constraints to enjoy
greater consensus even among agents of official culture with a history
of reflexive debunking. An excellent example is the Pentagon's formal
admission in 2021 that unexplained aerial phenomena do exist, after
decades of denying this fact. Consensus constraints held in place for
decades, requiring unknown phenomena to be officially nonexistent,
are now loosening. Through the sheer persistence of the phenomena,
yoked to the growing willingness of human witnesses to speak of its
presence in their lives, prior coherence constraints have slowly unwound.
New consensus takes shape, subject to continuous revision. Storylines
focused on larger realities once considered absurd make their way into a
growing consensus as credible, if not fully comprehensible as rational or
consistent with traditional assumptions about what's real, or could be,
or should be. Shape-shifting aerial events that appear and disappear on
the spot still don't "make sense," yet slowly the very uncertainties in the
reports become part of new mythologies of possibility.

Ontological shock opens to aftershocks bringing different kinds of
questions. "Was it real?" morphs to "What does it mean, what does it

want, is this my calling, and now?" UFO witnesses more readily take note of *what was happening just before*—uncanny promptings from "nowhere" to look to the sky. The ancient Greeks understood that the *daimon*—call it pattern, character, soul, angel, alien, heart, or inherent image—brings wisdom through mysterious events that seem to pull us off course. New ways of being arise from new ways of seeing, as the poet W. H. Auden understood:

> The so-called traumatic experience is not an accident, but the opportunity for which the child has been patiently waiting—had it not occurred, it would have found another, equally trivial—in order to find a necessity for its existence, in order that its life may become a serious matter.[32]

Traditional logic, linear casual reasoning, and good-faith skepticism don't disappear; they continue to be useful for navigating routines in dreaming the everyday, with its continuous rhythms of forgetting and waking. Alive to "the formless foundation of chaos, of pure potential, upon which our thoughts and world rest," Kastrup dares to wonder if "we may be able to re-sculpt the formless potentials into broader, richer, more beautiful, meaningful, and transcendent art."[33]

11

The Matter of Pascagoula

The renowned 1973 Pascagoula incident is one of the most thoroughly researched cases in UFO history. New evidence keeps turning up, including eyewitness accounts that support key aspects of the original descriptions by Charles Hickson and Calvin Parker. Most of these witnesses say they hesitated to come forward for the same reason the two men considered keeping quiet: fear of not being believed, ridiculed, and ostracized. Witnesses of high-strangeness events usually don't realize they aren't alone in dealing with an encounter that upends everything they take as real. They understand a huge downgrade in social standing is likely if they talk about what happened.

Calvin Parker never stopped being willing to talk candidly about the experience that changed his life, but he was done arguing with people who didn't mean him well or care about facts. He figured lying low was his best hope for a peaceful life. During a long phone conversation about the case, Calvin invited me to continue talking over home-cooked red beans and rice in Pascagoula. Also on the menu: a chance to find out about newly surfaced witnesses who had avoided the harsh glare of publicity in the immediate aftermath of the encounter.

Was the Pascagoula abduction case opening up again, five decades later? Maybe it never really closed. The day before boarding a plane for south Mississippi, I learned that retired captain Glenn Ryder, one of the last police officers to investigate the case from the start, had just died at age 86. With the passing of Charles Hickson in 2011, Calvin was the sole primary witness to the extraordinary events of an autumn night that rocked his world. These new witnesses could change everything.

October 11, 1973. Around seven o'clock on a humid south Mississippi night. The sun has dropped from sight, and a waxing gibbous moon is climbing from the east. Calvin Parker is sitting at the edge of a pier just off Highway 90, fishing with his coworker Charlie Hickson. That day, Calvin had begun work at a local shipyard, slamming metal with a sledgehammer. Casting his line into the muddy Pascagoula River, he notices an old coast guard ship anchored across the water.

How in the world does a massive steel ship manage to float? This is what he still remembers thinking. *What keeps something that heavy from sinking to the bottom?* Pondering his questions, Calvin notices hazy blue lights flashing against the water. "I'd already told Charlie we were

Fig. 11.1. Calvin Parker and Charles Hickson described a craft suddenly appearing behind them as they fished from a pier that no longer exists. This was their view of the Pascagoula River on the evening of October 11, 1973, when an eerie blue light flashed against the water and they turned around to determine its source.

trespassing, now I was fixing to say he would need to pay my way out of jail,"[1] Calvin recalls. But the lights aren't from a police cruiser.

"We both turned around and looked, and all of a sudden a real bright spotlight just hit us with a beam brighter than you can imagine. I blinked, and when I opened my eyes, I knew we had trouble, and not with the law. Three stocky creatures with no necks and thick shoulders were on us, each about five-six feet tall with wrinkly gray skin. My blood ran cold as I looked over at Charlie. He had gone pale; his mouth was wide open and he didn't say a word. They had legs, but the creatures glided above the ground and moved with lightning speed. Couldn't make out their faces because the light was nearly blinding. They had clawlike hands shaped like mittens. Two of 'em got hold of Charlie, one grabbed myself and floated me toward a craft that was shaped kind of like a football, maybe thirty feet in length and eight to ten feet top to bottom. The craft was hovering about two feet over the high weeds. I felt a sharp pinch in my left arm like an injection because my body got all relaxed. I tried looking for Charlie but couldn't turn my head. It was like I was weightless and frozen at the same time."

At the doorway, the light coming out of the craft is as bright as Calvin has ever seen. "It was as bright as a welder's arc," he says. The light seems to pour directly out of the walls. "This creature carries me in and makes a turn to the left, heading down a hallway before a second turn to the right into an examination room with a glass table at a 45-degree angle," Calvin says. "The way the thing moved, I'm thinking this is some kind of robot. The creature lay me on the table, and then it sidles up against the wall and kind of shuts down. As I looked at the ceiling, some kind of device about the size of a deck of cards comes down and stops about a foot and a half from my head. It starts rotating and going click-click-click-click, four times, and then it shoots back up into the ceiling."*

---

*The first commercially viable computerized axial tomography scan (or CAT scan) was marketed in England in 1972. This technology was unknown to Hickson and Parker in 1973 in Pascagoula.

Charlie reported a similar procedure: "Then I saw it: something that resembled a big eye seemed to come out directly from the wall. . . . The 'eye' came closer and stopped about six inches from my face. . . . The eye lingered there for a while then started to move down my body and returned to move over my entire body. No pain, no sensation."[2]

Then a new creature resembling a humanoid female comes in. Right off, Calvin notices the middle fingers of each hand are considerably longer than the others. The being comes over and places her left hand on Calvin's cheek and pushes down on his jaw with the other hand, then inserts one of her lengthy digits down his throat, "right past the little hang-me-down deal in the back of my throat [his uvula]. This got me choking and gagging and my nose bleeding. Then she quickly removed her finger, and I heard telepathic thoughts in a female voice, 'We mean you no harm.' Well, it was a little late for that.* She started making a low moaning sound like an alligator in mating season—*goonk-goonk*— and right away the big ugly robot sitting in the corner came alive and jumped up like a jack-in-a-box. That thing went and grabbed me by the arm and injected me with something else, then took me back out of the craft and stood me up at the same location they had first taken hold of me. I was facing the river with my arms stiff and stretched out, like I'd been bit by a rattlesnake."

Charlie remembers being glided back out through the same opening and "being moved toward the place they had taken me from. My feet were touching the ground. When they released me I fell when my legs gave way." Looking up at Calvin standing with his arms outstretched, Charlie sees "more terror on Calvin's face than I have ever seen on anyone's."[3] Charlie starts to crawl toward his friend and rises to his feet before reaching him, and tries to help relax Calvin's frozen arms. Hearing a zipping sound, Charlie turns and sees the blue flashing

---

*It is hard to describe the ironic tone with which Calvin said "Well, it was a little late for that," in his lifelong deep-Mississippi accent.

lights and almost instantly the craft is gone. Calvin remembers it going straight up and disappearing from sight.

They stand in stunned silence for what seems eternity. Charlie speaks first. "Well. The damage is done. Let's sit and talk about this for a minute."

"There's really nothing to talk about, Charlie."

"We got to tell somebody."

"Hell no, we don't," Calvin says. "Nobody needs to know about this. What we need to do is get up tomorrow and go to work." Calvin had no intention of losing his new job at the local shipyard alongside family friend Charlie, 42, who had recommended him for a full-time position. Calvin and his fiancée, Waynette, are due to marry in two weeks. He is not looking to become unemployed.

They debate telling or keeping quiet. Charlie favors informing the proper authorities—what if an invasion was underway? Calvin comes down on the side of keeping it all quiet—let's get back to normal. Charlie comes up with a compromise: If Calvin doesn't want to say anything, Charlie will just say Calvin passed out.

"I didn't want to tell anyone so I let him make the call," Calvin remembers. "Mostly I was terrified they might return and start up with us again."

Gathering their fishing equipment, they walk over to Calvin's new Rambler Hornet parked about 100 yards from where the craft had hovered. The windows on the passenger side are shattered (from exposure to the craft, they reason). The glass falls out when they open the door. The car won't start, and Calvin keeps cranking until the engine turns over. Heading onto the highway, Charlie tells Calvin to stop at a nearby pay phone, where Charlie calls Keesler Air Force Base. The receptionist says to call their local authorities because Project Blue Book has shut down and the air force no longer takes UFO reports. "I'm thinking we've still got time to keep all this to ourselves," Calvin tells me.

Charlie puts another dime in and dials the sheriff's department. The deputy who takes the call seems amused. "Come on over and we will talk about it," he tells Charlie. Calvin's first request upon arriving at headquarters: Give me a polygraph test. It was determined that both men are too wrought up for the lie detector, but the request is noted. After telling their stories separately at the sheriff's office, Calvin and Charlie are now exhausted but still highly agitated. When a deputy asks Charlie to tell his story again, Charlie snaps, "Well, this will be the third time!"[4] The request is repeated, and Charlie recounts what happened at the river. By the end of his story, the sheriff promises Charlie he can soon go home. He and his team excuse themselves on the pretext of going for coffee. Offered a cup, Charlie declines. As the men leave the office, Calvin is brought in and left alone with Charlie.

They have no idea Sheriff Fred Diamond has hidden a voice-activated tape recorder in a drawer. If the two are trying to pull a fast one, the tape will find them out and they'll be in serious legal trouble.

CALVIN: I got to get home and get to bed or get some nerve pills or see the doctor or something. I can't stand it. I'm about to go crazy.

CHARLIE: I tell you, when we through, I'll get you something to settle you down so you can get some damn sleep.

CALVIN: I can't sleep yet like it is. I'm just damn near crazy.

CHARLIE: Well, Calvin, when they brought you out—when they brought me out of that thing, goddamn it, I like to never in hell got you straightened out.

CALVIN (his voice rising): My damn arms, my arms, I remember they just froze up and I can't move. Just like I stepped on a damn rattlesnake.

CHARLIE: They didn't do me that way.

CALVIN: I passed out. I expect I never passed out in my whole life.

CHARLIE: I've never seen nothin' like that before in my life. You can't make people believe it . . .

CALVIN: I don't want to keep sittin' here. I want to see a doctor.

CHARLIE: They better wake up and start believin' . . . they better start believin'.

CALVIN: You see how that damn door come right up?

CHARLIE: I don't know how it opened, son. I don't know.

CALVIN: It just laid up and just like that those son' bitches—just like that they come out.

CHARLIE: I know. You can't believe it. You can't make people believe it—

CALVIN: I paralyzed right then. I couldn't move—

CHARLIE: They won't believe it. They gonna believe it one of these days. Might be too late. I knew all along they was people from other worlds up there. I knew all along. I never thought it would happen to me.

CALVIN: You know yourself I don't drink.

CHARLIE: I know that, son. When I get to the house I'm gonna get me another drink, make me sleep. Look, what we sittin' around for. I gotta go tell Blanche. What we waitin' for?

CALVIN (panicky): I gotta go to the house. I'm getting sick. I gotta get out of here.[5]

The recording convinces Sheriff Diamond that Charlie and Calvin are telling the truth, describing real experiences. It's a while before the two even know the tape exists, let alone get to hear it. They do notice their interrogators are suddenly more respectful. Late into the longest day of their lives, Charlie and Calvin are finally free to leave.

When he gets home that night, Calvin fears contact with the creatures and the craft might have left him contaminated. To be on the safe side, he gets into a hot shower and pours a bottle of bleach over his head and body. He puts his clothes and shoes in a paper bag and throws it in a dumpster.

Charlie and Calvin arrive at work early the next morning after a sleepless night. The parking lot is filled with news media vehicles and general pandemonium. Word has definitely gotten out. Things start moving fast.

Somebody at the shipyard suggests they should head over to Keeler Air Force Base and get tested for radiation. Calvin recalls, "I thought 'Thank God' and hopefully there is nothing wrong with us and we've not exposed half of Mississippi."[6] They're met by six men wearing white suits who announce "all clear" when radiation detectors find no danger.

Sheriff Diamond tells reporters he believes "something" had happened to the men because they were "scared to death and on the verge of a heart attack."[7] Says Captain Glenn Ryder, "If they were lying to me, then they should be in Hollywood."[8] By 8:15 p.m. the previous night, Pascagoula police report more than 100 calls describing sightings. Asked at midnight about the number of UFO calls, a police spokesman simply replies, "We don't have an adding machine that goes that high."[9] Larry Booth, operator of a gas station near the landing site, tells police he'd seen a UFO with "a flashing blue light" headed east toward Alabama.[10]

Astronomer J. Allen Hynek, the air force's former UFO consultant, is soon on the scene to interview Calvin and Charlie and law enforcement officials. He also listens to the secret tape several times. "There is no question in my mind that these men have had a very terrifying experience," he tells the media throng outside the sheriff's office. "Where they [the creatures and craft] came from is a matter of conjecture. But the fact that they are here on this planet is beyond a reasonable doubt."[11]

Unreasonable doubt makes the scene as well. Enter Philip J. Klass, an aviation magazine editor famous for his signature efforts to safeguard reality from the dangerous rumors advanced by crackpots, frauds, and opportunists peddling UFO yarns. In his many media appearances, Klass had made it known that with sufficient investigation of the proper type, all unexplained sightings would be shown to have ordinary explanations. Given the strangeness of close-encounter reports, the bias of professional debunkers often passed as objectivity.

Klass joined the controversy, demanding the Pascagoula duo submit to polygraphs. When the witnesses passed with flying colors, he objected that the chosen licensed polygraph operator lacked sufficient experience. When the two passed second tests administered by a more experienced examiner, Klass changed course yet again, saying polygraph results aren't reliable in any event. Calvin subsequently took a voice stress analysis that showed no signs of deception. Klass had nothing to say about that, instead resorting to blanket assertions of fraud. Calvin's claim of suffering a nervous breakdown was "obviously" faked. It was clear to Klass that Calvin had chosen to undergo the considerable expense of hospitalization, requiring him to miss work and lose income, to cement an elaborate hoax.

Calvin tells of crossing paths with Klass at a restaurant related to a planned joint TV appearance about the Pascagoula incident. When a reporter asks Klass why he had backed out of doing the TV show, Klass declares himself a scientist who only deals in facts and can't be expected to appear on the same panel with—he doesn't call them backwater Mississippi yokels, but the implication is hard to miss. Calvin has heard enough:

> I now informed Klass that he had never asked me anything about what had happened to us. How come he could accuse me of hoaxing this event without ever having contacted me or asked me any questions. If he was a scientist, he should not have done this. It was at this point that I became very irritated by this man. I did not like being called a liar and he didn't like it when I called him a fake scientist. At this point I lost my temper somewhat with Philip Klass and told him in no uncertain terms what I thought of him. Needless to say, we were asked to leave the restaurant before our food arrived.

The ride home was very quiet, and I was very hungry. This was my first and last meeting with Philip Klass.[12]

Following this dustup, Klass sent Calvin and Charlie letters repeating his hoax allegations and stating they were free to prove him wrong. "Neither of the principals, nor Hickson's lawyer," Klass eventually disclosed, "ever wrote or called to challenge my conclusion."[13] Podcaster Jimmy Akin, respected for covering all sides of these kinds of controversies with fairness, finds Klass's response ridiculous:

According to Calvin they did dispute [Klass's] hoax theory to his face. . . . But even if they hadn't, the claim that they didn't write him or call him would have basically zero weight as evidence. You just don't have to answer all your critics, and if you don't it doesn't show them to be right . . . To put it politely, Klass was an arrogant, egocentric and unscrupulous individual. I don't have time in this episode to document these claims but they have been well founded and documented by others. For now, just consider what kind of egomaniac you'd have to be to say, "Well, after I published a criticism they never wrote or called me to dispute it, so that's evidence that the criticism is true." . . . I get criticized all the time, and I have better things to do than waste my time writing and calling people of ill will to privately dispute what they've said.[14]

Klass continued dogging witnesses until his death in 2005. This was his bird-flipping good-bye to his adversaries:

To ufologists who publicly criticize me, . . . or who even think unkind thoughts about me in private, I do hereby leave and bequeath: THE UFO CURSE:

No matter how long you live, you will never know any more about UFOs than you know today. You will never know any more about what UFOs really are, or where they come from. You will never know any more about what the U.S. Government really knows about UFOs than you know today. As you lie on your own death-bed you will be as mystified about UFOs as you are today. And you will remember this curse.[15]

It is hard to imagine a more striking example of the kind of emotion-driven animus that often underlies the reasoning of self-styled debunkers, as distinct from genuine skeptics.

On the day of my Pascagoula trip, I woke at 4:30 to the hooting of an owl from the pitch darkness outside my bedroom window. Booked to fly more than 3,000 miles on three planes in a single day, I was happy to consider the owl a good omen. When I gave my class report on UFOs as a sixth-grade student, nobody could have convinced me that decades later I'd be traveling long distances to ask questions about the ways and means of a phenomenon that *doesn't officially exist*. A phenomenon that routinely breaches the separation between the subjective, psychological world inside our mind and the objective, physical world "out there." And does this with a genius for goading two exclusionary partisan camps to duel with take-no-prisoner certainty for one side of the divide. It gets perfect strangers at social gatherings to line up with conflict-ing absolute views: from eye-rolling rationalists who reflexively dismiss everything related to UFOs to sci-fi and tech-savvy enthusiasts equally certain UFOs could only be extraterrestrial visitors in nuts-and-bolts machines.

America's Deep South doesn't get much deeper than Pascagoula. Where it does, it's called the Gulf of Mexico.

The young reference librarian at the Pascagoula Public Library greets me at our agreed hour and shows me to a work area with several expand-ing folders plump with original news clippings and documents. A batch of books is neatly stacked. I had told her by phone I'd like to see every-thing they had on the case.

"Not many people come here to research the Pascagoula incident," she says. Her voice is smoky Patsy Cline with a side of coffee brandy.

"You're glad somebody's doing it."

"Yes. I am." Then a pause. "Do you think they told the truth?"

I tell her yes. If she and I had the same experience, we'd believe it.

"Me too," she says. Another pause. "I hope you crack the case," she says with a smile and a wave. Then she disappears into the Young Adult Fiction section. The game's afoot, as Sherlock Holmes said. Over the next two hours I identified several eyewitnesses who stayed silent in 1973 and agreed to speak around the time Calvin surfaced with his memoir decades later. Condensed summaries of witness reports follow.

Louis Lee

Mr. Lee had come to a public gathering in January 2019 to hear Calvin speak when his book *Pascagoula: The Story Continues* was published. Calvin didn't know Lee when he came up to him and said he had seen the object in the same area where the abduction had taken place. Lee had been an employee of the same shipyard where Calvin and Charlie worked. He was operating a crane on the Pascagoula River the night the famous incident occurred. He recounts to Calvin what he had seen.

"I was looking at the river and I see this object and I had never seen anything like this . . . I had to stop looking because they were giving me instructions about what lever to pull and everything. I took my eyes off of it, but it was kinda like round, like egg-shaped, with blue/silver ray lights, egg-shaped kind of round, right over the Pascagoula River."[16]

Lee remembers Charlie coming back to work, and as the contro-versy grew he decided he didn't want to be part of the hubbub. Lee kept the sighting to himself for more than 45 years.

Judy Branning

At the same book event, Ms. Branning came forward to say she'd seen a bright white light that she and friends first thought was an airplane "fixin to crash" not far from where she later learned Calvin and Charlie were fishing. From UFO investigator Philip Mantle's interview with Branning: "It had a disk-like shape but had a rounded top. It was a very bright white light and nearly blinded them. She also said that when it was close, their car motor died, and the radio went crazy. . . . It passed right over their car. She thought it was just a few feet . . . above their car . . . . The others in the car were terrified."[17]

Joey Nelson

A 25-year-old pool player from Mobile, Nelson was traveling on US 90 on October 11 when he and his passengers saw "a giant orb of light in the sky" resembling a blimp. "Nobody said anything," he recalls. Then a "small orb of light was emitted from the giant orb" and "It got right in my face and was very close and began to click and flash lights. . . . We were almost in shock about what was going on." Then it "zoomed out of the sky like you wouldn't believe and nobody could say anything. The three of us were almost like paralyzed."

Inexplicably, Nelson and his passengers found themselves traveling back in the direction from which they had started. "We went back to one of the places in Pascagoula and had a game and then for some reason came back to Mobile."[18] They heard about Parker and Hickson the next day.

Maria and Vernon Blair

A young married couple, Marie and Vernon Blair were down by the Pascagoula River that night waiting for a boat to come in, related to Vernon's work in the fishing industry. Marie noticed blue lights hovering and circling in the sky. "The object would move all over the sky and gave the impression that it did not know where it wanted to go."[19] Marie spots "something come out of the water and it was like a person and I told him [Vernon] there's somebody out there. Vernon responds, "Oh come on there ain't nobody out there."[20] Marie describes the "person" as "grey looking like the skin diver's suit."[21]

She tells Vernon she wants to report it. He says everybody would make her out to be crazy. So she keeps it to herself for decades, even though the knowledge disturbs her greatly. When Vernon is close to death in 2019, he tells Maria there's something she needs to know. He records this video on his cell phone in the hospital shortly before dying:

> I lied all them years saying I didn't see what my wife saw. I did see it; I just didn't want to admit it because I was afraid how people would look at me. But I saw exactly what she described, as an object, a person, a humanoid in the water, that I kept telling her that was a porpoise, but it was not a porpoise, it was a humanoid figure that was in the water, and it made a splashing noise. And I also saw the blue lights when they came down and the people, whatever, a humanoid leaving us, not, not coming to us but leaving us. I don't remember seeing them come to us, but I remember them leaving us and I saw them go back across the river to their spaceship or whatever it was. But that's as much as I remember, and I hope you get this on the record because this is all that's maybe left of me. I hope my wife understands, bye.[22]

The Underwater UFO

Marie Blair says she watched a blue-lit craft dive into the water. She variously describes the being in the river as a *person*, a *humanoid*, and an *alien*. Noting records that show military officials had studied underwater lights and contact with a submerged moving object, researcher Irena Scott speculates that the object encountered not only by the Blairs but by Charlie and Calvin "could be both a submarine and a flying object. It could also suggest that both underwater and flying UFOs were active at the same time during these events."[23] UFOs have been widely reported to move into, through, and out of water without apparent displacement or impact. "Flying saucers have demonstrated a penchant for bodies of water, diving into rivers and reservoirs around the world," John Keel reports. "The majority of the best-known UFO contacts have taken place on beaches and river banks.[24]

My mind was reeling from all the details. Keel had warned that those who track UFOs can be "driven insane when their minds are unable to translate the signal properly."[25] He didn't define "properly" but Nietzsche didn't hedge: "If you gaze long enough into an abyss, the abyss will gaze back into you."

It wasn't until I noticed the librarian watching me stare into space that I realized how deep into the material I had gotten. "Looks like you might be finding some interesting stuff," she says. Vernon Blair's deathbed confession had caught me short—along with Joey Nelson's unexplained change of course after being transfixed by a flashing orb of light. The librarian has thrown me a lifeline.

"There are witnesses very few people know about" is my reply. The common pattern in the stories practically shouts. All the witnesses had surfaced at the same time Calvin Parker had surfaced, after his long time in the wilderness of self-imposed silence. They had checked out when Calvin disappeared. Now Calvin was back. And with him came the witnesses, more than the few described here.

A wild thought landed. What if half of Pascagoula had seen what happened that night and kept it to themselves, not wanting to stand out and end up as a *cognitive minority*? I stifle a laugh that could have cleared the room. Calvin had told me he and Waynette would be home all afternoon. I'm welcome to head out there any time. I thank the librarian for all her help. She winks and gives me a thumbs-up. Mission accomplished. But not the final one. I need to know where

Fig. 11.2. Standing at a commemorative site established by the city of Pascagoula, Calvin Parker points the author to where Parker and Hickson were fishing the night they were captured by three robotic creatures that emerged from an unexplained craft.

Calvin had been, all the years he was away. And I didn't just mean what town.

"Yes, I hid out for sure," Calvin says. We're sitting on his screened-in porch overlooking the inlet where his fishing boat is docked. He and Waynette live in a quiet neighborhood adjacent to vast greenery that could pass for a forest. "I wanted to put the whole deal behind me from the start. Before the encounter I was left to mind my own business, but that all changed. I couldn't do a simple thing like go to the store without everyone asking me a lot of questions. Not long after the encounter,

I had a full nervous breakdown. I left town, moved around a lot."

Looking into the distance, he continued, "I even started going by an alias, calling myself Randy so nobody would be asking Calvin to tell his story. I paid a price for keeping it all inside—I didn't know how big a price it was until the day I realized Waynette was right. It was time to write the book."

They'd gone to a wake to pay respects to a neighbor and friend. Calvin mistakenly signed the guest book using his real name. This got folks asking him to tell his story on the spot. "Waynette and I felt a man's memorial service was the wrong place for that, so we went to leave. Sitting in the car outside, she turns to me and said, 'Calvin, you need to write the book.' A publisher had already reached out and I'd been putting him off. I needed to get the story out. That meant starting with my wife. All she knew was what she had heard from the media. For nearly 45 years, I had never told her what had happened. She trusted I'd tell when I was ready. Just try keeping a secret like that from your wife for that long."

His time on the run had run out. Being on the lam from having to be *that* Calvin Parker was a reasonable strategy, until the logic of it ran out, like a battery drained of charge. *"So long Randy, been weird to be you."* Fitting that Calvin would be reborn as himself at a man's funeral.

I had come to Pascagoula with questions bordering on the ultimate, aiming to track down new details about extraordinary happenings nearly five decades earlier. I'd found plenty. Multiple witnesses had intersected with strange phenomena around the time Calvin and Charlie had been by the river. As for origins, some prefer the extra-terrestrial hypothesis; others cite dimensions beyond time-space. How are the two scenarios different, at the level of experience? At minimum, these events defy physics and axioms—assumed laws that refuse to stay put. Most often the events include powerful and unexplained intuitions that seize ordinary people at their very depths.

Simultaneous contradictoriness, underworld symbolism, event-level reality, all crossing and tangled in ways that feel somehow more real than real.

An alien storyline with its own logic and vernacular punches a hole in our storyline. We, in our storyline, speaking to them: "Who or what are you, where are you from, what is your purpose in coming here?" They, in their storyline intersecting ours, speaking back: "We've got pretty much the same questions for you."

It's my last day in Pascagoula. I'm glad for a break from thinking about hazy blue lights streaming from a football-shaped craft across a body of water known by legend as "the singing river." Uncanny creatures with long, probing fingers that "mean no harm." Drivers who don't remember changing course on the highway after being transfixed by orbs of light. Happiness is watching squirrels leaping across branches in trees. Rose-breasted grosbeaks in flight. Potato salad brought by a woman called April who lives across the street. And Calvin's own red beans and white rice.

What the philosopher said about the astonishment that there is something rather than nothing, it never really wears out. Some truisms turn out to be true, sometimes truer-than. That there is *anything at all*—surely this is the hidden pulse that joins the endlessly varied, wildly rambunctious shapes and colors, sounds and touches that bestow the continuous creativity of this cosmos that is our home. Normal or supernormal, extraordinary or mundane, I'll go with Walt Whitman:

> And I say to any man or woman, Let your soul stand cool and composed between a million universes.[26]

Calvin picks up his cell phone and speaks to the programming: "Put on Otis Redding." The singer tells of sitting in morning sun all day through evening, watching ships come in and roll back out. "The blues is like old country," Calvin says, almost absently. "It's all life story."

I keep pondering the question that popped for young Calvin in 1973, as he sized up that old coast guard ship. Exactly how do big, heavy steel ships manage to stay afloat? He didn't know he was chewing on a quandary that preoccupied ancient alchemists: What is matter, and can it be transformed? Then young Calvin quickly finds himself floating, *being floated* into a luminous oval-shaped chamber, or maybe an alchemical vessel. The matter of Pascagoula.

I ask him what it's been like to not be believed—to be so radically *disbelieved*.

"You know what? I appreciate the people who doubt," Calvin says with a smile. "I would have doubted if I hadn't gone through it for myself. You've got to have doubters. The ones that don't open to it, they'll never accept without experiencing, at least not without setting aside prejudice and looking into it with a fair mind, like the sheriff did with Charlie and me. I don't know exactly what happened out there. I do know *something happened*."

Calvin Parker died on August 24, 2023, less than two months before the city of Pascagoula's long–planned fiftieth anniversary commemoration of the riverside happening that might not have become known if his friend Charlie Hickson hadn't insisted they had an obligation to go public. When I would ask Calvin to recount the basic details of the incident, I was struck never to notice significant additions or deletions. He came to appreciate doubters, but not because he sought their seal of approval; to the contrary, he would shake his head with amusement that Philip Klass and fellow debunkers never tired of claiming he and Charlie had faked the terror and panic heard in the jailhouse conversation secretly taped by the sheriff.

As I worked on this book, I envisioned the possibility that Calvin and Emily Trim of Ariel might someday compare notes on their long periods of self-imposed exile before each decided to return to their primal experiences, Emily as artist, Calvin as author of a book he agreed to write only if the publisher would not change even errors of spelling and punctuation. As for the new Pascagoula witnesses who came in from the proverbial cold to breathe new life into the events of Pascagoula in 1973, I applaud their grit in answering "the call" to go meet Calvin at the local bookstore.

Epilogue

When the *New York Times* broke the news in 2017 about "The Pentagon's Mysterious UFO Program," two widely held assumptions became suddenly more credible. Assumption number one: After decades of denying any interest in, or activity related to, unidentified flying objects (now rebranded as unidentified aerial phenomenon, or UAPs), the U.S. government was now confirming the existence of a well-funded, covert program dedicated to investigating not only UAPs but also their paranormal and psychic correlates. Assumption number two: Disclosure—the long-heralded revelation of definitive proof—was almost certainly at hand. The UFO phenomenon would finally yield its tightly held secrets. We would soon know what UFOs are.

The first assumption was a fact, not just plausible but obvious to anyone capable of reading and comprehending plain English. The *Times* story confirmed a congressional appropriation of just under $22 million beginning in late 2008 and lasting through 2011. The money was used for management of the program, research, and assessments of the threat posed by UAPs. As described in chapter eight, the funding went to Robert Bigelow's company, Bigelow Aerospace, which hired subcontractors and solicited research for the program.

The second assumption was less universal and closer to a hope; a new incarnation of the most enduring hope of UFO stalkers for the nearly eight decades since Ken Arnold stepped onto the runway tarmac after his famous flight. The longevity of this hope couldn't have been obvious to all readers of the *Times* disclosure, especially readers relatively new to UFO reporting and those coming to the subject cold. In a very real sense, the *Times* story succeeded in resetting the metaphoric UFO clock. If the story had come out when I was preparing my sixth-grade classroom report, I would have found it logical that such a government program had likely reached definitive conclusions. Whatever rationale existed for hiding the facts in the first place, it was likely just a matter of time before those facts came out.

Here's the thing. I'm not 12 anymore. This isn't my first season as a viewer of the UFO Disclosure Chronicles series. Definitive Disclosure has been imminent for quite some time, almost as long as Sisyphus has been pushing his mythological rock to the top of the hill—*success at last!*—only to find the rock always falls back to the bottom by its own weight. At times, disclosure expectations call to mind Samuel Beckett's famous play *Waiting for Godot.* The characters wait expectantly for the arrival of Monsieur Godot, never realizing what has become obvious to the audience: the wait is in vain, Godot will not come.

And yet—there was nothing resembling absurdist theater in Laurance Rockefeller's determination to effect greater government transparency regarding Roswell. In one sense, his mission failed. But in an equally valid sense, Rockefeller helped move the ball farther down the playing field. No doubt partly as a consequence of that effort, today there are UFO developments regarding transparency and disclosure that resemble milestones more than the millstones of past dashed hopes.

For example, on June 25, 2021, a report of the Office of the Director of National Intelligence that focused on 144 observations of unidentified aerial phenomena found that 143 of the sightings defied explanation. The admission that all but one sighting remained unexplained was widely hailed as the first official acknowledgment that at least some UFOs (now rebranded as UAPs) are genuinely "unknown aerial phenomena." A follow-up report in August 2022 stated that of 366 newly identified UAP reports, 171 remained unexplained, and some appeared to demonstrate "unusual flight characteristics or performance capabilities and require further analysis."[1]

Of specific relevance to disclosure stalwarts is the controversy surrounding what has come to be known as the Admiral Wilson Memo. In 2002, physicist Eric Davis, who holds security clearances with the U.S. government, supposedly held a private, two-hour meeting in a parked car with Admiral Thomas Wilson. The setting has been described as being like a scene from a Robert Ludlum novel. An 11-page memo supposedly written by Davis after the meeting has Wilson telling Davis about his discovery of deeply hidden programs linking the Pentagon to attempts to reverse engineer a recovered craft that was believed capable of operating in air, sea, and space or perhaps even in other dimensions. The program manager allegedly concluded that the craft was not man-made.

The memo was leaked from a seemingly unlikely source—the estate of deceased Apollo astronaut Edgar Mitchell, the sixth man to walk on the moon. About a decade earlier, in the 1990s, I came to know Mitchell when I worked as an editor of the *Noetic Sciences Review*.* This magazine was published by the Institute of Noetic Sciences, a nonprofit organization founded by Mitchell in 1973. The Institute's aim was to take a science-based approach to investigating mind-matter interactions, evaluating evidence for the survival of consciousness beyond physical death, and finding out how we can extend the kinds of extraordinary human capacities such as those chronicled in chapter eight.

In numerous conversations in person and by phone, Mitchell told me he believed there have been ET visitations with crashed craft and alien bodies recovered. In media interviews, Mitchell discussed the

---

*I was delighted when Mitchell agreed to my invitation to visit my son's California elementary school in 2008, where he spoke movingly about the Apollo 14 mission. I can still hear the silence of the student body as Mitchell described the moment he looked back at our blue-and-white planet floating in the background of deep black space—suddenly experiencing the universe as more than random, chaotic movement of a collection of molecular particles. All at once he became convinced that our universe is intelligent, harmonious, and purposeful.

notes of the alleged Wilson-Davis conversation. But he and I never discussed the topic, and I had no hint that the disputed memo would be found in his personal archives.

After the leak, Wilson denied any such meeting took place, and because the content of the memo covers classified information, Davis has refused to confirm or deny anything related to such a meeting or memo. The only undisputed detail seems to be their mutual non-corroboration.

In the wake of the hotly contested but never corroborated claims, meanwhile, has come a new generation of provocative rumors about recovered crashed spacecraft and aliens (dead and alive, based on different reports). It is alleged that these findings may have been handed off to aerospace corporations for safekeeping and efforts to hack the technology and that people with direct knowledge are ready to come forward so long as they receive immunity of sorts. In 2022, congressional legislation was drafted to include a secure method for authorized reporting ("safe harbor" or "whistleblower" provisions) for UAP-related matters. Legislation containing these provisions was signed into law on December 23, 2022. Current or former government employees or contractors are now free to submit UAP-related information to the Pentagon UAP office and through that office reach also the congressional armed services and intelligence committees.

Indeed, new dynamics are in play, at least new at the surface level of the UFO narrative. As we learned from the literary scholar Angus Fletcher in chapter one—and let's never forget we are dealing with *stories* here—a defining characteristic of an allegory is that it "says one thing and means another. It destroys the expectation we have about language, that our words "mean what they say."[2] An allegorical work goes along saying one thing in order to mean something beyond that one thing, in order to imply something or many things not stated in the primary or surface story.

A second defining characteristic of pure allegory, Fletcher notes, is that its formal, or literal, surface level doesn't explicitly demand to be interpreted for hidden meanings, for it often makes "good enough" sense by itself. This to say that based on a straight reading of the plain words of the *Times* story, it does seem reasonable, perhaps even plausible, that Big Disclosure is finally nigh. "But somehow this literal surface suggests a peculiar doubleness of intention, and while it can, as it were, get along without interpretation, it becomes much richer and more interesting if given interpretation."[3]

The art and practice of interpretation—deciphering meanings—descends from a Greek god named Hermes. Like his ally Proteus, Hermes is the personification of a type known as Trickster. In mythologies ranging from the Native Americans to the Greeks, the Chinese, the Japanese, and the Siberian and Semitic peoples, a figure known as the Trickster appears again and again in characteristic adventures and ordeals. The complexity of Trickster is demonstrated in his capacity to manifest at the same time as creator and destroyer, giver and taker, one who dupes and is invariably himself duped. "Laughter, humour and irony permeate everything Trickster does,"[4] writes the anthropologist Paul Radin in his classic account on the subject, *The Trickster*. Remnants of Trickster motifs in medieval jesters; in the modern clown and Punch and Judy plays; in the carnival festival, where, for a specific period of ritual time, the hierarchy of social roles reverses (mayor and garbage collector, prince and pauper); and, most assuredly, in the modern debate about unidentified flying objects.

Yet each time Trickster gets himself into some abysmal jam, his ability to turn the tables restores him to his savior nature. Jung warns that modern consciousness has for the most part lost touch with Trickster, but Trickster has not forgotten how to find us. In the final analysis, the theme of disclosure is not immune from the twists and turns that come with so much of the high-strangeness multiplicity of the UFO phenomenon. To be clear: the "presence" of Hermes and his ally Proteus takes nothing away from our ability to follow any part of the UFO controversy at the surface (literal) level of the daily news, including developments related to disclosure. To the contrary, these mythic elements bring *more* to the picture by making clear that things are not always what they seem with the UFO phenomenon. There are always secondary levels of interpretation, and these additional readings (think of them as *soundings*) take nothing away from happenings at the surface level. Given a choice between comprehending more or less of the richness, depth, potency, and yes, *complexity* of these phenomena—why would we opt for less?

Up to now, I have alluded to *daimons* without really defining the term or the territory. The notion of the daimonic is complex because it proliferates from a multitude of cultures, including different religious and philosophical frameworks. As my explorations near an end, the significance of daimonic reality comes more clearly into view as a "missing link" of sorts to many facets of UFO phenomena, especially those involving high strangeness.

The commonplace Christian idea of a creature with horns and pitchfork represents the daimon as demonized, and this stereotype stems from equating the daimonic with fallen angels. This likeness shows that the demonic and the angelic are closely related, and it shows that, in Greek myth as well as in Hebrew religious myths, daimons could be either good or evil. Daimon is the larger category that precedes the dichotomous division according to virtue; in fact, the word derives from the Greek *daíomai,* meaning "to distribute or to divide." The daimon is a distributor, usually of destinies; hence the frequent equivalence of daimon with fate, soul, necessity, or in the main idea of these pages, calling.

From earliest usage, the daimon had religious and spiritual significance decidedly referring to the otherworld; daimons were intermediaries understood to be guardians of the human species. All persons were guided by their guardian angel, in this case, a daimon, none more celebrated than Socrates's daimon. When Socrates was tried for corrupting the youth, Plato and other friends demanded to know why he refused to fight the charges. Socrates listened to, and reached, so to say, a negotiated settlement with his daimon, or, in a different cultural context, he heeded the voice of the Impersonal as a "force of nature" larger than his self-importance. James Hillman sets the frame:

> We must attend very carefully . . . to catch early glimpses of the daimon in action, to grasp its intentions and not block its way. The rest of the practical implications swiftly unfold: (a) Recognize the call as a prime fact of human existence; (b) align life with it; (c) find the common sense to realize that accidents, including the heartache and the natural shocks the flesh is heir to, belong to the pattern of the image, are necessary to it, and help fulfill it.[5]

The significance of these ideas became clearer as I looked into changes in how close-encounter witnesses refer to themselves and are described within UFO culture. It isn't clear when the term *experiencer* was first used to designate and account for the full range of close encounters with nonhuman beings generally referred to as aliens. In his book on the 1992 M.I.T. conference on abductions, journalist Courtlandt Bryan writes that during the conference, experiencer evolved into the "favored identification for an individual who has endured an abduction."[6] Recently I learned from Karin Austin, executive director of the John E. Mack Institute (an organization spearheading numerous initiatives aimed to further Mack's scientific and philosophical inquiries) that the definition of experiencer has continued expanding to include those who have encountered:

> [A] broad spectrum of exotic phenomena that many people have either directly experienced or can personally relate to in some way: out-of-body experiences, near-death experiences, meditative visions, psychedelic journeys, premonitory dreams, telepathy, precognition,

transcommunication [often called mediumship] and of course
UFO-related sightings. All of these mystifying occurrences manifest
on a continuum of consciousness. Ephemeral as they are, they often
leave lasting impressions within the human psyche and precipitate
the onset of major life changes for the person involved.[7]

This broader context speaks to what we have learned about the
full experience of Kenneth Arnold, who kept to himself for many
years the fact that the nine objects he witnessed appeared to be blue-
white, streaming, pulsating, seemingly alive, and somehow fundamentally connected with a larger dimensional world, "the world where we
go when we die." Arnold's daughter Kim would report that a ball
of light would appear in their family home shortly after her father's
famous sighting.

The broader context also reframes Betty Hill's experience to include
poltergeist-like effects in her home in the aftermath of whatever she and
her husband Barney had encountered late at night on a lonely stretch
of road in 1961. In the course of writing this book I have many times
paused to ponder how the contemporary UFO controversy might have
unfolded if the actual facts of the Arnold and Hill encounters had been
told at the time the cases were widely discussed.

Obviously, there's no going back; yet from where things stand today,
we can proceed as we have all along, as empiricists committed to tracking the evidence where it leads. And for the moment, Karin Austin
brings fresh insight.

Speaking broadly to "the experiencer perspective," Austin reports
that for many individuals:

[T]here are moments in certain contact encounters that are very
physical and tangible in the way human beings have evolved to
define reality through our five senses. For instance, we can feel the
coolness of a Being's skin when we touch them, or we sometimes

wake up with visible corroborating marks on our body from medical procedures performed by the Beings during an encounter. There is also at least one account of an experiencer who, in waking-state consciousness, tracked a Being's movement through the bodyweight depressions it made in her duvet (it straddled her legs and torso as it traversed the distance between the footboard and her chest).

In other moments, a contact encounter can feel like being transported beyond space-time into a nonlinear dimension that vibrates at a higher, faster frequency than our own. In this "other place," reality is not experienced as dense matter, but as molecularly "alive." This shifted state of being does not make the encounter any less real than our normal material state of physicality. It's just different. These distinctions in description and classification are a hot-button issue for many experiencers who are desperate for a new scientific, referential language that can be used to articulate a new definition of reality that manifests on a continuum of matter and consciousness.[8]

Jung was well aware of the ancient thinking about daimonic reality. Even though he framed his voluminous writings to accord with the prevailing materialist bias of our age, philosopher Bernardo Kastrup's speculations in chapter nine make clear that Jung concluded that archetypes are endowed with personality at the outset; they manifest "as daimones, or personal agencies," and they are not mere "figments of the imagination," as rationalism would have us believe.[9] Just as Jung held that a primary purpose of dreams is to compensate for unnatural psychic conditions (usually excessive rationality), the contemporary British writer Patrick Harpur takes Jung's ideas further, first, by defining as daimonic realities UFOs and abductions, fairies, mass-audience visions of the Virgin Mary, phantom animals, mysterious orbs and poltergeist events; and second, by proposing that the purpose of these events (which notoriously confound mind and matter, spiritual and physical, fact and fiction) is to "subvert the same modern worldview which discredits them."[10]*

My purpose is to emphasize that the UFO phenomenon with its many facets and dimensions is a call from the cosmos to expand our paradigms of science and society to accommodate human experiences and inquiries too long precluded by physicalist and materialist faith-based assumptions that declare transcendent experiences taboo. Science already welcomes some transcendent subjects with open arms; for instance, the widely accepted higher mathematics of quantum physics that refer to a deep structure of reality we cannot easily imagine or place in our everyday experience. Only rank prejudice and deeply engrained bias stand in the way of a broadened, more relevant, and more encompassing science recognizing that the deep structure of reality applies no less to fundamental experiences of the human spirit and imagination.

Yet even with a wider and more expansive purview, the remit of science is to reveal what nature *does* and how it *behaves*; science is not configured to determine what nature actually *is*. Interpreting the meanings of nature's doings, probing the being of nature, this is the province of philosophy, religious studies, psychology, anthropology, literature, and other tributaries of the humanities. Outside the academy lie storytelling around campfires and water coolers, at wedding receptions and resting points on hiking trails, anywhere and everywhere humans join to allow for common inquiry about the meaning of it all. As the late evolutionary theorist Steven Jay Gould celebrated with such clarity in his book *Rocks of Ages: Science and Religion in the Fullness of Life*, the genuine

---

*The authors of *Skinwalkers at the Pentagon* observed that when teams of visitors with military backgrounds visited Skinwalker Ranch to investigate the site's anomalies and brought with them a regimented, rationalist perspective, the unpredictable, seemingly intelligent "phenomena" of the ranch appeared to respond by generating ominous and often terrifying effects. Conversely, such effects tended not to manifest for visitors who came with an attitude of respect and humility.[11]

articles of sensory empiricism and faith are not enemies but two different, yet complementary, ways of knowing.

Ultimately, the province is our multiple ways of knowing and being.

I am encouraged to learn from scientist Colm Kelleher that new initiatives are in the works at the Bigelow Institute for Consciousness Studies, building on Robert Bigelow's success in expanding the paradigm of UFO research, as chronicled in chapter nine. And I'm heartened by reports from religions and philosophy scholar Jeffrey Kripal that the Archives of the Impossible project at Rice University is moving with dispatch to flesh out the idea of psychical and paranormal phenomena as "the still unacknowledged, unassimilated Other of modern thought, the still unrealized future of theory, the fleeting signs of a consciousness not yet become a culture." Their collaboration shows it is not only desirable and necessary but possible to join different quests that, especially in contemporary academia, are typically sequestered by professional specialization, divergent belief systems, and garden-variety fiefdom protection.

Kelleher and Kripal are far from alone. Across the current intellectual landscape we see promising signs that other thinkers willing to cross the divide between the physical world and the "metaphysical world" understand that for science to continue to ignore the effects of non-ordinary phenomena on the worldview of countless individuals throughout the world will surely lead to more of society viewing science and scientists with disdain and distrust. A shift is underway toward a more integral scientific context conversant with William James's radical empiricism, with new conversations between and beyond conventional disciplinary lines, as envisioned by Stephen J. Gould and others.

The following survey gives a sense of this emerging horizon.

Citing the apparent ability of UFOs to manipulate time and space, Jacques Vallée asks whether UFOs are "windows" rather than "objects," and then tells us "UFO occupants are not extraterrestrials" but "denizens of another reality."

Peter Rojcewicz says UFO phenomena "raise the question of whether or not an event takes place in an intermediate realm which doesn't manifest exclusively in a physical objective way or leave a trace."[12]

Fred Alan Wolf suggests that because such events "have both a partial and temporal physical manifestation," they are happening in a "realm of reality that doesn't fit into material physics" but does accord with quantum physics, "which doesn't describe the realm of subjective experience or the realm of objective experience" but rather the "realm of imaginal experience that is potential material experience."[13]

John Mack held that the trauma caused by the phenomena is often mistakenly blamed on childhood abuse. Kenneth Ring has said such abuse and other unresolved life trauma is responsible for the greater ability to perceive extraordinary phenomena. He calls experiencers "encounter prone" and raises the possibility that their visionary psyches may be early signs of an emerging evolutionary stage in human development.

In a similar vein, Fred Alan Wolf proposes that such "imaginal realm bleed-throughs into our normally seemingly separated minds are an evolutionary trend leading us to a single one-mind experience of our SELF, the whole universe and nothing else."[14]

Whitley Strieber says he ponders whether the UFO phenomenon as a whole "may simply be what the force of evolution looks like when it acts upon conscious creatures."[15]

Our world consists of three known dimensions, with time constituting a fourth. A growing number of scientists and science writers speculates that the 90 percent of matter that can be neither seen nor detected suggests that so much dark matter may exist in parallel dimensions or alternate realities, normally invisible and undetectable to us. Some versions of string theory propose that there exist either eleven or twenty-six such dimensions.

"The quantum theory of parallel universes is not some troublesome, optional interpretation, emerging from arcane theoretical considerations," writes Oxford physicist David Deutsch in his book *The Fabric of Reality*. "It is the explanation—the only one that is tenable—of a remarkable and counter-intuitive reality."[16]

"In other words," says science writer Marcus Chown, "physicists are increasingly accepting the idea that there are infinite realities stacked together like the pages of a never-ending book. So there are infinite versions of you, living out infinite different lives in infinite parallel realities."[17]

The idea is gaining traction. "We physicists no longer believe in a Universe," says Michio Kaku. "We physicists believe in a Multiverse that resembles the boiling of water. Water boils when tiny particles, or bubbles, form, which then begin to rapidly expand. If our Universe is a bubble in boiling water, then perhaps Big Bangs happen all the time."[18] Max Tegmark agrees: "The concept of the multiverse is grounded in well-tested theories such as relativity and quantum mechanics. It fulfills both the basic criteria of empirical science: it makes predictions and it can be falsified. Scientists have discussed as many as four distinct types of parallel universes. The key question is not whether the multiverse exists but rather how many levels it has."[19]

Author Richard Grossinger brings this keen insight:

UFOs present humanity with a dilemma, indicating less interstellar travel than the need for a new physics of dimensionality or a different relationship between mind and matter. They offer a material glimpse of something that is fundamentally immaterial and/or interdimensional. They begin in matter somewhere, but convert to energy before their coordinates can be captured and identified. In this regard, ambient phenomena cannot be reduced to hardware, nor does the sky have an intrinsically objective basis of being. Information transcends classification.[20]

And then there's Michael Murphy's speculation, covered in chapter eight and repeated here because I find the metaphor of the frog so compelling. Regarding reports by shamans, yogis, and ordinary people of interactions with departed entities, some UFO encounters, and reports by rock climbers of disembodied entities that tried to communicate with them, Murphy asks:

> Are those "somethings" aspects of a greater existence, distorted perhaps by the subject's perceptual filters? Are they first glimpses of a "larger earth"? To a frog with its simple eye, the world is a dim array of greys and blacks. Are we like frogs in our limited sensorium, apprehending just part of the universe we inhabit? Are we as a species now awakening to the reality of multidimensional worlds in which matter undergoes subtle reorganizations in some sort of hyperspace? Is visionary experience analogous to the first breathings of early amphibians? Are we ourselves coming ashore to a "larger earth"?[21]

These issues and challenges are not the stuff of what Thomas Kuhn called "normal science." The possibilities here envisioned seem closer to science fiction, with ideas whose plausibility stems partly from anomalies that raise doubts about a prevailing paradigm. As anomalies accumulate, more scientists begin taking discrepancies seriously. And they keep doing what brought them to scientific inquiry in the first place: seeking stories with greater explanatory power.

Physicist Max Tegmark is already there. "Space appears to be infinite in size," he writes. "If so, then somewhere, everything that is possible becomes probable, no matter how improbable it is."[22] Somewhere, like over Mount Rainier in 1947? Pascagoula in 1973? Ruwa, Zimbabwe, in 1994?

An epilogue marks the ending of a book, much like the assimilation stage signals the culmination of a rite of passage. In his account of the hero's journey, Joseph Campbell speaks of the protagonist's inevitable return to ordinary society following a supernatural adventure. Sometimes the hero may have to be brought back by assistance from without. "That is to say, the world may have to come and get him,"[23] Campbell writes—or her, as with Emily Trim.

In initiation ceremonies throughout the world, the first step is to separate the novice (the initiate) from the world they know; literally, "they are seized by their guardians and carried off into the forest."[24] Indeed Emily was "seized" by what she saw, especially the eyes of the black creature that cavorted outside the astonishing craft that had suddenly appeared. She quickly found herself in the transitional stage, a confusing betwixt-and-between liminal zone personified by parental certainty that "it" had not happened, and what therefore "did not happen" was not to be discussed. She remained in this painful marginal reality long after her family had returned to Canada. Though no longer physically in Africa, Emily remained there psychologically, until the arrival of a letter inviting her to return to Ariel and, inevitably, to the experience that remained frozen in time.

In this way, the invitation constituted "assistance from without" for Emily to begin the process of completing a rite of passage she had no real idea was underway. We almost never recognize a phase or stage of life as a "cycle" symbolic of anything, until we're on the far shore and realize there was significance to events that couldn't be recognized at the time because life is urgent and desperate when we are in its throes. This was true for Emily the day she opened and read the letter. "The world" had come to get her, and she was ready to be gotten.

Campbell speaks of the hero as returning with a "boon," a reward of insight to be shared with the community that had remained behind. Emily had first to be handed the boon, and this took the form of words from the village's sacred teacher, Duke.

"There are spiritual messages that you have to deliver," he told

Emily, who at first didn't understand. "You don't have to keep it for yourself," Duke emphasized. "Yes," Emily said. Seeing that she was soft-spoken and perhaps hesitant, Duke got more specific. "If they don't hear you speaking, maybe you have to shout. The significance of children is that they are not yet exposed to the world and they communicate better with the spirits and nature. If you want a message to be delivered, it has to be delivered to children because the child grows with the message." Since finding her voice, Emily has also grown closer to her parents, who have had their own shift. Life is not just a natural process; it is besides, and even more, a mystery.

For Calvin Parker, a long period of living in the margins of his community and his very being came to an end when, as serendipity would have it, he mistakenly signed his true name on a funeral registry. With the stroke of a signature, Calvin Parker was back. He might have disappeared again but for the words of his wife, Waynette, as they sat inside their car in the parking lot. "Calvin, you need to write the book." Her words to Calvin, Duke's words to Emily: rescues from without that moved two different people in similar situations to look within.

Duke's boon to Emily was permission to speak freely, and her boon to the community was to share her extraordinary talent as a visual artist, which had taken seed when she drew the first of many pictures of what she had seen on the playground.

As for Calvin, he'd had several opportunities over the years to write a memoir about his experience. He turned them down because he was sure a publisher would insist on making him sound "like a writer." The only way he would agree to write would be to have a publisher's guarantee not to change a word of what he wrote, not even correcting misspellings. It was as if he would agree to give up being "Randy" and become Calvin only if it was clear to one and all this meant being precisely himself.

◄o►

As I was writing this epilogue, I received from Karin Austin a photo of a page of handwritten notes by John Mack, in which he voiced his personal sense of mission and power, as well as his fears and vulnerabilities. The notes were written in 1991, before he had authored either of his two books on abductions, four years before Harvard's inquisition into his research ended with the university affirming his intellectual and academic right to "inquire freely." This led me to reflect once more on the last day of his life, when Mack was crossing a thoroughfare in London on foot. His American instinct told him to look to the right. In England, for a pedestrian heading south, westbound traffic comes from the left. Mack was struck by a vehicle and was pronounced dead two hours later.

For no clear reason, I also thought of Mack's colleague and friend, the astronomer Carl Sagan, whose TV series *Cosmos* I had watched devotedly so many years earlier. What Sagan had seemed to find the most stupendous and mind-boggling was the degree to which the majesty of our cosmos appeared greater the farther its distance from "the pale blue dot" we call home. I was struck that Sagan rhapsodized "the cosmos" as something that starts *way out there*, far above our heads, in galaxies and nebulae far, far away. Whenever he pointed to the photo mockup showing Earth as little more than a pinprick in the vastness of space, I got the impression he found the scale deeply satisfying. Our profound insignificance against the vastness of the cosmos, which starts far above our heads and keeps going farther and farther away. I didn't know Sagan, and I acknowledge that's simply my take.

I can say for sure that's not my sense of the cosmos. I have described my own experiences that changed my sense of death, and life; my sense of where and what we are. Cosmos is everywhere, and it starts here. I also spoke of my friend Mary Payne, who stood on the beach in Hawaii. Her words ("Why didn't he listen?") had reached me in ways neither of us could explain. In ways that had changed us both. Many years after Hawaii, I got a phone call from Mary when her health was in serious decline. I asked how she was doing.

"You know I'm sick again," she said. Somewhere between a statement and a question. She wasn't sure I knew.

"Yes," I said. "How sick?"

"I'm dying."

"How's that going?"

She laughed hoarsely. "I'm giving it everything I've got. You know me, always thorough."

"No stone left unturned," I said. "Word is they give dying-with-diligence trophies."

"Please, stop." We were both cracking up. Then, silence.

"I was wondering if you would come for a visit."

"How about tomorrow?" I said.

"But do you have plans?"

"Yes, my plan is to visit tomorrow, if there's a slot in your busy social schedule." More laughter. We agreed on a time.

"Well, I need to get back to dying," she said with a cough. Sounding tired.

"I'll see you tomorrow," I said. "It'll be grand."

"Yes, and you know what grand is for me," she said.

I knew it well. Grand was one of Mary's favorite words. It meant: as good as it gets.

After Hawaii, we had talked a lot about the fear of not existing as the primary fear underlying all others. To the extent that identity is assumed to be produced within the body and to depend upon the body for its survival, death is going to be dreaded, resisted, fought off. We talked about death as passage from one state of consciousness to another. About the body and personal identity interfacing with boundless awareness, a place of resonance between field and form. I had told her that my fear of death and dying had disappeared in Hawaii.

These many years later, Mary wanted to know: Am I still unafraid?

"Still," I said.

"You heard what I said on the beach," Mary said.

"Sure did." The room got quiet. She could see I had something to say.

"You know all the times in your life that were miserable, and still you trusted being?"

"Yes, many times," Mary said. Her face softened.

"Has trusting being ever let you down?" Her face lit up. She shook her head, smiling in a way that said, *Never.*

I smiled back, *Keep that up.*

Notes

INTRODUCTION

1. Murphy, 1.
2. Vallée, *Passport to Magonia*, 7.
3. Vallée.
4. Vallée, 7–8.
5. Vallée, 8.
6. Vallée.
7. Heinlein, *Stranger in a Strange Land*.
8. Friedlander, *Recentering Seth*, 64–5.
9. Kripal, *Authors of the Impossible*, 211.
10. Vallée, *Dimensions*, 290–1.
11. Esbjörn-Hargens, "Our Wild Cosmos."
12. Levoy, *Callings*, 2.
13. Levoy, *Callings*, 2.
14. Jung, *Flying Saucers*, 16.

I. WORDING, METHOD, SOURCES

1. Blumenthal, *The Believer*, 21.
2. Strentz, "An Analysis of Press Coverage," 24.
3. De Filippi, "UFOs: Another World in our Own?"
4. Freud, *The Uncanny*, 2.
5. Vallée, *Dimensions*, 9.
6. Grosso, "Transcending the ET Hypothesis," 9–11.
7. Campbell, *Hero*, 30.
8. Jung, *Flying Saucers*, 6.

2. WHAT KENNETH ARNOLD REALLY SAW

1. Jung and Kerenyi, *Essays*, 7.
2. Strentz, "An Analysis of Press Coverage," 24.
3. Campbell, Hero, 4.
4. Strentz, "An Analysis of Press Coverage," 24.
5. Jacobs, *The UFO Controversy in America*, 37.
6. Jung, *Flying Saucers*, 6.
7. Maccabee, 21–22.
8. Maccabee, 24.
9. Maccabee, 24.
10. Maccabee, 24.
11. Harris, *UFOs: How Does One Speak*, 1–32.
12. Kripal, *Secret Body*, 318.
13. Kripal, 318.
14. Berger, 6.
15. Jacobs, *The UFO Controversy in America*, 38.
16. Fletcher, *Allegory*, 2.
17. Fletcher, 3.
18. Fletcher, 2.
19. Fletcher, 79.
20. Vallée, 1988, 285.
21. Vallée, 1988, vii.
22. Kripal, 2017, 318.
23. Vallée, *Dimensions*, 49–51.
24. Jacobs, *The UFO Controversy in America*, 38.
25. Kastrup, *Meaning in Absurdity*, 113.
26. Kastrup, *Brief Peeks Beyond*, 12.

3. A MODERN SAGA TAKES SHAPE

1. Fawcett and Greenwood, *The UFO Coverup*, 213.
2. Ruppelt, *The Report*, 13–14.
3. Good, *Above Top Secret*, 146.
4. Steiger, 214.
5. "Letter—J. E. Lipp to Brigadier General Putt, Project 'Sign' No. F-TR-2274-IA Appendix 'D.'" Biblioteca Pleyades, accessed November 19, 2022.
6. Steiger, 213.

7. Jacobs, 50.

8. Keyhoe, *The TRUE Report*, 7.

9. Keyhoe, *The Flying Saucers Are Real*, 73.

10. Kottmeyer, "Entirely Unpredisposed," 3.

11. Kottmeyer, 4.

12. Hayward, *Shifting Worlds*, 8.

13. Hillman, *Healing Fiction*, 203

14. Campbell, *Hero*, 31.

15. Watzlawick, 101.

16. Watzlawick, 29.

17. Hillman, *Healing Fiction*, 55.

4. MORNING IN ZIMBABWE

1. Nickerson, *Ariel Phenomenon*.

2. Nickerson.

3. Nickerson.

4. Nickerson.

5. Nickerson.

6. Blumenthal, *The Believer*, 209.

7. Nickerson.

8. Nickerson, *Ariel Phenomenon*.

9. Nickerson.

10. Nickerson.

11. Nickerson.

12. Campbell, *Hero*, 590–60.

13. Nickerson.

14. Levoy, "Sacrifice: The Shadow," 221.

15. Nickerson, *Ariel Phenomenon*.

16. Nickerson.

17. Nickerson.

18. Blumenthal, *The Believer*, 212.

19. Campbell, *Hero*, 62.

20. Clark, *Extraordinary Encounters*, 67.

21. Dunning, *1994 Ruwa Zimbabwe*.

22. Nickerson, *Ariel Phenomenon*.

23. Nickerson.

24. Nickerson.

25. Colin, *Ella*, 2.

26. Nickerson.

5. DETECTING SIGNALS OF TRANSCENDENCE

1. Campbell, 11.

2. Berger, 53.

3. Berger, 4.

4. Berger, 3.

5. Berger, 5–6.

6. *Close Encounters of the Third Kind*, directed by Steven Spielberg.

7. Berger, 7.

8. Strieber, *Solving the Communion Enigma*, 57.

9. Campbell, 388.

10. Campbell, 30.

11. Berger, 55.

12. Bryan, 432.

13. Campbell, 58.

14. Levoy, *Callings*, 2.

6. THE ROCKEFELLER DISCLOSURE INITIATIVE

1. Elizondo, "UFOs regularly spotted in restricted U.S. airspace."

2. Vallée, *Passport to Magonia*, 154.

3. Vallée, *Passport to Magonia*, 154.

4. Cameron, *Records*.

5. Cameron.

6. Cameron.

7. Cameron.

8. Cameron.

9. Cameron.

7. THE ALIEN ABDUCTION IMPASSE

1. John Mack, letter to author, February 28, 1992.

2. Blumenthal, *The Believer*, 89–91.

3. John Mack and the author in conversation, 1989.

4. Blumenthal, 195.

5. Blumenthal, 10.

6. Wolf, *The Dreaming Universe*, 227–28.

7. Hynek, comments from a recorded telephone interview with the author, November 1985.

8. Hynek, 31–34.

9. Bryan, 13–14.

10. Bryan, 15.

11. Bryan, 15.

12. Jacobs, *Secret Life*, 308.

13. Bryan, 25–26.

14. Bryan, 16.

15. Bryan, 139.

16. Jacobs, *Secret Life*, 22.

17. Readers interested in scientific investigation of the possibility of reincarnation are urged to consult Ian Stevenson, *Twenty Cases Suggestive of Reincarnation: Second Edition, Revised and Enlarged* (Charlottesville, VA: University of Virginia Press, 1980), and Leslie Kean, *Surviving Death: A Journalist Investigates Evidence for an Afterlife* (New York: Three Rivers Press, 2017). Kean's book also explores contemporary mediums who seem to defy the boundaries of the brain and the physical world, and apparitions providing information about their lives on earth.

18. Jacobs, *Secret Life*, 23.

19. Jacobs, *Secret Life*, 23.

20. Miller, 10.

21. Miller, *The Picaresque Novel*, 10.

22. Bryan, 32.

23. Lommel, *Consciousness Beyond Life*, 105.

24. Jacobs, *Secret Life*, 23.

25. Jacobs, *Secret Life*, "A Note to the Reader."

26. Jacobs, *Secret Life*, 28.

27. Jacobs, *The Threat*, 120.

28. Watzlawick, 24.

29. Watzlawick, 29.

30. Kastrup, *More than Allegory*, 17.

31. Keel, *Operation Trojan Horse*, 42.

32. Jacobs, *The Threat*, 19.

33. Vallée, *Dimensions*, 143–44.

34. Dr. Garry P. Nolan, email to author, March 28, 2022.

35. Jacobs, *The Threat*, 133.

36. David Jacobs, "The End of History," David Michael Jacobs's website. Accessed December 15, 2022.

37. David Jacobs, "The End of History," David Michael Jacobs's website. Accessed December 15, 2022.

38. Ouellet, 134.

39. Hall, *Hill Radar–UFO Connection Weak*.

40. Hall, 13.

41. Thompson, Richard L., *Alien Identities*, 162.

42. Kripal, "Shooting Down Souls."

43. Bryan, 271.

44. Mack, *Abduction*, 2009, 17.

45. Mack, *Abduction*, 1994, 421.

46. Blumenthal, *The Believer*, 284.

8. WHO DO WE THINK WE ARE?

1. Pritchard, A. et al., *Proceedings*.

2. Bryan, telephone conversation with author, 1992.

3. Hopkins, telephone conversation with author, 1992.

4. Hopkins, telephone conversation with author, 1992.

5. Grosso, "Transcending the ET Hypothesis."

6. Maclehose, *Presidential Addresses*.

7. Langer, *Counter Clockwise*, 12.

8. Murphy, *The Future of the Body*, 3.

9. Thurston, *The Physical Phenomena of Mysticism*, 146–48.

10. Passage from an unpublished draft of *The Future of the Body* by Michael Murphy, who revised the passage before his book went to press. I include the longer, unpublished version here with appreciation for Murphy's kind permission to do so.

11. Murphy, *The Future of the Body*, 27.

12. Passage from an unpublished draft of *The Future of the Body* by Michael Murphy.

13. Murphy, *The Future of the Body*, 214.

9. THE BIGELOW FACTOR

1. Jerome Clark, "The Last Decade," *IUR* 5, no. 2 (March/April 1990): 20.

2. Vallée, *Dimensions*, xi.

3. Jeffrey Mishlove, "Researching the Paranormal with Colm Kelleher," web interview, *New Thinking Allowed*, January 15, 2022. Accessed March 26, 2022.

4. Kelleher and Knapp, *Hunt for the Skinwalker*, 89.

5. Kelleher and Knapp, 90.

6. Lacatski, Kelleher, and Knapp, *Skinwalkers at the Pentagon*, xiv.

7. Sarah Scoles, "Inside Robert Bigelow's Decades-Long Obsession with UFOs," *Wired*, February 24, 2018.

8. Jeffrey Mishlove, "Researching the Paranormal With Colm Kelleher," web interview, *New Thinking Allowed*, January 15, 2022. YouTube. Accessed March 26, 2022.

9. Kelleher and Knapp, 75

10. Lacatski, Kelleher, and Knapp, 17.

11. Lacatski, Kelleher, and Knapp, 39.

12. Lacatski, Kelleher, and Knapp, 45.

13. Keel, *Operation Trojan Horse*, 1.

14. Keel, 328.

15. Vallée and Davis, 3.

16. Vallée and Davis, 5.

17. Vallée and Davis, 7.

18. Helene Cooper, Ralph Blumenthal, and Leslie Kean, "Glowing Auras and 'Black Money': The Pentagon's Mysterious U.F.O. Program," *New York Times*, December 16, 2017.

19. Cooper, Blumenthal, and Kean, *New York Times*.

20. Office of the Director of National Intelligence, *Preliminary Assessment: Unidentified Aerial Phenomena*, June 25, 2021.

21. Kuhn, *Structure of Scientific Revolutions*, 41–42.

22. Lara Logan. "Bigelow Aerospace Founder Says Commercial World Will Lead in Space." *60 Minutes*, May 28, 2017.

10. MUSING ON THE FUTURE OF REALITY

1. Vallée, *Passport to Magonia*, 2020, 8.

2. Kuhn, *Structure of Scientific Revolutions*.

3. Dunne, *Mr. Dooley.*

4. Kastrup, *Why Materialism is Baloney*, 17.

5. Kastrup, *Brief Peaks Beyond*, 12.

6. Kastrup, *Brief Peaks Beyond*, 13.

7. Kastrup, *More Than Allegory*, 136.

8. Kastrup, *Why Materialism Is Baloney*, 2.

9. Kastrup, *Meaning in Absurdity*, 109.

10. Blumenthal, *The Believer*, 287.

11. Jung, *Flying Saucers*, 6.

12. Kastrup, *Decoding Jung's Metaphysics*, 34.

13. Kastrup, *Decoding Jung's Metaphysics*, 35.

14. Hillman, *A Blue Fire: Selected Writings*, 23.

15. Kastrup, *Decoding Jung's Metaphysics*, 35.

16. Kastrup, *Meaning in Absurdity*, 82.

17. Kastrup, *Decoding Jung's Metaphysics*, 62.

18. Kastrup, *Decoding Jung's Metaphysics*, 63.

19. Kastrup, *Decoding Jung's Metaphysics*, 63.

20. Kastrup, *Decoding Jung's Metaphysics*, 68.

21. Kastrup, *Decoding Jung's Metaphysics*, 69–70.

22. Kastrup, *Meaning in Absurdity*, 3.

23. Kastrup, *Meaning in Absurdity*, 32–33.

24. Kastrup, *Meaning in Absurdity*, 35–36.

25. See: Gröblacher, S., Tomasz Paterek, Rainer Kaltenbaek, Časlav Brukner, Marek Żukowski, Markus Aspelmeyer, and Anton Zeilinger. "An Experimental Test of Non-Local Realism" *Nature*, 446 (April 19, 2007): 871–75.

26. Kastrup, *Meaning in Absurdity*, 40.

27. Kastrup, *Meaning in Absurdity*, 29.

28. Kastrup, *Meaning in Absurdity*, 87–88.

29. Kastrup, *Meaning in Absurdity*, 88.

30. Kastrup, *Meaning in Absurdity*, 96.

31. Kastrup, *Meaning in Absurdity*, 65.

32. Hillman, *Soul's Code*, x.

33. Kastrup, *Meaning in Absurdity*, 97.

11. THE MATTER OF PASCAGOULA

1. Calvin Parker, conversation with the author. May 8, 2022. This is the source of all quotes of Calvin Parker unless specifically linked to another source.

2. Parker, *The Closest Encounter*, 26–27.

3. Parker, *The Closest Encounter*, 29.

4. Parker, *The Closest Encounter*, 41.

5. Blum, *Beyond Earth*, 14.

6. Parker, *The Closest Encounter*, 65.

7. "Expert Says UFO for Real." *Tulsa Tribune*, October 15, 1973, 7B.

8. "Expert Says UFO for Real." *Tulsa Tribune*, October 15, 1973, 7B.

9. Givens, Murphy. "Incident is retraced week after happening." *Mississippi Press*, October 18, 1973, 13.

10. "UFO Beings Take Fisherman Hostage." *Mississippi Press*, October 12, 1973, 4.

11. *Tulsa Tribune*, October 15, 1973, 7B.

12. Parker, *Pascagoula—The Story Continues*, 365.

13. Klass, *UFO Abductions*, 19.

14. Jimmy Akin, "#128: Hickson-Parker UFO Abduction," November 20, 2020, Jimmy Akin's Mysterious World, podcast, 01:14.

15. Moseley and Pflock, *Shockingly Close to the Truth*, 230.

16. Parker, *Pascagoula—The Story Continues*, 48.

17. Parker, 51–52.

18. Parker, 61–64.

19. Parker, 39.

20. Parker, 36.

21. Parker, *Pascagoula—The Closest Encounter*, 41.

22. Parker, 46.

23. Scott, *Beyond Pascagoula*, 53.

24. Keel, *Disneyland of the Gods*, 79.

25. Keel, *Operation Trojan Horse*, 329.

26. Walt Whitman, "Song of Myself," in *Leaves of Grass*. Philadelphia: Rees Welsh, 1882.

EPILOGUE

1. Matthew Gault, "Pentagon's New UFO Report: 247 New UAPs Just Dropped," *Vice*, January 12, 2023.

2. Fletcher, *Allegory: The Theory*, 2.

3. Fletcher, *Allegory: The Theory*, 2.

4. Radin, *The Trickster*, xxiv.

5. Hillman, *The Soul's Code*.

6. Bryan, *Close Encounters of the Fourth Kind*, 16.

7. Karin Austin, personal communication with the author.

8. Karin Austin, personal communication with the author.

9. Harpur, *Daimonic Reality*, 1.

10. Harpur, xvi.

11. Lacatski, Kelleher, and Knapp, *Skinwalkers at the Pentagon*.

12. Bryan, *Close Encounters of the Fourth Kind*, 443.

13. Wolf, *The Dreaming Universe*, 13.

14. Bryan, *Close Encounters of the Fourth Kind*, 443.

15. Strieber and Kripal, *The Super Natural*, 116.

16. Deutsch, *Fabric of Reality*.

17. Chown, *The Universe Next Door*, 97.

18. Kelleher and Knapp, *Hunt for the Skinwalker*, 277–78.

19. Kelleher and Knapp, 280.

20. Private correspondence with the author, December 3, 2023. Grossinger develops this idea in his forthcoming book, *Homeopathy as Energy Medicine: Information in the Microdose*, Inner Traditions, Healing Arts Press, 2024.

21. Passage from an unpublished draft of *The Future of the Body* by Michael Murphy

22. Kelleher and Knapp, 246.

23. Campbell, 207.

24. Madhi, Foster, and Little, *Betwixt & Between*, 69.

Bibliography

Berger, Peter L. *A Rumor of Angels*. New York: Knopf Doubleday Publishing Group, 1970.

Blum, Ralph and Judy Blum. *Beyond Earth*. New York: Bantam Books, 1974.

Blumenthal, Ralph. *The Believer: Alien Encounters, Hard Science, and the Passion of John Mack*. High Road Books: Albuquerque, 2021.

Broad, C. D. *Religion, Philosophy, and Psychical Research*. New York: Harcourt Brace, 1953.

Bryan, C. D. B. *Close Encounters of the Fourth Kind: Alien Abductions and UFOs— Witnesses and Scientists Report*. London: Weidenfeld & Nicolson, 1995.

Cameron, Grant. "Records from the Clinton OSTP Related to UFOs, Extraterrestrial Intelligence and the Laurance Rockefeller Initiative." Last modified July 26, 2022.

Campbell, Joseph. *The Hero with a Thousand Faces*. Princeton: Princeton University Press, 1949.

Chown, Marcus. *The Universe Next Door*. New York: Oxford University Press, 2002.

Clark, Jerome (2000). *Extraordinary Encounters: An Encyclopedia of Extraterrestrials and Otherworldly Beings*. Indiana University: ABC-CLIO, 2000.

Colin, Sid. *Ella: The Life and Times of Ella Fitzgerald*. London: Elm Tree Books, 1986.

Darrach Jr., H. B., and Robert Ginna. *"Have We Visitors From Space?" LIFE*, April 7, 1952.

De Filippi, Sebastiano. *"UFOs: Another World in our Own? A few scattered thoughts on the semantics of an acronym and epistemological paradigms."* Position paper. Center for Theory and Research, Esalen Institute, Big Sur, CA, 2021.

Deutsch, David. *The Fabric of Reality*. New York: Penguin, 1998.

Didion, Joan. *The White Album: Essays by Joan Didion*. New York: Farrar, Straus and Giroux, 2009.

Dunne, Finley Peter. *Mr. Dooley in Peace and in War*. Independently published, 2021.

Dunning, Brian. "The 1994 Ruwa Zimbabwe Alien Encounter." Podcast. Archived from the original on September 17, 2021. Retrieved September 17, 2021. https://skeptoid.com/episodes/4760.

Esbjörn-Hargens, Sean. "Our Wild Kosmos!: An Exo Studies Exploration of the Ontological Status of Non-Human Intelligences." Accessed July 15, 2022.

Fawcett, Lawrence, and J. Greenwood. *The UFO Coverup*. New York: Prentice-Hall, 1984.

Fletcher, Angus. *Allegory: The Theory of a Symbolic Mode*. Ithaca, NY: Cornell University Press, 1964.

Freud, Sigmund. *The Uncanny*. New York: Penguin Books, 2003.

Friedlander, John. *Recentering Seth: Teachings from a Multidimensional Entity on Living Gracefully and Skillfully in a World You Create but Do Not Control*. Rochester, VT: Bear & Company, 2022.

Good, Timothy. *Above Top Secret: The Worldwide UFO Coverup*. New York: William Morrow and Co., 1988.

Grosso, Michael. "Transcending the ET Hypothesis." *California UFO* 3, no. 3 (1998): 9–11.

Hall, Richard H. "Hill Radar–UFO Connection Weak." A report on an article published in *MUFON UFO Journal* no. 140. Accessed December 22, 2022.

Halprin, Daniel J. *Intimate Alien: The Hidden Story of the UFO*. Stanford: Stanford University Press, 2020.

Harpur, Patrick. *Daimonic Reality: A Field Guide to the Otherworld*. Ravensdale, WA: Pine Winds Press, 2003.

Harris, Paolo Leopizzi. *UFOs: How Does One Speak to a Ball of Light?* San Antonio: Anomalist Books, 2011.

Hayward, Jeremy W. *Shifting Worlds, Changing Minds*. Boston: Shambhala Publications, 1987.

Heinlein, Robert. *Stranger in a Strange Land*. New York: Penguin Classics, 2016.

Hillman, James. *Healing Fiction*. Barrytown, NY: Station Hill, 1983.

———. *A Blue Fire: Selected Writings of James Hillman*. New York: Harper & Row, 1989.

————. *The Soul's Code: In Search of Character and Calling.* New York: Random House, 1996.

Hynek, J. Allen. *The UFO Experience: A Scientific Inquiry.* Chicago: H. Regnery Company, 1972.

Jacobs, David M. *The UFO Controversy in America.* Bloomington: Indiana University Press, 1975.

————. *Secret Life: Firsthand Documented Accounts of UFO Abductions.* New York: Simon & Schuster, 1992.

————. *The Threat: The Secret Alien Agenda.* New York: Simon & Schuster, 1998.

Jung, C. G. *Flying Saucers: A Modern Myth of Things Seen in the Sky.* Princeton: Princeton University Press, 1978.

————. *The Undiscovered Self.* London: Routledge, 2009.

Jung, C. G., and Carl Kerenyi. *Essays on a Science of Mythology.* Princeton: Princeton University Press, 1973.

Kastrup, Bernardo. *Meaning in Absurdity: What Bizarre Phenomena Can Tell Us About the Nature of Reality.* Winchester, UK: IFF Books, 2011.

————. *Why Materialism Is Baloney.* Winchester, UK: IFF Books, 2014.

————. *Brief Peeks Beyond: Critical Essays on Metaphysics, Neuroscience, Free Will, Skepticism and Culture.* Winchester, UK: IFF Books, 2015.

————. *More Than Allegory: On Religious Myth, Truth and Belief.* Winchester, UK: IFF Books, 2016.

————. *Decoding Jung's Metaphysics: The Archetypal Semantics of an Experiential Universe.* Winchester, UK: IFF Books, 2019.

————. *The Idea of the World: A Multi-disciplinary Argument for the Mental Nature of the World.* Winchester, UK: IFF Books, 2019.

Kean, Leslie, "The Pentagon's Mysterious U.F.O. Program," *New York Times,* December 16, 2021, 1.

Keel, John A. *Disneyland of the Gods.* Lilburn, GA: IllumiNet Press, 1995.

————. *Operation Trojan Horse: The Classic Breakthrough Study of UFOs.* San Antonio, TX: Anomalist Books, 2013.

Kelleher, Colm, and Knapp, George. *Hunt for the Skinwalker: Science Confronts the Unexplained at a Remote Ranch in Utah.* New York: Paraview Pocket Books, 2005.

Keyhoe, Donald. *The Flying Saucers Are Real.* New York: Fawcett Publications, 1950.

————. *The TRUE Report on Flying Saucers.* New York: Fawcett Publications, 1967.

Klass, Philip J. *UFO Abductions: A Dangerous Game*. Buffalo, NY: Prometheus Books, 1989.

Kottmeyer, Martin. "Entirely Unpredisposed." *Magonia* 35 (January 1990), 3–10.

Kripal, Jeffrey J. *Authors of the Impossible: The Paranormal and the Sacred*. Chicago: The University of Chicago Press, 2010.

———. *The Flip: Who You Really Are and Why It Matters*. New York: Penguin Books, 2019.

———. *Secret Body: Erotic and Esoteric Currents in the History of Religions*. Chicago: University of Chicago Press, 2017.

———. "Shooting Down Souls . . . Good Luck with That: Some Paradoxical Thoughts on the UFO Phenomenon from a Historian of Religions." November 18, 2023. SOL Foundation Initiative for UAP Research and Policy Symposium at Stanford University. Lecture.

Kuhn, Thomas S. *The Structure of Scientific Revolutions*. Chicago: University of Chicago Press, 1970.

Lacatski, James T., Colm Kelleher, and George Knapp. *Skinwalkers at the Pentagon*. Henderson, Nevada: RTMA, 2021.

Langer, Ellen J. *Counter Clockwise: Mindful Health and the Power of Possibility*. New York: Ballantine Books, 2009.

Levoy, Gregg. *Callings: Finding and Following an Authentic Life*. New York: Three Rivers Press, 1997.

———. "Sacrifice: The Shadow in the Calling." In *Being Called: Scientific, Secular, and Sacred Perspectives*, edited by D. B. Yaden, T. D. McCall, and J. H. Ellens, (215–224). Santa Barbara, CA: Praeger, 2015.

Maccabee, Bruce. *Three Minutes in June: The UFO Sighting that Changed the World*. CreateSpace Independent Publishing Platform, 2017.

Mack, John. *Abduction: Human Encounters with Aliens*. New York: Charles Scribner's Sons, 1994.

———. *Abduction: Human Encounters with Aliens*. New York: Charles Scribner's Sons, 2009.

Maclehose, R. *Presidential Addresses to the Society for Psychical Research, 1882–1911*. Glasgow: University Press, 1912.

Madhi, Louise Carus, Steven Foster, and Meredith Little, eds. *Betwixt & Between: Patterns of Masculine and Feminine Initiation*. La Salle, IL.: Open Court, 1987.

Miller, Stuart. *The Picaresque Novel*. Cleveland: The Press of Case Western Reserve University, 1967.

Moseley, James. W., and Karl T. Pflock. *Shockingly Close to the Truth: Confessions of a Grave-Robbing Ufologist*. Amherst, NY: Prometheus, 2002.

Murphy, Michael. *The Future of the Body: Exploration Into the Further Evolution of Human Nature*. New York: Jeremy P. Tarcher/Putnam, 1992.

Nagel, Thomas. "What Is It Like to Be a Bat?" *The Philosophical Review* 83, no. 4 (1974): 435–50. https://doi.org/10.2307/2183914.

Nickerson, Randall, dir., prod. *Ariel Phenomenon*. Documentary film, written by Randall Nickerson and Christopher Seward. String Theory Films, 2022.

Ouellet, Eric. *Illuminations: The UFO Experience as a Parapsychological Event*. Charlottesville, Virginia: Anomalist Books, 2015.

Parker, Calvin. *Pascagoula—The Closest Encounter: My Story*. West Yorkshire: Flying Disk Press, 2018.

———. *Pascagoula—The Story Continues: New Evidence & New Witnesses*. West Yorkshire: Flying Disk Press, 2019.

Pritchard, A., D. Pritchard, J. Mack, P. Kasey, C. Yapp, eds. *Alien Discussions: Proceedings of the Abduction Study Conference*. Cambridge, MA: North Cambridge Press, 1994.

Radin, Paul. *The Trickster*. New York: Schocken Books, 1972.

Ring, Kenneth. "Near-Death and UFO Encounters as Shamanic Initiations: Some Conceptual and Evolutionary Implications." *ReVision* 11, no.3 (Winter 1989): 14–22.

Ruppelt, Edward J. *The Report on Unidentified Flying Objects*. New York: Ace Books, 1956.

Scott, Irena McCammon. *Beyond Pascagoula: The Rest of the Amazing Story*. West Yorkshire: Flying Disk Press, 2020.

Stacy, Dennis. "The Contactee Era." In *Phenomenon: Forty Years of Flying Saucers*, by John Spencer, edited by Hilary Evans, 121–133. New York: Avon Books, 1988.

Stewart, R.J. *The Elements of Creation Myth*. Longmead, England: Element Books, 1989.

Story, Ronald D. *The Encyclopedia of UFOs*. New York: Doubleday, 1980

Strentz, Herbert. "An Analysis of Press Coverage of Unidentified Flying Objects, 1957–1966." PhD diss., Northwestern University, 1970.

Stieger, Brad. *Project Blue Book: The Top Secret UFO Files that Revealed a Government Cover-Up*. Newburyport, MA.: MUFON (Red Wheel/Weiser), 2019.

Strieber, Whitley. *Solving the Communion Enigma: What Is to Come*. New York: Penguin Publishing Group, 2012.

Strieber, Whitley, and Jeffrey J. Kripal. *The Super Natural: A New Vision of the Unexplained*. New York: TarcherPerigee, 2016.

Thompson, Keith. "The UFO Encounter Experience as a Crisis of Transformation," in *Spiritual Emergency: When Personal Transformation Becomes a Crisis*, edited by Stanislav Grof and Christina Grof. Los Angeles: Jeremy P. Tarcher, 1989.

Thompson, Richard L. *Alien Identities: Ancient Insights Into Modern UFO Phenomena*. Alachua, FL: Govardhan Hill Publishing, 1993.

Thurston, Herbert. *The Physical Phenomena of Mysticism*. London: Burns, Oates and Washbourne, 1952.

Vallée, Jacques. *Passport to Magonia: From Folklore to Flying Saucers*. Chicago: Henry Regnery Co., 1969.

———. *Dimensions: A Casebook of Alien Contact*. Chicago: Contemporary Books, 1988.

———. *Passport to Magonia: From Folklore to Flying Saucers*. Brisbane: Daily Grail Publishing, 2020.

Vallée, Jacques F., and Eric W. Davis. "Incommensurability, Orthodoxy and the Physics of High Strangeness: a 6-layer Model for Anomalous Phenomena." *Proceedings of the International Forum "Ciência, Religiao e Consciência,"* Fernando Pessoa University, Porto (Portugal) 23–25, pp. 223–239 (October 2003).

Van Lommel, Pim. *Consciousness Beyond Life: The Science of the Near-Death Experience*. New York: Harper Collins Publishers, 2010.

Von Glasersfeld, Ernst. "An Introduction to Radical Constructivism." In *The Invented Reality: How Do We Believe What We Believe We Know?*, edited by Paul Watzlawick. New York: W.W. Norton, 1984.

Watzlawick, Paul. "Self-Fulfilling Prophecies." In *The Invented Reality*, edited by Paul Watzlawick. New York: W.W. Norton, 1984.

Whitaker, Bill. "UFOs regularly spotted in restricted U.S. airspace." *60 Minutes interview with Luis Elizondo*. Broadcast August 29, 2021, on CBS.

Wolf, Fred Alan. *The Dreaming Universe*. New York: Simon & Schuster, 1994.

Index